AF771333

The Japanese Economy and the Way Forward

The Japanese Economy and the Way Forward

Rameshwar Tandon

palgrave
macmillan

© Rameshwar Tandon 2005

All rights reserved. No reproduction, copy or transmission of this publication may be made without written permission.

No paragraph of this publication may be reproduced, copied or transmitted save with written permission or in accordance with the provisions of the Copyright, Designs and Patents Act 1988, or under the terms of any licence permitting limited copying issued by the Copyright Licensing Agency, 90 Tottenham Court Road, London W1T 4LP.

Any person who does any unauthorized act in relation to this publication may be liable to criminal prosecution and civil claims for damages.

The author has asserted his right to be identified as the author of this work in accordance with the Copyright, Designs and Patents Act 1988.

First published 2005 by
PALGRAVE MACMILLAN
Houndmills, Basingstoke, Hampshire RG21 6XS and
175 Fifth Avenue, New York, N. Y. 10010
Companies and representatives throughout the world

PALGRAVE MACMILLAN is the global academic imprint of the Palgrave Macmillan division of St. Martin's Press, LLC and of Palgrave Macmillan Ltd. Macmillan® is a registered trademark in the United States, United Kingdom and other countries. Palgrave is a registered trademark in the European Union and other countries.

ISBN-13: 978–1–4039–4778–9 hardback
ISBN-10: 1–4039–4778–3 hardback

This book is printed on paper suitable for recycling and made from fully managed and sustained forest sources.

A catalogue record for this book is available from the British Library.

Library of Congress Cataloging-in-Publication Data
Tandon, Rameshwar.
The Japanese economy and the way forward / Rameshwar Tandon.
p. cm.
Includes bibliographical references and index.
ISBN 1–4039–4778–3 (cloth)
1. Japan–Economic conditions–21st century. 2. Japan–Economic conditions–20th century. 3. Japan–Economic policy–21st century. 4. Japan–Economic policy–1945- I. Title

HC462.95.T3697 2005
330.952–dc22 2004057666

10 9 8 7 6 5 4 3 2 1
14 13 12 11 10 09 08 07 06 05

Printed and bound in Great Britain by
Antony Rowe Ltd, Chippenham and Eastbourne

Dedicated to old friends:

Professor Kiyoshi Kojima
Emeritus Professor, International Economics
Hitotsubashi University, Kunitachi city, Tokyo

Professor Hitoshi Hirakawa
Professor, Graduate School of Business
Nagoya University, Nagoya

Masahiko Takeda
Manager, International Department
Bank of Japan, Tokyo

Professor Peter Drysdale
Director, Australia Japan Research Centre
Australian National University, Canberra

Professor Hugh Patrick
Stern School of Business
Columbia University in the city of New York, NY

Professor Kazuo Sato
Department of Economics
Rutgers University, New Brunswick, NJ, USA

Contents

List of Figures

List of Tables

Acknowledgements

A Senior Fellowship awarded by the Indian Council of Social Science Research, New Delhi, made the work for this study on Japan possible. I offer grateful thanks to the Membership Secretary and Chairman for supporting my research work over the past several years. I still remember the unlimited time and effort they spared for helpful discussions.

While it is customary to thank several people for their help, I particularly record my indebtedness to those without whose assistance it would have been very difficult to complete this study. For reading several chapters and making valuable comments and suggestions, special mention should be made of the following social scientists in various countries over a number of years: Professor Sir Hans Singer of IDS, Sussex, Neelambar Hatti of Lund University, Kiyoshi Kojima and Jurio Teranishi of Hitotsubashi University, Tokyo, H. Akiba of Niigata University, Hitoshi Hirakawa of Nagoya University, Ikuya Fukamachi of Kumamoto University, Ali M. El-Agraa of Fukuoka University, Kyushu, and Masahiko Takeda of the Bank of Japan, Tokyo.

During preparation of the final manuscript, useful comments were made by Professor R.L. Varshney of the Indian Institute of Foreign Trade, New Delhi, Professor Sandwip K. Das, Sunanda Sen, I.N. Mukherjee of Jawaharlal Nehru University, New Delhi, P.C. Verma of the Institute of Economic Growth, Delhi, Jagdish Srivastav of FICCI, New Delhi, and Charan Wadhva of the Centre for Policy Research, New Delhi.

For extensive discussions and dialogue on various issues, my thanks go to several old friends in the University and Institute here: Professor I.D. Gupta, Mohamed Muzammil, Arvind Awasthi, Rakesh Awasthi, R.T. Tiwari, Roopam Bachhil, S. Bharti and Usha Saxena.

At the Indian Institute of Management, Lucknow, I thank Professor Pritam Singh, S.B. Mathur and K.G. Sahdevan for prolonged and helpful discussions. My grateful thanks are also due to the staff of several libraries in India and abroad in Singapore, Hong Kong and Japan.

Lastly I offer grateful thanks to the International Institute of Special Education, Lucknow, for providing excellent infrastructural facilities for this work.

RAMESHWAR TANDON

List of Abbreviations

ACU	Asian currency unit
ADB	Asian Development Bank
AFDC	Asian Finance and Development Corporation
AFIC	Asian Finance and Investment Corporation
APEC	Asia Pacific Economic Cooperation
ASEAN	Association of South-East Asian Nations
BA	Bankers' acceptance
BB	Brokers, Broker (that is, Nilson Sogo-Shoken-Japan Mutual Securities and Nilson Tento Shoken-Japan OCT Securities
BIS	Bank for International Settlements
BOJ	Bank of Japan, Tokyo
CAPM	Capital asset pricing model
CB	Convertible bonds
CD	Certificate of Deposit
CP	Commercial Paper
DAC	Development Assistance Committee
DCF	Discounted cash flow
EPA	Economic Planning Agency
FB	Financing Bill
FED	Federal Reserve Board
G-5	Group of Five (France, Germany, Japan, UK and USA)
G-7	Group of Seven (France, Germany, Japan, UK, USA, Italy and Canada)
G-10	Group of Ten (France, Germany, Japan, UK, USA, Italy, Canada, Belgium, Sweden and the Netherlands)
GIF	Global Infrastructure Fund
IBF	International banking facility
IDA	International Development Association
IDM	Inter-Dealer Market
IFC	International Finance Corporation
IPO	Initial public offering
IR	Internal rate of return
JAIDO	Japan International Development Organization
JASD	Japan Association of Securities Dealers
JASDAQ	Japan Association of Securities Dealers, Automated Quotations
JETRO	Japan External Trade Organization

JOM	Japan offshore market
JSF	Japan Securities Finance Co.
JSRI	Japan Securities Research Institute
KSE	Kyoto Stock Exchange
LTD	Large-scale time deposits
MMC	Money-market certificate
MITI	Ministry of International Trade and Industry
MOF	Ministry of Finance
NEEDS	Nikkei Economic Electronic Data System
NSE	Nikkei stock average
NYSE	New York Stock Exchange
ODA	Official Development Assistance
ODR	Official discount rate
OECD	Organization for Economic Cooperation and Development
OECF	Overseas Economic Cooperation Fund
OED	Option expiration day
OOF	Other official flows
OPEC	Organization of Petroleum-Exporting Countries
OSE	Osaka Stock Exchange
OTC	Over the counter (stocks)
PAFTAD	Pacific Trade and Development Conference
PECC	Pacific Economic Cooperation Conference
R&D	Research and development
REEF	Real effective exchange rate
SAF	Structural adjustment facility
SEA	Security and Exchange Act (USA)
SEL	Security and Exchange Law (Japan)
SII	Structural impediments initiative
SIMEX	Singapore International Monetary Exchange
SML	Security market line
SQ	Special quotation
TB	Treasury bills
TIFFE	Tokyo International Financial Futures Exchange
TOPIX	Tokyo Stock Exchange Price Index
TSE	Tokyo Stock Exchange
TTB	Telegraphic transfer buying
TTS	Telegraphic transfer selling
TXC	Transaction costs
WIDER	World Institute for Development Economic Research

1

Japan's Problem in the New Millennium

Looking towards the new century from the vantage point of 2002, handling the repercussions of the collapse of the bubble economy of Japan is indeed a serious problem. The downslide started in 1989, but stagflation, affecting the economy for the last several years, has turned into the most serious recession in an industrial country since the 1990s. To the problems posed by the duration and severity of this crisis should be added the continued ineffectiveness of several fiscal injections, along with liberal monetary policies.

While several medium-run projections suggest that future growth might remain very slow due to the rapid ageing of the population, questions are now being raised about the true extent of the fiscal stimuli required. These issues, along with several recession-related weaknesses, would propel public debt to a level of 150 per cent of GDP. Of course, the country's future prosperity, or lack of it, will strongly affect the prosperity of the world economy. In Japan there has been growing support for fiscal consolidation and monetary tightening, associated with the IMF programmes, but Japanese institutions continue to advocate several Keynesian policy measures.[1]

In recent research, the rediscovery through the Japanese crisis of the 'recession' economics of J.M. Keynes has helped to rescue his 'liquidity trap' hypothesis from earlier objections. Of course, despite Keynes's own doubts as to its empirical relevance, his 'limiting' case is regarded as suggesting a more general threat to stability in a low-inflation international environment.[2]

Three major problems have been focused on in recent studies:

1 What are the most important reasons for the extremely disappointing performance over the last decade?

2 What policies could the authorities adopt to restore higher rates of growth in the short to medium term?
3 What is the outlook for Japan's longer-run future and for its unique economic 'model'?

What went wrong?

When Japan's 'bubble' economy burst in 1991, the shortfall in the stock market and land values made economic downturn inevitable. A decade of stagnation has had wide-ranging effects. The Japanese full employment record has been eroded; in 2001–2, unemployment was above US levels for the first time since the war. There has also been a marked deterioration in the country's public finances. The OECD put the structural budget deficit for 2002 at 7 per cent of GDP and, more importantly, if one includes the accounts and the balance sheets of other financial and non-financial institutions, the overall debt ratio would rise to over 190 per cent.[3] If allowance is made for unfunded pension liabilities, this would be pushed above 200 per cent, since several assets held by the public sector are of doubtful value.

The business cycle downturn, which started with a burst in the asset-price bubble, produced one of the longest recessions in post-war history and greatly weakened the legendary Japanese manufacturing competitiveness; for example, since the second quarter of 1994–95, after a short recovery, the shortfall between growth of exports and growth of markets was 4.5 per cent, and not all of this due to an overvalued currency.

More alarming is the fact that, almost a decade later, the Japanese economy has yet to recover. Except for 1996, when annualized growth touched 5 per cent, GDP growth since 1991 has averaged less than 1 per cent per year and has been continuously negative from 1999 to 2002. In contrast, during the last four decades Japan was the premier growth economy, with the world's highest saving rates and an endless capacity to adapt to the latest industrial technology; Japanese GDP grew at 6–12 per cent during the 1950s and 1960s, and also 4–5 per cent during the 1970s and 1980s. Even today these basic virtues of private industry and thrift and a highly skilled labour force in hi-tech manufacturing remain intact, but during the whole of 1995 domestic aggregate demand (both private investment and consumption) failed to recover.

The build-up of deflationary pressures in Japan was aggravated by continued decline in asset prices, and also decline in personal, corporate and financial sector balance sheets. From the peaks in 1991, the price of commercial land has fallen by 85 per cent and the price of urban residential land declined by more than a third, further pushing the downward momentum. The aggregate net worth of all households has shrunk by a third since 1991, dampening consumer spending. By mid-1995, the accumulated debts on bank balance sheets were an estimated ¥42 trillion ($420 billion), roughly equal to 10 per cent of Japanese GDP.[4]

Moreover, for several years, domestic credit extended by banks was stagnant in view of the declining capital base of the banking system. Consumer and business confidence has fallen because of the 5 per cent unemployment, along with falling wages. The problems in the financial sector need to be studied afresh. The concentration of bad debts in smaller financial institutions, for example regional banks, credit unions and mortgage institutions, increased their exposure to bank runs, as was the case in the Tokyo–Kansai area in 1995. These runs raised the issue of a systematic financial sector crisis, affecting the world financial markets. Moreover, negative spillover effects are issues of great concern in developing countries.

The Plaza Accord of September 1995 acknowledged the need for sizeable realignment of exchange rates among major currencies, with a view to rectify persistent imbalances in the external accounts of the major economic powers – the USA, Japan and Germany. During the first few years after the Accord, the yen exchange rate appreciated by about 50 per cent against the US dollar, from ¥250 before the Accord to less than ¥160 at the end of 1985. In Japan, one consequence was the 'Endaka' Fukyo (strong) yen recession.

In order to cope with the situation, several changes in the economy were undertaken when the government pushed through financial reforms, including liberalization of deposit interest rates. Of course, much of this restructuring movement was due to external pressures from the USA. The Bank of Japan repeatedly lowered its discount rate to a historical low of 2.5 per cent in February 1987 and it remained at this level until May 1989. It was widely hoped that growth of the economy would oblige Japan to rely more than previously on domestic demand, rather than on exports.

In fact, the contribution of exports to real growth of the national economy was 0.5 per cent in 1982 and 1.5 per cent in 1983, but it became negative in 1986–87. The decline in oil prices since 1985 partly compensated for the disadvantage of the yen's appreciation. The strong yen also induced a rapid growth in foreign direct investment outflows as the prices of overseas assets and manpower became cheaper in relation to their domestic counterparts. In this period there was strong growth in plant and investment equipment, along with economic overheating over this period due to visible wage increases and inflation in goods and service prices, leading to a rise in the prices of stock assets.

Creating a bubble economy

Economic theory that prescribes normal relationships between investments and asset prices (equity prices) helps us to view asset prices as a business cycle indicator. If a market is efficient, the equity price should reflect future earnings created by corporate investments. The deviation in asset prices from an investment-earning ratio – Tobin's average 'Q' – is regarded as a noise that results from market inefficiency, or expectation elements. As Ogawa found, after studying this relationship by measuring movements in average 'q' and marginal 'q' during this bubble period, there was significant noise during the period and it was related to the values of land assets owned by the corporate sectors.[5]

In the absence of inflation during mid-1980s, due to the low price of imports in terms of yen, including that of 're-imported' goods of Japanese firms now operating abroad, domestic demand expanded significantly. The consumer price index dipped in the early years of the 1980s, from 100 in 1980 to about 93 in 1982 and slowly climbed back to 100 and remained at that level until early 1988. This index reached 109 at the end of 1992.[6]

As a result, the trend of increasing surpluses in trade and current accounts continued until 1987, since the figures were much inflated by short-term J-curve effects of yen appreciation. Moreover, the lowering of interest rates led to a general increase in bond prices. In 1987, the government introduced a policy package of ¥600 billion ($40 billion or about 2 per cent of GDP) to stimulate the economy.

The movements in asset prices had two components – one was the improvement in economic fundamentals and the other was the bubble element. There was rapid expansion in corporate profits and also in the demand for office space in major cities. These changes were supported by low interest rates and strong growth in the money stock. The discount rate was lowered from 5 per cent in January 1986 to 2.5 per cent in February 1987 and was kept at this level until May 1989.

All these events in the late 1980s led to a climate that was ripe for wide speculation. The dramatic increase in the market values of financial assets made it easier for private firms to raise capital through equity finance, as convertible bonds, warrants and new stocks. The purchase of stocks became a popular pastime, but it was large institutional investors – banks and life insurance companies (45 per cent) and firms (25 per cent) – that held the bulk of outstanding corporate equities.[7]

Rising asset prices attracted speculative investments in equities and land purchases in search of capital gains, which reached about ¥500 trillion worth over 140 per cent of GNP in 1987. Over four years from 1986 to 1989, capital gains on land and stock assets surpassed gross domestic output produced during this period by more than 20 per cent. Low interest rates worked as leverage to expand selective investments in stock assets. During this period, financial institutions increased their asset holdings in equities and land through direct investments and loans to real estate developers. In 1987, the growth of loans to the real estate sector was twice as high as that of total loans. Since Japanese institutions used land as collateral for loans, rising land values provided a push to create credit through demand and supply-side factors.

The BIS regulations, by allowing financial institutions to count 45 per cent of their unrealized gains as a capital base, revised the ceilings for loan evaluation. Hence bank loans continued to grow at about 15 per cent per year during this period, twice as fast as growth in nominal GDP. It was suggested that appreciation of the yen, which reduces the profit margins of export-oriented industries, was likely to cause a fall in the Nikkei stock average of 225 leading Japanese firms, but as non-price factors became more important in international marketing, the yen's appreciation reduced export quantities less than it used to. The recent dominant view is that a strong exchange rate of an appreciating yen tends to induce a hike in the Nikkei stock average.[8]

The end of the bubble was triggered by changes in interest rates along with quality controls. The discount rate was raised in May 1989 – the first time in nine years – to 3.25 per cent, with a view to control inflationary pressures, caused by overheating of economic activities. In March 1990, it was raised again to 5.25 per cent – the level prevailing before the Plaza Accord. This high rate slowed down growth of real investment and investment in stock assets.

Lending to the real estate sector grew rapidly as the price of commercial land skyrocketed in the Tokyo–Osaka areas. The price hike started with commercial property in central Tokyo around 1983, while commercial property in Osaka and Nagoya led the price hike in 1987, followed by other regions in 1989. Reportedly Japanese land in the circumstances of the 'land bubble' was, at one time, valued by the real estate industry at four times the worth of all the property in the USA.[9] This meant that, on average, an identical area of land would cost 100 times as much in Japan as in the USA, as the former is one twenty-fifth the size of the latter. The domestic conditions further activated 'Japan money' on an international scale, since Japanese firms could obtain financial resources abroad more advantageously than before by using overvalued domestic collateral.[10]

After the Plaza Accord, foreign direct investment began to increase dramatically. As an OECD report observed, between 1985 and 1989 investment outflows from Japan increased about sixfold in dollar terms (or threefold in yen terms).[11] By the end of the 1990s, Japan became the largest home country of foreign direct investment.[12]

With the introduction of quantitative restrictions on bank lending to the real estate sector in 1990, the market was convinced that the liquidity squeeze was devised not only as a counter-cyclical measure, but also as a counter-bubble measure. This led to a reversal in expectations for asset price movements.

As P.N. Snowden recently observed, increasingly reflecting American monetary policy concerns, with the international overvaluation of the dollar, the relative stability of the (policy-determined) Japanese discount rate led to a declining interest differential in the years to 1985.[13]

The Plaza Agreement, involving an understanding that official foreign exchange intervention would seek to drive down the value of the US currency, was more successful in securing its objective than was the Louvre Accord to stabilize the dollar at exchange rates prevailing in early 1987. But some efforts to arrest the slide of the US currency were evident in Japanese short-term rates after 1985, and in relative rate settings during 1987 and 1988. Hence the suggestion that Japanese monetary policy in these years was trying to suppress the continuing rise in the yen, as Kazuo Ueda observed, and that episodes of increased currency were associated with subsequent monetary relaxation by the Bank of Japan.[14]

The BIS regulations on own capital worked negatively in this phase by restricting bank lending. During the expansion phase, part of the BIS regulations that govern tier 2 of own funds, helped accelerate bank lending through a revaluation of supplementary capital due to increasing latent gains of listed securities, Moreover, the regulations worked to discourage bank lending during the collapse in equity prices. Sawabe noted the destabilizing aspects of the BIS regulation; the corporate sector was deprived of 'indirect' financing through the banking sector due to the credit crunch raised by this BIS regulation.[15]

The monetary policy changes

Such aggressive bank lending to the real estate sector was the main background to asset inflation, and monetary policy changes after the Plaza Agreement also contributed. The Group of Five ministers and governors agreed that 'Policy coordination for redressing the large and growing external imbalances was important and that exchange rates should play an important role in adjusting external imbalances.' It was also suggested that some further orderly 'appreciation' of main non-dollar currencies against the dollar was desirable.

After the Plaza Agreement, the yen appreciated against the dollar from ¥240 in mid-1985 to ¥120 at the end of 1987, in spite of efforts to stabilize the markets and the exchange rates at ¥150–160 during most of 1987. Such a sharp appreciation of the yen was a heavy blow to the Japanese export industry; while the advantage of a strong currency over the long run was recognized, the economy had to face more immediate adverse consequences of deflationary effects.

With a view to mitigate the deflationary effects of the yen's appreciation and the reduced surplus, the BOJ (Bank of Japan) lowered the official discount rate five times up to early 1987, from 5 to 2.5 per cent. Due to reductions in the official discount rate, the deflationary effect of the yen's appreciation was reduced. Moreover, Japanese balance of payments was producing a large and growing current account surplus, which, as a ratio of nominal gross national product (GNP), reached 3.6 per cent in 1985. Hence international pressure on Japan to reduce its surplus was widely mounted.

By mid-1987, it was clear that the worst had been seen and that the economy had started on an upswing where domestic demand was the major driving force. It was at this stage that a special emergency fiscal package of ¥6 trillion was introduced, called by the critics as 'too large and too late', and it was just possible it also contributed to the build-up of successive demand for goods and services and also for assets. In the summer of 1987, it was clear that the economy had bottomed out and prices of some commodities, for example construction materials, began to rise. But the so-called 'Black Monday' in October 1987 made it difficult for the BOJ to tighten its monetary control, along with several emergency measures for extra injection of liquidity.

Collapse of the bubble economy

Since 1985, the government had issued frequent 'administrative guidance' to the banking sector to restrain loans to the real estate sector.

The major banks could circumvent government guidance by diverting their funds to the real estate sector, through their non-bank affiliates. The curbing of rising land prices in urban areas did not take place until the end of the 1980s and a fall began in 1991. Moreover, government overhauled the existing tax system with a view to increasing the withholding costs and discourage hoarding and also softened the zoning and construction code, which in the past imposed rigid regulations on its use for residential construction with a view to increasing the limits on floor space in urban residential areas.[16]

By spring 1989, the BOJ became alarmed by rising asset prices and began to raise the discount rate; it reached 6.0 per cent in five incremental stages over nine months. The last incremental increase of 0.75 per cent (from 5.25 to 6 per cent) took place on 30 August 1990.

Besides the interruptions caused by Black Monday in October 1987 and the quick recovery thereafter, the Nikkei stock average continued its high up to 38,915 at the end of 1989. From this high, it slipped in January, slid faster in February and began a heavy nosedive in March 1990. It went down to 14,309 in August 1992.

A rapid downturn in speculative investments weakened both demand and asset prices, creating a downward spiral. A World Bank study put the capital loss at ¥200 trillion (42 per cent of GDP in 1991) and more than ¥400 trillion (87 per cent of GDP) in 1992. After the bubble burst, the rate of decline in asset prices from April 1991 to October 1993 was much larger (a decline of 53.6 per cent in stock prices, 27.5 per cent in land prices) than the decline had been from November 1973 to March 1975 (a decline of 31 per cent in stock prices, 6.8 per cent in land prices), in severe stagnation after the first oil crisis.

The self-inflicted bubble burst in the early 1990s and created a larger collapse in the domestic asset market than had been caused by a major external supply shock two decades earlier. Such capital losses in the 1990s negatively affected output growth by dampening business investment and consumer spending.[17]

The model-based simulations in the above study showed that other things being equal, 25 per cent decline in stock prices will reduce Japanese GDP by 0.05 per cent in the first year in real terms and 0.16 per cent by the third year at all levels. A 25 per cent decline in land prices is estimated to have reduced Japan's real GDP by 0.4 per cent in the first year and 1.5 per cent by the third year.

In 1989, Japan's trade in current account surplus posted a heavy decline and the yen weakened against the dollar. Pressure and the prices slowly increased and a new 3 per cent consumption tax was introduced. In May 1989, the BOJ raised the official discount rate 0.75 points for the first time since August 1980 – following nine years of continuing decline – but most of the market participants ignored this increase since there was considerable inertia due to low interest rates. The bank raised the official discount rate twice in October and December 1989 to 4.25 per cent, and thus the feeling in the market was that a watershed had been created in interest rates.

In 1990, the Ministry of Finance asked the banks to contain the growth rate of their real estate-related lending to less than that of total lending. The year 1990 began with a 'triple decline' – decline in stock and bond prices and also in the yen rate. This triple decline triggered a fall in the prices of other assets – land, houses, condominiums and golf club membership.

With the Gulf crisis in August 1990, oil prices shot up; the Nikkei stock average tumbled 48 per cent from its peak, again due to the perception abroad of the vulnerability of the Japanese economy to oil shortages, but mainly due to the hopes of monetary tightening. In late August 1990, the official discount rate (ODR) was raised for the fifth time to 6 per cent with a view to prevent imported inflation from becoming 'home made'.

The prolonged recession

The 'normal' business cycle recession that began in April 1991 was lengthened by compounding structural and external factors. The monetary and fiscal tightening in 1989 led to a normal slowdown in credit creation and business investment. Equity prices began to drop drastically in 1990 and land prices in 1991 due to the quantity restrictions on bank loans to the real estate sector in 1990.

Among the biggest losers in the stock collapse were the financial institutions, which saw the value of their shareholdings greatly reduced after years of high asset growth. Before the collapse, commercial banks effectively used rising stock assets to meet the capital adequacy requirements of the Bank for International Settlements (BIS).

It was reported that the prospects for the big four security firms in Japan – Nomura, Daiwa, Nikko and Yamaichi – fell by more than 60 per cent in 1990 and small firms saw large declines of 80 per cent and more in 1990–91 and 1992; almost every broker except Nomura lost money. Big declines were observed in the volume of trade as the bear market doldrums set in.[18]

On per one estimate, the total capital losses in the Tokyo stock market up to the early months of 1992 were said to be as large as the entire capital valuation of the European stock markets altogether. With their capital base now eroded, many banks had to curtail their lending sharply, with a view to fulfilling the BIS requirements. A temporary recovery in stock prices in the second half of fiscal year 1992 as a result of the government's price-boosting measures made it possible for banks to use their capital gains to write off some business losses. The recovery trend halted in mid-1992 and substantial decline followed afterwards.

Moreover, rapid appreciation of the yen during 1993 lengthened the business cycle downturn (during this period the yen appreciated by more than 20 per cent against the dollar – 125.1–103.7 yen/dollar or by 25 per cent in real effective terms). There was no opportunity for export drive in the economy, but significant import penetration was widely observed of about 15 per cent in relation to GDP in real terms and there was a continuous leak of recovery to the rest of the world.

The burst in asset prices strengthened the yen and higher imports of goods led to the process of disinflation. This was another factor in the long recession that widened the output gap by dampening domestic demand and further deflationary pressure. This disinflation was also caused by supply factors, for example advances in deregulation in the distribution sector, a rapid rise in import penetration and the rise in consumers' price awareness. All these factors lengthened the recession by reducing corporate profits and employment activity. The current business cycle pattern forced several structural adjustments in the corporate sector downturn and such large-scale corporate restructuring led to widespread unemployment, further undermining the consumer demand. All these structural factors produced a pattern of stagnant income generation in the midst of a recovery in industrial production, thus making the short recovery during 1993–95 very fragile. Another rapid yen appreciation during the first six months of 1995 further affected the fragile recovery. Moreover, between December 1994 and September 1995, the yen appreciated by 27 per cent against the US dollar. This led to further serious problems.

The Japanese economy thus made the transition from a 'bubble period' of low interest rates, a strong yen, financial deregulation and overall business optimism, to a recession of high interest rates, a weaker yen, selective restrictions on real estate lending along with widespread pessimism.

Current formation of monetary policy

In the transmission mechanism of monetary policy, several variables play a role. The BOJ experienced difficulty in assessing the growth of the money supply during the period of financial deregulation. One issue was how to implement monetary policy when there was a sharp contrast between flow prices and asset prices. Moreover, it was also very difficult for the BOJ to correct external balance compatibility with other policy objectives.

While price stability is the final objective of monetary policy, the BOJ used the consumer price index (CPI) and wholesale price index (WPI) as pilot indicators to judge inflation. Of course, the experience of the 1980s led several researchers to question the implementation of monetary policy, focusing on general flow prices shown by the CPI and WPI in the late 1980s. The BOJ maintained an expansionary monetary policy due to the stability of general flow prices and several weaknesses of economic activities; the shift to lower growth reduced the corporate demand for credit and resulted in a sharp decline in overborrowing. The large-scale issue of government bonds, necessary to finance the accommodating monetary and economic policies, stimulated the development of the security market and decreased the predominance of indirect finance. The decline in the situation of overborrowing and indirect finance decreased the importance of credit in the monetary policy process.[19]

During the build-up of the speculative bubble, asset prices rose sharply. The BOJ also observed that monetary policy in the late 1980s contributed to asset inflation. The idea of making asset price stabilization an objective is widely disputed, since it is very risky as real factors also play a role.

It was suggested that monetary policy played a critical role in spurring residential construction and business fixed investment. The reduction in the official discount rate in 1986 and 1987 contributed to record low mortgage rates. Residential construction soared by 25 per cent in real terms during fiscal year 1987, with housing starts in 1987 surpassing the USA. Low interest rates also helped to spur business fixed investment which expanded by about 10 per cent during this period.[20]

Japan benefited from wealth effects related to falling interest rates over three years as the capitalization of the Tokyo Exchange more than doubled to ¥400 trillion (US $3.5 trillion), while the value of landholding in Japan rose by an estimate of ¥750 trillion (US $6 trillion). These increases are equal to about 60 per cent and more than 100 per cent respectively of Japanese 1987 GNP which, when combined, may make up the most significant wealth effect that any developed country experienced during the post-war period.

While low interest rate policy was maintained for a fairly long period, the incident of Black Monday on Wall Street in October 1987 was one of the issues that made the BOJ hesitant to raise the discount rate. In this way, euphoria in the financial and real estate markets was created, and similar tendencies in the USA and other developed countries fortified this tendency in Japan like the 'Zeitgeist' (spirit of the age).[21]

As Miyao recently observed, disturbances to the call rate equation are viewed as 'exogenous' monetary policy shocks. With the use of a simple VAR framework to measure effects of monetary policy in Japan, he suggests a possible structural break in the role of monetary policy in the 1990s, since the BOJ's monetary policy always begins with controlling interest rates in short-term money markets. Recent institutional discussions also suggest that the monetary base is 'endogenously' determined under the partially lagged reserve system. These characteristics of the actual operating procedures of the BOJ suggest that the call rate is treated as mostly exogenous and predetermined for the monetary base. The reserve requirement system is known as a mixture of lagged and contemporaneous reserve systems or 'two weeks lagged' and 'two weeks contemporaneous' arrangements in a given calendar month.[22]

Of course, the shift to lower growth reduced the corporate demand for credit and resulted in a sharp decline in overborrowing. The issue of government bonds stimulated the growth of the securities market and decreased the dominance of indirect finance. While the banks absorbed a major share of these bonds, this led to increases in money supply in the economy. The process of financial reform since 1985 reduced the effectiveness of the influence of inter-bank interest rate changes on broad-based lending by banks. The reforms helped in the creation of a more open and non-regulated financial market, with more flexible interest rates, as Okabe observed, 'the formula now employed in Japan is more aptly called a "money focused" monetary policy rather than a monetary targeting policy'.[23]

Moreover Suzuki recently observed, 'the policy attribute of the BOJ is, in my view, neither that of post-Keynesian discretionary fine-tuning nor that of a percent rule; an appropriate term may be "eclectic" gradually'.[24]

Money market interest rate changes

In fact 1981 was the turning point for innovative policy changes; in May 1981 the BOJ began to sell financing bills on the open market to absorb the liquidity surplus. The securities and bills operations are engaged between the BOJ and money-creating financial institutions and as against open market operations; they do not directly influence the money supply. The BOJ uses the security and bills operations (outright purchase of government bonds from financial institutions) as an instrument for creating additional base money in the economy, without disturbing the growth of the money supply.

The main reason for introducing open market operations was the development of open, less regulated financial markets, for example the market for certificates of deposit (1979), the Euro-yen market and introduction of the market for bankers' acceptance (1985), money market certificates (1985), commercial paper (1987), and the Tokyo offshore market (1986). The share of these open markets in the total money market increased significantly until the autumn of 1988, when the volume of the inter-bank market, especially the bills market, shrank as a result of increasing open market rates, compared with relatively stable interest rates in the inter-bank market. The decreasing volume of the inter-bank market reduced the influence of the BOJ on the money market rate and compelled the BOJ to deregulate the interbank market as from November 1988.[25]

The BOJ also observed in several reports that monetary policy in the late 1980s contributed to asset inflation and so a more careful watch would be kept on asset price movements. The fact that several experts disagreed with the idea of making asset price stabilization an objective, underlined their concerns that this commitment was very risky indeed, since monetary policy can explain only a part of the rise in asset prices during the late 1980s.

The BOJ liberalized the interest rate for commercial bills that was regulated earlier (abolition of quotation). Then the tight range of maturity for the collateralized call and bill markets was adjusted in order to realize more fine-tuning in the money markets. The maturity for collateralized calls was changed from overnight to three weeks into overnight to six days, and for bills from one to six months into one week to six months. Thus overlap in maturity between calls and bills was eliminated. In April 1989 the maturity for bills and the uncollateralized money market was extended to one year.

Further, the quantitative restrictions and quotation system for the uncollateralized call market were abolished and the maturity allowed for this market was extended from overnight to three weeks to overnight to six months to reinforce the arbitrage between the inter-bank and open markets. These measures led to doubling of inter-bank market volume during November 1998 to July 1989. As D. Batten recently observed, the November reforms allowed the BOJ to maintain the controllability of short-term interest rates during the ongoing financial reform process.[26]

Before the reforms, inter-bank transactions with a maturity of less than one month were mainly conducted in the call market and not in the bills market. For its bills operations, the BOJ relied on bills with maturities of two or three months. Hence the market players regarded the two-month bill discount rate as a policy target by mid-1988 and sometimes interpreted technical adjustments as being deliberate.[27]

As Suzuki (1989) observed, two and three months' bills operations by the BOJ revealed its interest rate view two or three months ahead. Under the new monetary control regime, the BOJ concentrated on the shortest maturities (overnight call rates) and one to three weeks' bill discount rates and left the rates of longer maturity instruments to move freely as per market expectations.

As for the open market interest rates, the BOJ could influence them through the mechanism of interest rate arbitrage between the inter-bank and open markets, but several other factors, for example differences in expectations and different characteristics of various segments of the open markets, determine open market interest rates. But the declining share of the inter-bank market in the total money market made it more difficult for the BOJ to influence interest rates on the open markets by the use of interest arbitrage. The last decade saw the introduction of an open market policy by the BOJ as an instrument to exert direct influence on the open markets.[28]

The BOJ has used various instruments in its open market policy, for example the sale of FBs with repurchase agreements (first in May 1980), CDs, purchases of CPs with repurchase agreements (first in May 1989) and purchase of TBs with resale agreements (first in January 1990). With a view to facilitate the open market policy of the BOJ, the Ministry of Finance introduced, in August 1989, three-month TBs, promoted development of the secondary market by increasing the number of TB issues from one to two when monthly issue volume exceeds ¥2 trillion, and expanded the issue of TBs in the fiscal year March 1990–91 to ¥9 trillion.

While the BOJ never set a target for any specific monetary aggregates, it has continued to disclose its quarterly projections for M2 + CDs since 1970, following the experience of excess liquidity and high inflation in the early 1970s. In this sense the BOJ has focused more on monetary aggregates since the mid-1970s. The growth rate of M2 +CDs has been brought down since then. In the early 1980s, the rate of inflation was significantly lower and stable.

The open market operations of the BOJ influenced the money supply through various channels. The existence of a direct mechanism has to be mentioned. When the BOJ sells TBs directly to the non-financial sector, the money supply is reduced. The result of these operations is a declining reserve position of the financial institution (decrease of deposits at BOJ), moreover the open market operations have wide-ranging consequences for supply and demand relations on the secondary markets of TBs and also for interest rates on this market. As for these transmission channels, the significant rise during the 1980s of prices of assets such as equities and real estate strengthened the importance of wealth effects.

Since the mid-1980s, doubts were expressed about the usefulness of monetary aggregates as prompted by progress in financial innovations, liberalization and rapid appreciation of the yen. The process of liberalization of interest rates made the effects of interest rate changes on private expenditures (direct channel) and the effects on asset values and on private expenditures (indirect channel) much more significant.

As Royama observed, new short- and long-term prime rate systems and the increased use by banks of funding instruments with money market-related interest rates inspired more effective changes in money market interest rates to lending and in the borrowing behaviour of the non-financial sector.[29]

In the BOJ policy of financial reforms several 'caveats' applying to the interpretation of the money supply since the mid-1980s were mentioned by observers such as Tamura and Nakao.[30] Doubts were expressed about the usefulness of monetary aggregates since the mid-1980s. Due to gradual liberalization of time deposit interest rates, the 'shift in' of funds to, and 'shift out' from, M2 + CDs became more active than before, leading to volatile movements in its growth. M2 + CDs were traditionally regarded as a set of financial assets, which could be used as a means of payment, but this feature also changed over time and hence it was more difficult for the BOJ to make accurate projections for M2 + CDs.

It was suggested that the BOJ never pursued a target for M2 + CDs; its official position has been expressed as 'conducting monetary policy, based on overall judgment that takes account of monetary aggregates as well as other indicators'. But since the late 1980s, the emphasis on M2 + CDs in deciding a policy framework was undermined. But the BOJ still emphasized the stabilization of money growth in the medium term. Hence both the money supply and the exchange rate (yen/dollar) were used as targets by the BOJ. Exchange rate stability and a sustainable external position should not be regarded as the ultimate objective of monetary policies; as convergence of policies of individual countries it is also a prerequisite. The BOJ wanted to achieve the goal of price stability by controlling growth of the money supply and on the other hand, by keeping the yen sufficiently strong against the US dollar to avoid imported inflation. As M. Hutchison observed, the BOJ did not rely fully on the internal track, but also focused systematically on the external track.[31] The increasing emphasis of the BOJ on interest rate management was obvious in the official ending of the 'window guidance' in June 1991, and thereafter the BOJ relied mostly on indirect credit control.

Official discount rate and market interest rate

The policy changes in the past were initiated by a change in the official discount rate, since short-term lending rates were linked to it for several years. At present, the BOJ can influence short-term lending rates in a timely manner through money market operations, even without changing the official discount rate. This is because the lending rates of financial institutions have become more sensitive to money market rates during the period of interest rate liberalization.

While money market rates cannot arbitrarily deviate from the official discount rate, this type of policy measure has influenced policy options and also given more manoeuvrability. Changes in the official discount rate are regarded as an instrument to be used when the BOJ wants to convey changes in monetary policy so that money market rates may be adjusted simultaneously.

The risks of a sharp increase in long-term Japanese interest rates are lower than in the USA, since the policy framework in Japan makes inflation less of a threat than in the USA. Japan also achieved remarkable progress in reducing its once massive government budget deficits to the extent that the currency remains strong. Rises in US dollar commodity prices are tempered in yen terms, and the enhanced competitiveness of exports from dollar-linked NICS in South Asia also helps to control inflationary pressures.

The peak of this economic boom was reached around April 1991 when the economy began to decline and continued the recession. The ODR was raised five times from 3.25 to 6 per cent between May 1989 and August 1990 to control overheating of the economy. In the late 1980s, private sector investment in production infrastructure was very vigorous, with 4.5 per cent increase in 1987, 17 per cent in 1988, 15 per cent in 1989 and 13 per cent in 1990, thus showing slow effects of changes in the official discount rate, under high liquidity in the economy.

But warnings in the latter part of 1989 did not influence the investment decisions of the BOJ in 1990. None except *The Economist* gave warning signals against this euphoria. The BOJ raised the discount rate in May 1989 to 3.25 per cent. The then Minister of Finance, R. Hashimoto, opposed this increase. The change of governorship of the BOJ in December 1989 helped the bank to raise the interest rate on its own initiative. The MOF was not happy with this increase, due to pressures from the US government. Under these boom conditions, the markets for the first time experienced the liberalization, largely supported by abundance of money; they simply went on to play a go–go game.

This aggressive capital investment was supported by the 'new' money created in the capital market at a low cost, due to the wide feeling that average growth rate of 5 per cent achieved during these five boom years showed true potential for growth in the future as well. The overcapacity present in several sectors was created from this distortion of reality. In the early 1990s, government tried four times to stimulate the economy with a total amount of $450 billion that included public investment for 160 billion and the tax cuts of 55 billion. But this did not produce the expected results, because the stock adjustment of equipment investment took a very long time; moreover, the yen showed upward tendencies in the early 1990s.

The first stimulus that mobilized during this time was larger than that after the Plaza Accord; in the earlier package, the total amount was ¥15 trillion that induced public investment of ¥7.5 trillion and tax cuts of ¥1 trillion. While in 1987, public investment growth rate on a GDP basis was 9.5 per cent, this time it was 16.7 per cent in 1992 and 14.5 per cent in 1993. The fiscal balance of Japan was not so inadequate in the past, if the surplus of the social security account is included. The OECD forecast was that Japan would have a deficit of 2.4 per cent of GDP in 1995, even if the social security account were included. The recent hard line of the Ministry of Finance was based on such a forecast. Hence the issues of trade surplus, a two-tier price mechanism between tradable and non-tradable goods, government regulations, the iron triangle among the politicians, bureaucrats and industries and the volatility of the yen rate, were still on the table.[32]

Sorting out financial mess of bad loans

The banking system in the early 1990s was facing several problems; securitization or disintermediation caused corporate clients to leave the banks and move to capital markets. Real estate financing was a new growing area; its financing replaced the declining corporate credits. Due to the increase in real estate values, the value of its collateral increased during this 'bubble' period. The banks and other non-bank institutions found that more credit could be extended on the basis of this more valuable collateral. Banks gave credit aggressively for 100 per cent collateral value due to their belief that the real estate price would rise indefinitely, which turned out to be a mere myth. The present value of several commercial buildings in large cities is 30–45 per cent lower than their values during the peak of the bubble. Some of the loans were caught by this decline in the value of collateral; the non-performing assets of banks were mostly in this sector, as real estate loans accounted for up to 20 per cent or more of total Japanese bank lending.[33]

These banking troubles were the legacy of the bursting of the share and property market bubble in 1991, followed by recession for several years. For these bad loans of banks, cooperative and housing finance companies, the official estimate of bad debts by mid-1995 was about ¥40 trillion ($400 billion). The amount of non-performing loans reported by the Mitsubishi Bank and Bank of Tokyo to the US authority, based on the US standard, was 2.5 times larger than that reported in Japan. The banks include only subsidiaries with more than 50 per cent stock holdings and related companies with 20–50 per cent stock holdings in their accounts for disclosure of their balance sheets: this excludes the coverage of non-bank financial institutions, mobilized by banks during the bubble period. Hence the official estimates of 'bad' loans were regarded as a 'lower' bound.

The MOF disclosed that as at the end of September 1992, the bad loans of the 21 leading Japanese banks (11 city banks, 3 long-term banks and 7 trust banks) amounted to ¥12,300 billion ($100 billion) as compared to ¥8000 billion ($64 billion) six months earlier. The accepted norm is that loans are regarded as non-performing when debtors are bankrupt and there is no possibility of recovering their capital or when they have not paid interest for six months.

As per MOF estimates, bad loans held by deposit-taking financial institutions at the end of September 1995 were ¥37.4 trillion. This figure does not include bad debts held by financial institutions already bankrupt, for example Cosmo Credit Union, Hyogo Bank and Kazoo Credit Union. A popular estimate of bad loans of these banks ran up to ¥30,000 billion ($240 billion). These figures do not include the troubled loans given by leading banks to regional banks and to non-bank affiliates, for example property finance corporations. In fact these banks reportedly lent ¥80,000 billion ($640) billion to their affiliating corporations who lent it to property developers (Tables 1.1 and 1.2).

While non-performing loans were loans to borrowers in legal bankruptcy, the 'restructured' loans were those for which interest was reduced to the level of the official discount rate. The restructured loans by different groups of institutions and their ratio to total loans extended at the end of September 1995 are given in Table 1.3.

Table 1.1 Details of bad loans (end of Sept. 1995, ¥100 million)

	*21 major banks**	*Other institutions†*	*Total*
Non-performing loans‡	129,710	114,590	244,300
Covered by collateral§	47,993	42,398	90,390
Covered by special reserve account	48,820	20,770	69,590
Unresolved	32,897	51,422	84,320 (A)
Restructured loans¶	103,890	25,710	129,600
Restructured loans except loans to 'Jusens'″	–	–	68,480
Normalized**	–	–	34,240
Covered by collateral§	–	–	12,669
To be non-performing	–	–	21,570 (B)
Restructured loans to 'Jusens'	–	–	61,120
Total bad loans	233,600	140,300	373,900
Assets possibly to be turned into losses held by 'Jusens'			77,000 (C)

Sum of 'unresolved amount' for deposit-taking financial institutions (A+B+C): 182,890.
* City banks, long-term credit banks and trust banks.
† Regional banks and other deposit-taking financial institutions.
‡ Loans to borrowers in legal bankruptcy and past due loans.
§ Covering rate is estimated to be 37%.
¶ Loans for which interest has been reduced to a level below the official discount rate.
″ Housing loan companies.
** 50% of restructured loans is expected to be normalized (except loans to 'Jusens').
Source: Ministry of Finance.

Table 1.2 Bad loans held by deposit-taking financial institutions (end of Sept. 1995, ¥100 million)

	Total	*Bad loans*		*Allowance for doubtful debts*	
		*Non-performing loans**	*Restructured loans†*	*Total*	*Special reserve account*
21 major banks	233,600	129,710	103,890	61,670	48,820
City banks	130,940	80,580	50,360	41,790	32,730
Long-term credit banks	39,700	21,160	18,540	10,380	8,420
Trust banks	62,960	27,970	34,990	9,500	7,670
Regional banks	77,350	54,960	22,390	18,680	12,840
Regional banks I	49,460	32,880	16,580	12,680	8,450
Regional banks II	27,890	22,080	5,810	6,000	4,390
Other financial institutions	62,950	59,630	3,320	15,180	7,930
Total	373,900	244,300	129,600	95,530	69,590

* Loans to borrowers in legal bankruptcy and past due loans.
† Loans for which interest has been reduced to a level below the official discount rate.
Source: Ministry of Finance.

Table 1.3 Ratio of restructured loans to total loans (end of Sept. 1995, ¥100 million)

	Total assets	*Total loans (A)*	*Restructured loans (B)**	*B/A (%)*
21 major banks	7,704,790	3,906,220	103,890	2.66
City banks	4,322,990	2,746,130	50,360	1.83
Long-term credit banks	873,290	545,290	18,540	3.40
Trust banks	2,508,510	614,800	34,990	5.69
Regional banks	2,681,600	1,845,830	22,390	1.21
Regional banks I	1,992,540	1,335,450	16,580	1.24
Regional banks II	689,060	510,380	5,810	1.14
Other financial institutions	2,638,920	1,291,080	3,320	0.26
Total	13,025,310	7,043,130	129,600	1.84

* Loans for which interest has been reduced to a level below the official discount rate.
Source: Ministry of Finance.

Of 21 major banks, trust banks as a whole showed very high restructured loans for total loans ratio of 5.7 per cent, compared to 1.8 per cent among city banks and 3.4 per cent among long-term credit banks.

For the stock of non-performing loans, it was reported that about 37 per cent of the total amount is covered by collateral; special loan-loss reserve accounts cover another 28 per cent. So 'unresolved' loss is around ¥8.5 trillion, about one-third of the ¥25 trillion of bad loans reported by deposit-taking financial institutions. The coverage rates of bad loans are estimated by an MOF survey of all banks in Japan and by the price of credits purchased by the Cooperative Credit Purchasing Corporation Ltd (Saiken Kaitori Kiko). At the end of March 1995, the average ratio of covered bad loans to total bad debts was about 40 per cent in both estimates.

As for the stock of 'restructured' loans, except for those made to (Ju-Sens) housing loan firms, half the amount (¥3.5 trillion) was to be normalized and 37 per cent covered by collateral and the potential loss projected at about ¥2.1 trillion. In the event that all the bad loans made by Jusens were attributed to parent banks as loan losses, they would amount to about ¥7.5 trillion. The total of non-covered bad loans to be dealt by deposit-taking institutions was put at ¥18.3 trillion ($183 billion). The official estimates of bad loans were regarded as very low due to the wide belief that these loans were under-reported, and estimates of bad debts were put at ¥50–100 trillion ($50 billion–$1 trillion).[34]

Table 1.4 Profits of deposit-taking financial institutions (first half of fiscal year 1995, ¥100 million)

	Operating profits	*Ordinary profits*	*Net profits*	*Latent gains of listed securities*
Major 21 banks	24,110	5,710	2,490	128,340
City banks	18,100	4,550	1,960	80,960
Long-term credit banks	3,270	620	290	25,040
Trust banks	2,740	540	240	22,340
Regional banks	9,610	5,020	2,200	59,090
Regional banks I	7,010	3,950	1,750	50,710
Regional banks II	2,600	1,070	450	8,380
Other financial institutions	7,460	–	–	15,950
Total	41,180	–	–	203,380

Source: Ministry of Finance.

On 28 August 1992 the government announced a comprehensive package of measures. This stimulus package amounting to ¥10,700 billion ($86 billion) or 2.2 per cent of GNP contained about ¥8600 billion earmarked for public investment projects, including procurement of land for public works projects.

A supplementary budget was necessary to implement some parts of the package. The long dispute between the ruling Liberal Democratic Party and the Opposition delayed approval until 10 December 1992. With a view to giving further impetus, the government announced on 13 April 1993 another package of ¥13,200 billion ($116 billion) or 2.8 per cent of GNP, only two weeks after the 1993 budget had been adopted. The new package was almost the same as the previous ones. The coalition government announced in September a ¥6150 billion ($59 billion) package for infrastructure spending, business loans and deregulation measures.

It was suggested that by mid-1995 about 30–40 per cent of total bad loans were already covered with accelerated transfers to loan-loss reserves and by liquidation through the CCPC, and banks' operating profits began to improve due to widening interest spread, created by several cuts in policy rates. Through seven stages, the discount rate was reduced from 6 to 1.75 per cent and another cut announced in October 1993 by 0.75 per cent when the rate was 1.75 per cent (Tables 1.4–1.6).

The MOF supported lowering the discount rate, since this would brighten the climate and also reduce the imperative to lessen the tax.

Table 1.5 Trends in non-performing loans held by the 21 major banks* (trillion yen)

	Fiscal year				
	1991	*1992*	*1993*	*1994*	*1995*†
Operating profits	2.4	3.2	3.2	2.8	2.4
Losses from disposal of non-performing loans of which:	0.7	1.6	4.1	5.5	2.0
Transfer to special reserve account‡	0.5	1.1	1.7	2.4	0.8
Losses from transfer to CCPC§	–	0.2	1.9	2.1	0.8
Non-performing loans¶	approx. 8.0	12.8	13.6	12.5	13.0
(Ratio to total assets, %) of which:	(1.13)	(1.93)	(2.09)	(1.96)	(1.68)
Unresolved amount	n.a.	5.8	5.1	3.2	3.3

* City banks, long-term credit banks and trust banks.
† First half of fiscal year 1995.
‡ Including ordinary redemption.
§ Cooperative Credit Purchasing Company Ltd.
¶ Loans to borrowers in legal bankruptcy and past due loans, end of fiscal year.
Source: Ministry of Finance.

But others argued that any shortfall in government revenue due to a cut in income tax could be financed either by an increase in consumption tax or an issue of deficit loans. As the OECD observed, a strong yen and declining inflation along with still weak land prices during 1993 provided the opportunity to give additional stimulus, without the risk of recreating the speculative bubble which accompanied the previous phase of monetary relaxation.[35]

The Economic Planning Agency announced prematurely in June 1993 that the Japanese economy had bottomed out. But it turned out that several events – large-scale business scandals of major construction companies, rapid exchange rate fluctuations, an unseasonably wet cold summer that affected the agricultural sector, many other natural disasters, for example earthquakes and typhoons, and political uncertainty of the new coalition government – would prolong the recession.[36]

Continuing negative effects of bad loans

In order to tackle the problems created by bad loans by banks, cooperatives and housing finance companies, the government set up several agencies such as the Cooperative Credit Purchase Company,

Table 1.6 Risk asset ratio of banks (end of fiscal year, the number of banks, numbers in parentheses, are as of the end of fiscal year 1993)*

%	Fiscal year			City banks	Long-term credit banks	Trust banks I	Regional banks I	Regional banks II
	1992	*1993*	*1994*†					
Average	9.30	9.71	9.03	8.87(9.68)	8.76(9.25)	9.38(10.47)	9.45(9.78)	8.68(9.12)
Over 11	1	2	1	0(0)	0(0)	0(0)	1(2)	0(0)
10–11	8	25	10	1(1)	0(0)	1(7)	8(17)	0(0)
9–10	52	45	40	2(10)	1(3)	4(0)	28(25)	5(7)
8–9	28	17	36	8(0)	2(0)	2(0)	18(12)	6(5)
Under 8	1	0	1	0(0)	0(0)	0(0)	0(0)	1(0)
Total	90	89	88	11(11)	3(3)	7(7)	55(56)	12(12)

* Banks that adopt the BIS criterion (8%).
† Based on a prompt report.
Source: Bank of Japan.

the Resolution and Collection Bank and the Housing Loans Administration.[37] Also the government tried to stimulate effective demand by fiscal and monetary policy measures – a balance sheet adjustment through economic development. But the performance of the economy during 1992–94 was so poor that it hardly affected the scenario.[38]

The process of dealing with these problem loans was very slow indeed. The government then tried to help the financial institutions in writing off the bad loans by widening the interest spread and thus creating a profit margin for lending operations along with the asset operations by official funds in support of equity prices.

Several observers held that it was the 'expected' capital gains, rather than dividend yield, that motivated these equity acquisitions. It was reported that the dividend yields of Japanese stocks were traditionally low, on average –1.2 per cent during 1980–86 and 0.5 per cent in 1988–92.[39]

A wider spread helped the banking sector to write off bad debts out of increased operating profits. From a macro point of view, the overall credit crunch in the economy continued for several years. As Otsubo suggested, even if the increased spread persisted and banks continued to pay off bad loans at the rate prevailing in 1995, financial institutions might not be able to wipe out a majority of bad debts before the turn of the century. The recent downgrading of Japanese financial institutions would raise their funding costs and narrow the spreads: while the growth in loans and discount extended by the banking sector were stagnant during 1995–96, this suggested a year-on-year growth of less than 1 per cent, thus dragging the growth of money stock that was increasing at about 3 per cent a year. Hence the financial sector had hardly been playing its core role of financial intermediation for credit creation during the last several years. Thus growth in the stock of 'high powered' money was offset by a decline in the money multiplier.[40]

Hence a resumption of consumption and investment expenditures in the economy was adversely affected, leading to a downward shift in the path of capital accumulation, along with more distortions in income distribution in the economy. In a report the EPA stimulated negative effects of the widened interest spreads. Assuming that a long-term interest rate, relevant for consumption, housing investment and plant/equipment investment decisions, rises in line with the postulated increase in the banks' lending rate, it was observed that an increase in spread of 0.5 percentage point lowered the real GDP by 0.14 per cent compared to the base case in the first year and by 0.41 per cent by the third year.[41]

The MOF suggested the idea of liquidating the collateral for bad loans and disclosing the amount of those loans held by financial institutions on a periodic basis. Thus the banks urged for a bail-out plan, modelled on the US government's rescue operations for the savings and loan industry. The idea was criticized by non-financial institutions, as it amounted to giving away taxpayers' money to these institutions. The original scheme for the CCPC as a private entity was initially capitalized at ¥8 billion ($64 million), the bulk of which was paid by the 21 leading banks.

This institution was envisaged as purchasing non-performing loans, rather than their collateral. Of course, it is the non-performing loans, rather than their collateralized assets, that the institutions will purchase. As far as banks are concerned, the sale transaction is a swap of assets between a bad debt of the original borrower and a good debt of the new institution. A fairly large portion of this (about 50 per cent) will be credited against corporate tax, to be paid to the government. The collateralized assets could be sold by the original debtors and their proceeds passed on to the CCPC, which would pass them on to the banks as debt repayment. It is not clear what should be done with the loans not sold by the end of the 10-year period. Hence banks themselves will lend to the new institutions to finance purchase of their own bad assets.

One advantage of this mechanism lies in the administrative concession of the government that allows banks to bypass Japan's slow foreclosure process and to realize immediate losses on bad debts. This might generate quick tax write-offs for lenders in difficulties.

It was suggested that the vigorous growth of Japan, as well as *keiretsu* linkage, through which non-performing loans were handled rather discreetly, spared the country from forming a secondary market for non-performing assets. The plan also includes a small organization to evaluate bad loans, besides the discount to be paid by the CCPC for these bad loans. This Price Appraisal Committee consists of neutral third parties, for example certified tax accountants and real estate appraisal. A general understanding was reported between the major participating banks and the MOF that the collateral will be valued generously, so as to provide an artificial floor for the property market.

Regulatory response

On 18 August 1992 the government announced a temporary rule change that allowed corporations to defer reporting stock-portfolio losses until the end of the fiscal year (March 1993); permitted other accounting innovations that conceal the impact of stock price and land price declines on reported assets; allowed banks not to report interest concessions as taxable income; directed the postal life insurance system to support the stock markets via funds provided to trust banks and sales of government-held shares of Nippon T and T and Japan National Railways and also used 'administrative guidance' to encourage institutional purchases of equities and discourage institutional sales of equities.[42]

The suggestion was made that the CCPC transactions involve direct use of public funds. Moreover, the repayments of loans provided to the CCPC were not guaranteed. No 'new' financing was involved in the above transactions. But if the burden was to be shifted to the general public, then a case could be made that public funds are being spent for bank rescue operations. Really the CCPC was set up to provide accelerated tax benefits to large banks without requiring them to write off losses directly. The banks were required to lend to the CCPC an amount equivalent to the value of their assets; if the assets were finally sold to the market from the CCPC with losses, banks would be held responsible for the losses.

This new arrangement did not require transfer of collateral ownership from the original debtors to the banks or the CCPC. It was difficult to speculate to what extent the property sector would be revitalized by CCPC operations. As far as Japanese banking regulations are concerned, all banks must hold tax-deductible loss reserves equal to 0.3 per cent of their total loans, and any amount of reserves beyond this limit was subject to income tax.[43]

It is not certain what would happen if a large portion of debt were not repaid to the CCPC; one possibility is that the domino effect would operate in a way that the CCPC would default its debts to the bank creditors in 5–10 years. Moreover, it was not clear where the responsibility for liquidating the collateral lies. The original banks may not wish to hold on to it, so long as the real estate market remains depressed.

It was also reported that several major real estate corporations were planning to create an institution to purchase collateralized real estate. It was envisaged that the collateral purchasing company, financed by property firms, would buy some of the collateralized properties for the loans purchased by the CCPC.[44]

As Leadbeater tersely observed, the new plan failed to address the issue of those non-bank financial institutions that are independent of major banks, which were very exposed in the real estate sector. As at the beginning of 1993, the non-banks (whether affiliated or not) and commercial banks had loans worth about ¥98,000 billion ($900 billion) and about 40 per cent of them were in the real estate industry.[45]

Moreover new institutions may operate exclusively as a bail-out for the major banks, leaving weaker banks insolvent, and hence many second-tier regional banks were doomed to disappear during the 1990s. For this likely structural transformation during the 1990s, the issue of bad loans was one important factor. Another factor in the current financial reform movement stemming from the Financial Reforms bill adopted by the National Diet in June 1992, was aimed at easing the segmentation of the Japanese financial system, which allowed the banks to engage in the securities business through subsidiaries.

A temporary recovery of the stock market in the second half of fiscal year 1993 provided banks with windfall capital gains that could be used as a source of financing loans to the CCPC. In several cases, the debtors wishing to liquidate their collateralized properties were not allowed to do so, as their creditor banks feared the properties were too underpriced to cover their debts.[46]

Hence the focus of the CCPC was on those bad loans collateralized by real estate. It was reported, during several weeks prior to the end of March 1993, that the first round of purchases were for 229 loans from those banks which wanted to shore up profits by the end of fiscal year 1992, with a face value totalling ¥682 billion ($6.2 billion) at a discount of 33.3. These purchases amounted to a mere 5.5 per cent of the officially announced total of non-performing debts held by the 21 leading banks in September 1992. Since the qualities of purchased loans were generally good, the discount rate was rather small and banks were able to remove the loans from their books and write off a small loss. As at the end of March 1993, bad loans of the 21 leading banks amounted to ¥12,775 billion ($116 billion), a 4 per cent increase in yen terms over six months.[47]

As Hugh Patrick recently observed, the harsh reality is that every big bank and indeed most other deposit-taking institutions have had serious bad loan difficulties. These range from loans to companies gone bankrupt, non-performing loans in which interest and principal payments are unpaid and substantially past due, loans which have been restructured at highly preferential low-interest rates and loans which are being serviced, but future payments are in doubt. Banks that have lent in urban areas, for example Tokyo and Osaka, have been most hard hit.[48]

While attempts to identify the scale of the problem are hampered by lack of disclosure, the first official estimate (March 1992) of 'bad' loans was not produced until October 1992, banks being asked to disclose data from the end of 1993. The coverage of data was extended to embrace all Japanese deposit-taking intermediaries – city banks, long-term credit banks, trust banks, regional banks and cooperatives. Private estimates of actual bad loans were substantially greater than the amounts announced by the banks and the MOF.[49]

The restructured loans on which interest was reduced began to feature in the data in September 1995. These changes improved the transparency of reporting; undisclosed contingent exposures, arising from the main banks and the *keiretsu* relationships, still remain a continuing source of concern, as does the decision to allow banks with effect from end March 1998 to value their securities holdings using either the traditional lower of cost or market valuation convention or acquisition cost.[50]

Of course, the stock price is crucial to banks, as their equity assets or their capital gains could be sold to raise money for loans to the CCPC. According to one estimate, it is 19,000, or above what the Nikkei stock average must maintain itself at to allow financial institutions to generate capital gains to recover 'bad' loans on a continual basis, without causing overall losses.[51]

But the recent performance was below this threshold and would make the scheme unworkable; for the fiscal year ending March 1994, upward revaluation of the grossly undervalued price of real estate assets held by banks was suggested as a one-off scheme. Stock market equity, one component of the portfolio, made a remarkable recovery in the second half of fiscal year 1993. This was caused by the government's stock-buying measures. The MOF instructed banks not to sell their stock market securities as a means of shoring up profits to the end of the mid-year accounting period (September 1992), as well as that of the next year, March 1993. Hence as long as overall prospects are uncertain, government intervention alone will not bring about a stable recovery in the securities market.

The emergency measures designed to reduce the pressure on banks' balance sheets, by providing them with a way to avoid appraisal losses at the end of the financial year, because of the fall in stock market prices, has backfired on the authorities.[52] Moreover, the list of restructured banks excluded also differs from year to year, and the picture was clouded by banks' loan exposure to the 'Jusen' housing loan companies, which dropped out of the figures in September 1996 on resolution of the Jusen crisis that involved the affected banks, collectively transferring ¥3686 billion to special accounts for loan-loss write-offs by end March 1996 and abandoning ¥614 billion of such loans outstanding.

Over time the disclosed amounts of bad loans have increased in the late 1990s, as even after write-offs, private estimates of actual bad loans have been substantially greater than amounts announced by the banks and the MOF. Based on the figures disclosed by the city banks, long-term credit banks and trust banks, 'bad' loans for the industry as a whole peaked at end September 1994, but restructured loans did not feature in the data, since data were not disclosed for the whole of the banking industry. Since November 1995, following the MOF's examination of banks' bad debts and restructured loans during the autumn of 1995, the total of bad loans outstanding fell from ¥38 trillion at end September 1995 to over ¥28 trillion at end September 1997 – a fall from just over 5 per cent of total loans to under 4 per cent. More important are the figures of estimates of 'unrecoverable' and 'unprovided for' loans, which fell from ¥18.6 trillion to ¥4.3 trillion over the same period.[53]

In autumn 1997 the MOF shocked the world with its estimates of bad and troubled loans – ¥76.7 trillion, triple the previous estimates and 12 per cent of total bank loans and credits, 12 per cent of loans of big banks, 10 per cent of loans of regional banks and 14 per cent of loans of second-tier banks. This reflected a new inclusion in the definition of bad loans – a category of loans currently being serviced, but in potential future danger. As a recent BOJ study estimated, about 85 per cent of such loans continued to be serviced, but future estimates depend on corporate borrower performance, in turn dependent upon the overall performance of the economy.

Only in 1997 did the regional banks and credit associations first disclose their bad loans. Over time, the definition of bad loans has become more comprehensive and clear, now approaching the US SEC definition. Each bank estimates its own bad loans; the presumption is that estimates of stronger banks are closer to reality than those of weaker banks. However, when weak banks collapsed later, audits revealed that the actual bad loans situation was far worse than the banks had announced even a short time earlier.[54]

Of course, the overall figures marked significant differences between industry types (city banks, long-term credit banks, trust banks, etc.). And within each group between individual institutions, when data were published by industry grouping for the period ending September 1995 (the overall figure of 5.4 per cent for proportion of total bad loans), contrasted with figures of 4.9, 7.3, 10.2, 3.7, 5.5 and 5 per cent for city banks, long-term credit banks, trust banks, regional banks and second-tier regional banks and cooperate groupings respectively.

In this scenario, three facts are important:

1. Most of the loans have some form of collateral backing of real estate. The issue is disposal value of the collateral. The actual losses banks have taken and will take are much less than the estimates of banks' bad loans.
2. It has been really very difficult for tax and legal reasons for a bank to actually write off a loan as bad. Most of the write-offs are in the form of 'provisioning' – increased allocation of profits and capital to bank loan-loss reserves.
3. While small until 1995, over time the cumulative amounts of actual write-offs have been huge and impressive. The 21 big banks between 1992 and 1998 wrote off ¥42.82 trillion, most of it (69 per cent) in the last three years and ¥12.14 trillion (29 per cent) in 1998 alone.[55] This was financed from operations projects, realized capital gains on securities holdings and modest capital accounts transferred. The immensity of this write-off is apparent in comparison with the amount of capital these banks had at their peak (March 1994) of ¥22.15 trillion.[56]

Hence due to the new disclosure rules in 1998, the decline in the South-East Asian countries, along with a shortfall in the local stock market as it ended the fiscal year 1997 below the 15,000 level, around which it remained in 2000 as well, compounded the financial problems. Despite making collective bad debt disposals for about ¥10.7 trillion and recording a collective pre-parent loss of ¥4.5 trillion, the top 18 banks still face an uphill battle to dispose of remaining bad debts, now estimated at ¥22 trillion during the next few years. Of special concern is their exposure in Asia, with estimates of non-performing loans ranging from ¥3 trillion to ¥6 trillion, up to half of which may necessitate a total write-off.[57]

The consensus view

The Japanese problem as defined in the media foresees a systematic financial sector crisis triggered by the collapse of a number of financial institutions that, in turn, will be caused by a lack of explicit policies to rescue banks from bad debts. In Japan, this anticipated crisis is expected to deepen and lengthen the recession.

The consensus view in the new century is that the Japanese problem only represents a worst case scenario and is not the most likely of possible outcomes. As the Japanese financial system is operating normally without any systematic credit crisis, the only problem is a large stock of 'bad loans' and a lack of consensus-based policy actions by the authorities. It is likely that the authorities will eventually be forced to mobilize ¥5–10 trillion ($50–100 billion) of public funds to protect deposits and loans in small financial institutions and Jusens. The simulation exercise for public bail-out assumes the size of the bail-out at 2 per cent of GDP, worth about ¥10 trillion ($100 billion) in 1996 currency. Of course, the BOJ has assets to enable it to supply more than sufficient short-term liquidity; on the US side, authorities have already made pre-emptive strikes against possible negative ripple effects by showing their determination to supply short-term equity on demand.[58]

Most likely form of public sector bail-out

Several observers have suggested that a systematic financial crisis is not impossible, if a substantial volume of bad loans had not been reported. Also looming are risks of further devaluation of property values, taken as collateral, and of a possible downturn in the stock market, which could wipe out latent gains. Suggestions have been made that more write-offs of these bad loans should be made against the backbone of an expanding economy, along with introduction of public funds for bail-out of small financial institutions. While there has been no consensus on whether to introduce public funds for a bail-out, it is still worthwhile preparing indicative scenarios, including some involving a type of financial crisis for public bail-out.

The BOJ and the government have been helping these insolvent institutions with special loans or donations from the Deposit Insurance Corporation. The BOJ, as lender of last resort, has also made special loans (Nichigin Tokuyu) to save these institutions over recent years. The size of bail-out ranges from 1.5 per cent of GDP in the UK case to 7 per cent in the Finnish case. In Japan's case bail-out would likely cost more than 2 per cent of GDP or about ¥10 trillion ($100 billion) against estimated ¥18.5 trillion in non-covered bad loans. The failures and bail-outs in the savings and loans (S and L) industry in the USA during the 1980s and early 1990s revealed that total cost to US taxpayers of cleaning up the debacle were estimated in 1991 by the Congressional Budget Office at more than $215 billion.[59]

In 1994, this estimate was lowered to about $150 billion by the same office. The bail-out consisted of the US government issuing implicit guarantees to cover future losses and then funding deposit reimbursements: in the US case, net outlays were financed through an increase in public expenditure and in fiscal deficit.

In November 1997, the government announced new criteria for bad loans and a new definition of the problem according to new criteria. The first category in the new criteria included normal performing loans, and the second included performing loans with some concerns for the future; the third and fourth categories were non-performing loans. The sum of the second, third and fourth categories amounted to ¥79 trillion. During 1994–97 banks used various measures to write off non-performing loans. Japanese banks realized *fukumi* to write off non-performing loans, besides using current profits. Banks also realized some of the gains from the falling stock prices of the 1990s to help write off bad loan losses.[60]

As Otsubo and Tsutsumi observed, the economic costs of a crisis in Japan will really be large. Growth averaged only about 1 per cent p.a. during 1991–99, with real long-term interest rates averaging a little below US rates and the real value of the yen surging in this period. The fiscal costs of restructuring would add to the structural deficit that was built up after long effort to combat the recession. This would add to the problem of a less favourable starting point from where to confront the problems associated with population ageing in the new century.[61]

When the yen appreciated to ¥80 per US dollar, export industries were widely affected. The stock price index declined below the 15,000 mark. Moreover, banks' *fukumi* declined and affected their balance sheets. Bank lending declined, adversely affecting several real sectors; the official discount rate was cut from 1.7 per cent at the beginning of the year to 0.5 per cent in June and a fiscal stimulus package was announced. Several researchers found the policy response of the government was 'long' delayed and 'less' than adequate. It was hoped that by solving the 'Jusen' problem by policing the burden on the banks, the major part of bad loans had been solved.

The authorities held that none of the 21 largest banks would be allowed to go bust. But the government would not be able to maintain the 'too big to fail' policy further and moral hazard among bank officials became prevalent after this policy was announced. By denying the seriousness of the problem, the government could not prepare a scheme that would inject fiscal funds to solve the problem with the help of the Deposit Insurance Corporation. This made it impossible to act decisively. All these mistakes prolonged the 'bad' loan problem and it finally erupted into a full-blown crisis in November 1997.[62]

Scenario analyses in recent research show that 'negative' domestic and foreign ripple effects could largely be contained and subsequent business cycle oscillations mitigated, once the authorities stepped in to supply short-term liquidity (with the government issuing bonds to support the operations), sufficient to keep short-term interest rates from rising in the initial years of the crisis. Even without the trigger of a financial sector crisis, coping with financial sector issues will leave the Japanese economy in a 'less' favourable position to confront the problems due to an ageing population.

2
Japanese Financial Deregulation – the 1980s

If miracles fill us with wonder, they can also breed envy when their beneficial glow falls outside our reach. Economic miracles are no exception. For Japan, this fall from grace inspired several observers to re-evaluate whether the Japanese approach to the economy is really distinctive or whether it has all along followed traditional wisdom. Does one gain a better grasp of what drives the Japanese economy by focusing on the ways it differs from textbook economic approaches? Of course, research concerns are not really unaffected by several burning problems in the economy. The fact remains that the rising economic power of Japan during the 1980s encouraged research into that sustained era of growth. If Japan could succeed against more developed economic powers, they must be doing something radically 'different' from their Western competitors.

For answers here, we must see how the Japanese financial economy developed during the last two decades, since banking and monetary policy played a significant role in determining the pace of financial liberalization during the late 1980s. For several years, Japan generated unprecedented trade and current account surpluses, extensively liberalized its international financial transactions and emerged as a major investor around the world. It was a bank-based system with underdeveloped stock and bond markets. Risk-averse savers had few alternatives to holding savings as deposits and rapidly growing corporations had to rely heavily on bank loans to finance their very high rates of fixed investments. The system was stable in that there were no new entries and virtually no failures or other exits.

As Hugh Patrick recently observed, the essence of the regulatory regime was to guarantee that banks could not fail; this was achieved by interest rate controls, with wide spreads between deposit and loan rates so that all financial institutions made profits.[1] Moreover, a 'convoy' system was maintained whereby the assets of all banks grew at about the same rate and in this system, interest rate competition was not allowed and other forms of competition were muted. Hence the tradition at the MOF afforded financial institutions the opportunity to serve the long-run interests of the Japanese economy, rather than allowing them individually to pursue more defined paths of self-interest. The strength of the Japanese financial system was thought to be the MOF's willingness 'directly' to guide financial institutions which strayed from desired activities. The financial system was not left to the vagaries of the market but, instead, was buttressed by various bureaucratic corrections.

The development of the main bank system epitomized the stereotype of large bank–big business relations. Although, in practice, most of the banking system's credit was lent to medium-sized and small business, the main bank system overcame problems of inadequate information and difficulties in analysing the new projects monitored, embodied in the process of rapid post-war development.[2]

The main bank monitored its main industrial clients, maintained de facto lending syndicates with them and had a special responsibility to provide financial and managerial assistance in times of trouble. While all big banks had some main bank clients, the major main banks were Mitsubishi, Sumitomo, Mitsui, Fuji, Sanwa and Dai-ichi-Kangyo, notably with relationships with their respective *keiretsu* members, and the Industrial Bank of Japan, with a wide range of main bank relationships.

While the BOJ targets short-run interest rates, this policy proved insufficient to control speculation in risky assets. As the experience after the mid-1980s showed, a single-minded concentration on short-term interest rates was rather misplaced in Japan. As recent researches have shown, Japanese monetary policies and bank regulations are unique to Japan, since the current Japanese banking crisis finds echoes in the US nightmare with its thrift. Perhaps as a result of continuing to operate in an overly cosseted sphere, Japanese financial institutions have lagged behind the West in developing and exploiting new financial instruments.[3]

Several factors in the early 1980s were responsible for growing pressures for reform of the pricing market for government bonds and for growth of the secondary market: for example, significant decline in public sector finances, along with a personal sector surplus. The operating practices in the primary market were put under strain due to the sheer increase in the volume of bonds that the underwriting syndicate of banks and other institutions were being asked to absorb. The build-up of Japanese government debt over the years forced several changes in the relationship between the BOJ and the members of government bond underwriting syndicate. Hence fears were expressed that the BOJ could no longer offer its generous rediscount facilities for government debt, without jeopardizing its ability to exert control. Moreover, 'resale' in the marketplace was prohibited until 1977 and would have resulted in capital losses being incurred due to low yields paid on the bonds.

Since the syndicate members had to hold bonds for a minimum of one year after which the BOJ would purchase them, the increasing budget deficits posed funding problems for the banks and their profitability was also affected due to the increase in the proportion of their investment portfolio held in low-yielding forms. Hence, by minimizing the cost of servicing the debt, government realized that the post-1975 situation would require modification in market procedures. The MOF came under increasing pressure to deregulate the financial system to allow market-determined interest rates, the creation of new financial instruments, the development of a competitive bond market, the breaking down of market segregation and in general, increased competition from all financial institutions and in all financial markets. However, the deregulation process has been steady, but very gradual, beginning in the late 1970s.

As M.J.B. Hall observed, the funding (cash reserve) burden of the banks as the main syndicate members would have to be elevated by making issues direct to general public and non-bank financial intermediaries and by allowing banks to call on the general public. Both measures would help to reduce the adverse impact on bank profitability that would otherwise result.[4]

For several years Japan had been moving to a competitive market-based system of banking and because of efficient markets, equity in regulation and competition was actively promoted. Of course, financial institutions were under great pressure to cut costs, increase efficiency and develop new financial products in order to compete. The government's desire to finance the budget deficits in a non-monetary fashion and to protect the banking system from adverse consequences led to diversification in the types and methods of bond flotations that inspired growth of the secondary market.

The new environment created new kinds of risks, with new opportunities and dangers of taking risks including interest rate risks for assets and liabilities, exchange rate risks and credit risks, since companies were also in a more competitive environment. In fact the costs and benefits of capital market finance versus bank finance are very much shaped by the realities of imperfect information, cost of generating information and principal–agent issues as well as ordinary transaction costs.[5]

The MOF was trying to reform the financial system with a view to eliminating the separation between the securities business and banking business. The freeing-up of long-term yield helped to promote growth of short-term open markets and also to exert more pressure to relax interest rate controls.

The main bank system played an important role in monitoring corporate behaviour and performance. The main banks are constrained from shirking in times of corporate adversity, by the reputation effect in their relationships with other main banks. The inter-bank market provides the BOJ with a primary instrument of monetary policy, by means of sales and purchases of commercial bills. Since the early 1980s, several Japanese corporations chose to rely more on the bonds and direct or indirect equity issues, rather than bank financing, but the Japanese financial system, based on functional separation of various types of financial institutions, has been in a state of transition, along with advances in financial technology; it was widely recognized that the traditional system had outlived its usefulness. Moreover, the internationalization of the Japanese financial system was adopted as a clear policy objective, while the financial markets were freed from formal restrictions on capital flows into and out of Japan, but the administrative guidelines to financial institutions about their activity were influential in redirecting certain transactions into certain areas. The banks were allowed to issue, at market rates, negotiable certificates of deposit (CDs) in 1979 and money market certificates in 1985, subject to restrictions on the amount and maturity of issues; the ceilings on the amount of issues were removed in 1987.

The demands for wider access to alternative sources of funds went hand in hand with a search for higher real returns, as corporate financial management gained in sophistication (the *zaiteck* phenomenon). Further deregulation of financial markets during the early 1980s enabled firms to supplement insurance company financing with bond financing during this period, but the BOJ's practice of window guidance of commercial banks' domestic credit activity persisted until early 1991. Of course, the banking lobby was in full swing following the fall of corporate loan demand and loss of depositors to other institutions, for example the post office, and their instruments offering higher real returns. Such a state of affairs led the banks to demand liberalization of their deposit and interest rates, removal of maturity restrictions on their deposits and power to offer new instruments, on which they could pay competitive rates. They also sought the ability to diversify their customer base which would require removal of constraints on domestic activities for some and on foreign activities for all and additional freedom to allow them to improve risk management.[6]

Of course, new hedging and funding opportunities would have been welcomed by domestic intermediaries operating in Japan, with a view to diversifying portfolio risks.[7] The Foreign Exchange and Foreign Trade Law (December 1980) formalized the principle that all external transactions may be freely carried out, unless otherwise specified. Two measures in the law were crucial: integrating the domestic money market with international money markets, for example authorization for Japanese banks to borrow and lend foreign currencies freely, subject to prudential guidelines, and for Japanese companies to finance themselves abroad through foreign currency denominated loans.

During 1983–84 several measures were taken to reinforce Japanese banks' capability to cope with the strains in world financial markets and prudential guidelines on banks' international banking practices were strengthened. The city banks' subsidiaries were allowed to issue bonds abroad to increase their parent banks' funding source for lending abroad. The Euro-yen lending by Japanese banks was liberalized completely. The yen–dollar swap limits for foreign banks operating in Japan were revised by 20 per cent and the limit on overall foreign exchange positions of foreign banks was doubled to $1 million.[8]

During 1984–85, further changes were implemented, for example abolition of the real demand principle (requirement to undertake trade or securities transactions for forward exchange transactions by residents); introduction of foreign commercial paper and foreign CDs in Japanese markets, elimination of notification requirements on sale of yen-denominated securities, for example government bonds, and relaxation of rules for issue of Euro-yen bonds.

As Allen Frankel and Paul Morgan suggested, the succession of regulatory reforms that followed the introduction of unregulated rates (CDs in 1979) caused the interest costs of banks to become increasingly sensitive to movements in the market interest rates. Of special importance to this change was the 1985 introduction of money market certificates that yield interest rates based on CD rates with a specific formula according to denomination.[9]

The dramatic rise in export of Japanese capital provided a major boost to the securitization movement, which facilitated a rapid increase in off-balance sheet financing and a revival in bond insurance. Of particular interest is the rise of private financial institutions as shareholders of other corporations. In 1985, Japanese investors purchased $59 billion of foreign equity, accounting for three-quarters of the country's capital outflows. Japan was investing its surplus liquidity in negotiable financial instruments and there were no major equity purchases; only $1 billion out of $59.5 billion was invested in overseas equities.

During 1985, the importance of Japanese securities firms increased further and the big four – Nomura, Daiwa, Nikko and Yamaichi – were the top 20 leading managers of fixed interest and convertible Eurobonds, but they did not achieve similar distinction as leaders of floating rate note issues.[10] Japanese securities firms continued to play an active role in recycling Japan's trade surplus and investing surplus savings abroad; for the later half of the 1980s, Japanese banks and securities firms dominated the international financial stage.[11]

Unlike banks in the USA and UK, Japanese banks are legally allowed to own equities of other private corporations (subject to a 5 per cent limit). No doubt, corporate stock ownership has undergone a most dramatic turnaround in Japan – the *keiretsu* banks, insurance companies and non-financial business own each other. The interlocking shareholdings became an effective means of guaranteeing corporate control within the *keiretsu* groups, eliminating any possibility of hostile takeover by foreign investors.[12]

International transactions

For the policy of allowing foreign exchange transactions, the administrative fiat became increasingly costly to administer and a need to simplify the procedures led to the enactment of the December 1980 Foreign Exchange Law. The MOF retained some control in areas crucial to regulation of the domestic market, such as issue of yen-denominated bonds, regulation of unauthorized foreign exchange banks and residential bank accounts abroad. The Euro-yen markets are the markets on which yen-denominated financial assets are traded outside Japan. Trading is conducted through the medium of Euro-currency instruments (Euro-yen deposits, Euro-yen CDs, Euro-yen CP and loans and bonds). The Japanese banks have the largest share in Euro-yen transactions under the framework of the new law. Restrictions on capital flows were further eased, for example abolition of restrictions on the amount of foreign currency (including Euro-yen liabilities) that could be converted into yen assets by the financial institutions (June 1984), easing the requirements for both resident and non-resident firms in the Euro-yen bond market, eliminating withholding tax on Euro-yen bonds for non-residents (April 1985) and allowing the introduction of new types of Euro-yen instruments such as zero-coupon, deep discount and floating rate bonds. The markets flourished in the early 1980s because of the relative advantage they enjoyed vis-à-vis the domestic market; for example, Euro-yen transactions were free from domestic controls such as interest rate controls and legal reserve requirements.

One result of these measures was a growth in the size of the Euro-yen bond market related to the domestic yen-denominated bond market and Euro bonds. The liberalization of international capital transactions made Tokyo an important international banking centre. As far as the non-resident issue of Euro-yen bonds is concerned, the first major development was in March 1979, when foreign governments and international organizations with a previous good record in issuing yen-denominated foreign bonds in Japan were added to the list of institutions eligible to make such issues. The range of eligible issuers was further expanded in December 1984, when foreign private corporations, state and local governments and government agencies were added to the list. Moreover, the guidelines relating to non-resident Euro-yen bond issues were released in line with the May 1984 Joint Group report and the standard for eligibility of the issuer. The non-resident private sector firms with a minimum credit rating of A were unconditionally eligible to make Euro-yen bond issues, just like non-resident public sector bodies.[13]

Further liberalization of issuance eligibility criteria occurred in July 1993 when foreign institutions without a credit rating were allowed to issue Euro-yen bonds. In 1996 the criteria were abolished in respect of non-resident Euro-yen bond issues in Japan; this also applied to resident issues of Euro-yen bonds outside Japan.

These measures led to several new trends in the economy, for example:

1. The financial cost structure responded to regulation of interest rates;
2. Relaxation of business boundaries enabled the firms to forge ties with other firms and set up a bankers' bank, and
3. New financial areas were developed by the firms.

In the early 1990s, the drive was towards reforming Article 65 by allowing the banks and securities firms to enter each others' business through wholly owned subsidiaries.

Other measures were the sanctioning of a diversification in products of foreign bank issues of Euro-yen bonds (June 1986), the introduction of a system of blanket approval (April 1995), the abolition of the lock-up period during which time sale of Euro-yen bonds to Japanese residents is prohibited, and relaxation of eligibility criteria for use of the shelf registration system.

Further measures to stimulate supply were taken in July 1985, when criteria for issue of resident Euro-yen convertible debentures were relaxed. The new system from July 1987 meant that all Japanese companies rated AA and above, with net assets of over ¥55 billion, could unconditionally issue straight Euro-yen bonds by public offer in the Euro-markets. For all other respective residents, and Euro-yen bond issuers, the size-related requirements had to be satisfied.[14]

Since July 1992 the criteria for resident Euro-yen bond issues were further relaxed; the minimum rating requirement for a company to issue yen-denominated convertible bonds was BBB and Japanese companies with a credit rating of A were eligible to issue straight and with warrant Euro-yen bonds. The net asset requirements were eased for other prospective issuers. From January 1996, the issuance eligibility criteria for resident issues of Euro-yen bonds outside Japan were completely abolished.

Liberalization also occurred through sanctioning of a more diverse set of products and by relaxation of restrictions, limiting flow back into Japan. While issuance of dual currency bonds was recognized in June 1985, the lock-up period was also cut from 180 to 90 days in April 1986 and 60 days in April 1996.[15]

Several measures for trade in Euro-currency instruments were also taken; for example, the ban on short-term Euro-yen lending to non-residents was lifted in June 1983, and the non-prudential limits on overseas yen lending were abolished in April 1984. The issue of Euro-yen CDs was authorized in December 1984, medium and long-term Euro-yen lending to non-residents was authorized in April 1985 and the Euro-yen CP market was established in 1987, with restrictions on non-resident issues being abolished during fiscal year 1995.

The method by which Japanese banks raised effective yields above nominal rates involved the use of compensating balance requirements. Throughout the 1980s, the reliance on compensating balances declined steadily from 45 per cent for surveyed loan contracts in 1980 to

25 per cent in 1990. But asset inflation later led to the dilemma whether to induce a further shift by loan customers away from the now profitable balance arrangements or to maintain the arrangement at the cost of overly intensive use of bank capital during a period when capital allocation was the primary factor in Japanese bank operations.

As a result of all these measures, a free market in yen-denominated Euro-currency instruments developed; while inter-bank transactions were free, in principle, 'administrative' guidance prohibited medium or long-term Euro-yen borrowing by domestic branches. As far as Euro-yen lending was concerned, loans to non-residents were free of controls for those institutions not required to provide notification. As for Euro-yen lending to Japanese residents, only short-term loans were regulation free, but medium and long-term loans were subject to advice for voluntary restraints until May 1989.

The third area of liberalization that was to stimulate activity in the Euro-yen market was the setting up of an offshore Tokyo market. It was meant to promote expansion in Euro-yen transactions and yen internationalization. But outstanding claims stood at $400 billion by the end of 1988, due to a lack of appeal vis-à-vis the other offshore centres of London, New York, Singapore and Hong Kong. While transactions are free of interest rate controls, reserve ratio requirements, deposit insurance requirements and withholding taxes, participants' inability to trade securities (only loans and deposits are authorized) and their liability to corporate and local taxes and stamp duty, render participation relatively unattractive.[16]

The role of the market mechanism during the 1980s deregulation and liberalization affected so many areas that the financial markets were significantly transformed so that the Japanese financial structure adapted to international standards. Moreover, the greater role of the market mechanism, along with the remaining regulations on the types and maturity of bank assets and liabilities, have increased the exposure of financial institutions to interest rates and other risks. A booming Tokyo stock market assisted the Japanese bank market capitalization. While the American banks showed low share price multiples in 1989, the capitalization of the 13 largest Japanese banks added up to $500 billion compared to $95 billion for the 50 largest US institutions.

The increased ease of access to more deregulated Euro-markets led more and more Japanese firms to conduct their financial transactions outside Japan. With a view to revitalizing the domestic corporate bond market, the MOF introduced a bond rating system in 1985 and relaxed the eligibility requirements for issuing unsecured bonds without collateral, and the number of firms that issue bonds domestically increased from 60 before February 1987 to 200 by 1990.

The collateral requirements for unsecured bonds were further eased and the disclosure for firms issuing secured bonds was simplified. The operations for inter-bank markets were progressively deregulated during 1989–90 to ensure the progress of inter-bank market operations by maintaining the depth of the market and increasing the arbitrage opportunities with other markets.

Liberalization of foreign yen-denominated bonds

When reconstructing the financial system, the MOF and MITI rejected the Anglo-Saxon belief in the ability of private capital markets to allocate financial resources efficiently.

The yen-denominated foreign bonds may be divided into two classes – those issued by public offer (Samurai bonds) and those issued by private placement (Shibosai bonds). A first amendment issuance rule (February 1981) for the Samurai bond market was carried out in April 1984. The range of eligible issues was expanded to include those with an AA credit rating for first-time public offer. In December, the standard determining the eligibility of private sector issues was changed again; further revisions of the standard were carried out in April 1985 and 1986 to match divisions made to the standard, applying to Japanese companies in the domestic 'straight' corporate bond market.[17]

From July 1992, access to the Samurai bond market was extended to all foreign borrowers, with an investment grade credit rating. In January 1996, for resident issues of Euro-yen bonds outside Japan, issuance eligibility criteria were abolished. The liberalization of the Samurai bond market also took place through official recognition of a more diversified set; for example, dual currency bond issues were authorized in November 1985. Later in April 1997, foreign commercial banks were allowed to issue Samurai bonds for the first time; CITICORP availed itself of this new opportunity then.

In the Shibosai bond market, a standard for eligibility was established in July 1983 and relaxed again in April 1984 and also in April 1986, when a formal rating system was introduced.

The need for an interest rate control-based system was felt because there was no efficient bond market. Several observers suggested that the catalysts for financial reform emerged from the real sector of the economy. There were few alternatives to devise a means of diverting personal savings from financing industrial investment to financing budget deficits.

These changes expanded the capacity of the yen-denominated foreign bond market in Japan. Yet it became unattractive to issuers, compared with the Euro-yen bond market. The market began to decline in 1986, though popularity of Shibosai issues in the first half of 1986 ensured that this segment of the market actually grew during the year, and by the end of the first quarter of 1987 the share of Euro-yen bonds in international bond issues shot up to 14 per cent from 1 per cent in 1984. The control over government bond markets changed with deregulation, and between 1984 and 1990 a healthy growth in these bond markets was observed.[18]

Towards the end of the decade, several steps were taken by the MOF to promote financial futures trading, including the establishment of future markets for the yen–dollar exchange rate and Euro-yen and Euro-dollar interest rates. The deregulation measures also spread to public sector financial institutions which control huge volumes of liquidity, but were not allowed to invest in foreign securities.

Reacting to steep yen appreciation, the MOF in August 1986 placed a ceiling of investment in foreign securities from 10 to 30 per cent of the assets of the life insurance and non-life insurance companies. Similar relaxations were made for non-bank financial institutions.

By the late 1980s, deregulation had reached a point of no return. With a view to creating a short-term security in the market, the MOF started issuing six-month treasury bills (TBs) in 1987, but despite the active role of the BOJ, the pace of growth of this market was very slow indeed.[19]

Internationalization of foreign exchange markets

An important liberalization measure was abolition of the 'real demand rule' in April 1994. This control was to prevent exchange rate volatility due to speculation by ensuring that there was an actual transaction whenever a bank engages in a forward exchange transaction.

Another significant step was the abolition of yen conversion limits in June 1984. It involved setting up ceilings on the amount of yen the banks could secure through conversion of foreign currency. This was undertaken after the Joint Group recommendations that it should be scrapped to help internationalize the foreign exchange market. Since occasional easing of restrictions on residents' holdings of foreign currency deposits abroad, one step related to the types of foreign exchange transactions sanctioned.[20]

Liberalization of interest rates

With the move to floating exchange rates and the inflationary consequences of the first oil price shock, the BOJ gave high priority to price and exchange rate stability in later years. After the second oil price shock in 1979, the BOJ quickly reduced money growth to suppress inflationary pressures. Several structural changes in the economy led to demands for deregulation at home. Hence monetary policy in the early 1980s evolved from the credit control system of regulated interest rates to monetary control with flexible interest rates. These changes were supported by extensive financial and foreign exchange liberalization during the 1980s.

Several changes were also observed in the financial positions of different sectors in the economy – the public sector deficits shot up, along with the personal sector, but corporate sector deficits began to decline. During the mid-1980s easy monetary policy was followed with a view to preventing further appreciation of the yen. The decline in public sector finances created pressures for reform of the primary market for government bonds and growth of secondary markets. The operating practices in the primary market were under heavy strain, because of the sheer increase in the volume of bonds that the underwriting syndicate was being asked to absorb.

Hence the funding burden on the banks could be reduced by making issues direct to the general public and non-bank financial intermediaries and by allowing banks to sell on to the general public. Both measures would help to reduce adverse impact on bank profitability. Hence the authorities' desire to finance the budget deficit in a non-monetary fashion and to protect the banking system from adverse consequences led to diversification in the types and methods of bond flotation.[21]

As per the Action programme, the MOF began in October 1985 further deregulation of interest rates. Banks were allowed to pay whatever rates they liked on time deposits of an initial term of three months to two years, with a minimum denomination of $1 billion. In October 1987, all large (over ¥100 million) time deposits with a minimum of one month were freed from interest rate controls.

The BOJ increased money growth significantly from 1987 to 1989. Historically low levels of interest rates emerged, credit conditions were eased and bank loans increased sharply. All these measures still left small 'time' deposits and all demand deposits subject to regulation. The authorities slowly lowered the qualifying threshold for payment of freely determined rates that came down to ¥3 million in November 1991. This was followed by complete liberalization of all time deposit rates in June 1993, with interest rates on demand deposits being liberalized in October 1994.

All these circumstances made it possible for an economic boom, starting in 1986 to last for a long time, and resulted in asset price inflation in subsequent years from the fourth quarter of 1985 to 1989; stock prices rose sharply by 25.5 per cent and land prices in the six largest cities rose by 27 per cent.

In March 1985 the sanctioning of issues of non-negotiable money market certificates was the first official step to liberalize large deposit rates since the Joint Group agreement of 1984. By October 1987, banks' funding limits had been removed, the minimum denomination was down to ¥10 million and the initial term could run from seven months to two years, but the interest rates remained in place until November 1990. The minimum denomination constraint was abolished during 1992, paving the way for full liberalization of interest rates by the end of June 1993. As a result of these measures, by the end of September 1990 the share of city bank deposits on a deregulated interest rate basis rose to 65 per cent of total deposits, compared to 16 per cent at the end of March 1986.[22]

The deepening of the domestic financial market

In view of the monetary targeting system with flexible interest rates, the BOJ also changed its intermediate targets of monetary policy in 1978 from lending by financial institutions to the corporate sector to a broadly defined money stock. Further, more importance was given to inter-bank market rates for reserves, in particular the call rates and two-month discount rates as primary instruments for money market operations to achieve desired monetary objectives.

During the 1980s, significant deepening of the Japanese money market was achieved by liberalizing operations on existing markets, creating new markets and securing close-up integration with overseas markets. The inter-bank market (with claims of more than ¥50 trillion) bulk of transactions had to pass through one of the six moneybroking firms (Tanshi) up to December 1990. These are call money markets, and only those institutions which have accounts at the BOJ were allowed to borrow in the call money market; all transactions took place on a secured basis and rates were fixed under the quotation system.[23]

The process of rate liberalization culminated in the scrapping of the rate quotation system in April 1979; afterwards, all transactions were to be done on a free rate basis. Since November 1995, the Federation of Bankers' Association of Japan has published, on a daily basis, a yen-TIBOR (Tokyo inter-bank offered rate) that is, a reference rate for Japanese money markets.

Government also sought to promote growth of the call market by expanding the range of transactions that take place in the market and the number of eligible participants. The first policy led to introduction of two six-day calls in April 1979 and two three-week calls in August 1985, along with 'unsecured' trading. Moreover, growth in the numbers eligible to participate in the markets was achieved by allowing city banks to make call loans (April 1981) and then by readmitting securities companies to the call markets as borrowers.

As far as deregulation of interest rates is concerned, in June 1978 the rates on bills with an outstanding maturity of over one month were liberalized. As one-month bills had been traded on a 'free' rate basis since November 1978, this meant that by October 1979, all bill rates had been liberalized.[24]

The third element of the inter-bank market was the deepening of the Tokyo dollar call money market achieved through deregulation of transactions in foreign currency, removal of restrictions on the maturity of transactions and a rapid growth in the number of active participants in the markets. Since the December 1980 amendments to the Foreign Exchange Control Act, this market functioned as a convenient place to invest surplus foreign currency balances or raise short-term foreign currency loans.

As for the open money market and the liberalization of negotiable CD market, one development after the inauguration of this market in May 1979 was an increase in the ceiling placed on the amounts the financial institutions could raise from CD issues in April 1980 (it took effect in April 1981); the ceiling was raised from 25 per cent of net worth for Japanese banks to 50 per cent of net worth. The ceiling on issuance was extended slowly through further increases in January 1983, January 1984, October 1985, April 1986 and April 1987 and the limit was finally removed in October 1987.

Due to ongoing financial liberalization in the domestic market and the offshore yen market, it became more difficult for the BOJ to control short-term interest rates. In November 1988, the BOJ reformed the domestic money markets by altering the intervention procedure for the money market. With this reform, interest rates on shorter maturity, overnight call rates or one-, two- and three-week discount rates are more appropriate indicators of the BOJ policy stance.[25]

An important development in the CD market was admission of securities companies as traders in June 1985. As for the Gensaki bond market, there was growth in the ceiling on Gensaki selling by city banks from ¥5 billion to 20 billion; under the MOF policy, all corporations are eligible to engage in transactions in the Gensaki bond market. The non-financial corporations were the largest lenders, with securities companies being largest borrowers. The liberalization of capital transactions under the 1980 amendment to the law led to further growth in the market share of non-residents.

As for the new money markets, a yen-denominated bankers' acceptance (BA) market was created; in June 1985, treasury bills first issued in February 1986, a commercial paper market in November 1987 and a market in cash-secured bond borrowing transactions sprang up in January 1986, duly leading to a proper bond repo market.

The creation of a yen BA market was a direct outcome of US–Japan yen–dollar meetings, with a view to deepening the short-term money market in Japan and also help towards internationalization of the yen. The market is open to financial institutions and corporate entities (resident and non-resident) and original sale of eligible bills is limited to authorized foreign exchange banks which underwrite the bills. The TB issues started in 1986 in the form of issues of six-month maturity discount bonds. The TBs differ from other short-term government securities, for example foreign exchange fund bills, since they cannot be underwritten by the BOJ and are issued through the competitive price-bidding system to institutional investors. Recently the minimum size of issue was slowly reduced from ¥100 million to ¥50 million in April 1987 and to ¥10 million in April 1990. But it was observed that this militated against further use of the yen as a reserve currency and the development of efficient money market operations in short-term government securities. Hence the internationalization of the yen and of Japanese financial markets was impeded.[26]

By the end of January 1987, TBs accounted for 17.5 per cent of ¥71 trillion of open money market claims outstanding, with most of the trading occurring in Gensaki form.[27] The next open money market to be set up was commercial paper (CP) in November 1987. It was delayed due to objections that the principle of collateral in markets would be isolated, thus adversely affecting the growth of the bill market. Moreover, a rating system was introduced in December 1988 to determine eligibility of issues; the firms had to have over ¥33 billion in net assets and their debt was to be rated in the rating classes.

Today borrowers in the CP markets are highly rated corporations, securities companies, non-bank financial intermediaries and even foreign investment banks. Merrill Lynch launched a ¥100 billion issue in March 1998 and the lenders are institutional investors. The minimum issue size is ¥100 million and maturity can extend up to nine months.

The last open money market in Japan (market in cash-secured bond borrowing transactions) emerged in January 1996, following the MOF's elimination of restrictions imposed on the payment of interest by banks against cash collateral posted by borrowers of bonds.[28]

Bank financing of industry

In the second half of the 1980s, Japan enjoyed above-trend growth and near zero inflation. These conditions resulted in a significant decline in the country-risk premium and a marked upward adjustment in growth expectations which boosted asset prices, fuelled by credit expansion. At the same time, Japanese banks were considered among the strongest in the world. During the same period, the pace of financial liberalization accelerated which spurred price competition and also prompted banks and other depository institutions to take greater risks, including increased lending to the real estate sector. With a rise in land prices, these institutions loosened the credit standard and the government curtailed total bank lending to the real estate sector and the banks' asset growth was adversely affected.

Hence the banks played a key role in financing Japan's post-war industrialization, as in 1980 manufacturing industry accounted for more than 50 per cent of total lending. The fact that commercial banks hold about 20 per cent of outstanding corporate equity in Japan is one indicator of this; while in the USA commercial banks hold virtually no corporate equity.[29] This traditional relationship weakened in the late 1980s.[30]

Manufacturing firms relied so heavily on equity finance at the peak in 1989 that about 70 per cent of their funds were provided by equity issues (including convertible and warrant bonds), compared with only 25 per cent in the first half of the decade. These firms substantially increased their investments in financial assets in the first half of the 1980s, over 70 per cent of their funds were used to finance the fixed investments; by 1989, this ratio came down below 50 per cent and investment in financial assets was more than 40 per cent of funds invested.

In the early 1990s, this trend was abruptly reversed, as the slump in stock market prices forced firms to cut back equity finance. As Takeda and Turner observed, the ratio of financial assets to liabilities in the manufacturing sector (0.6 in the early 1980s) rose steadily during the decade to above 1 by 1988. The traditional financial positions of industrial companies (net financial liability incurred to finance real assets) were thus reversed.[31]

For corporations this opened up the seductive possibility of financial arbitrage. The greatly intensified financial market activity of non-financial companies (financial engineering or *zaitech*) made an important contribution to corporate profits and also guaranteed earnings for the banks. Hence there was a sharp decline in non-financial companies' non-operating losses, as gains on financial investments began to offset interest payments. This non-operating loss rebounded to ¥2.2 trillion by fiscal year 1991, as corporations were squeezed by losses on securities investments and higher interest payments.[32]

It was recently suggested that the traditional placement of funds in fixed-term bank deposits had gradually been eroded over the last several years; while investments in equities steadily became more important, by the end of the decade equity investments accounted for about one-half of corporate financial asset holdings before declining sharply in 1990, as equity prices dropped.[33]

Two important consequences followed. First, that it increased the sensitivity of the financial corporate sector to equity price movements. During the boom years, the accumulation of a large amount of financial assets gave the non-financial corporate sector the impression that it had a big cushion to soften the impact of adverse developments in its core business. Moreover, it also made it more difficult for firms to refund heavy redemption of convertible and warrant bonds due in the early 1990s – especially 1993–94. According to a November 1991 estimate, ¥24 trillion inconvertible and warrant bond redemptions were due during 1992–95.[34]

As later experience showed, it was simply impossible to roll over these debts with similar low interest paper, and corporations were burdened with more expensive debt financing. The authorities announced several measures in August 1992 to sustain the equity market and to contain the ramifications of any weakness. In the second half of August 1992, the stock market showed a remarkable recovery that was sustained for a few months. However, the levels reached in this recovery were much below the levels at which it could be attractive to exercise most warrant or convertible options. According to one estimate, the issue yields on equity-linked paper reached 4.75 per cent in the first half of 1991, compared with less than 1 per cent in 1989.[35]

A second consequence was that larger firms had less need of bank loans, forcing the banks to seek more business from small firms. This change affected most large city banks, the share of their loans going to small firms rising from less than half in the early 1980s, to about three-quarters by the end of the decade. Hence these small firms, without a main bank patron, could borrow more readily and more cheaply.[36]

As the BOJ report observed, banks have tried to expand their margins by increasing lending to smaller companies and individuals and by raising the ratio of long-term lending. But quantitative expansion, without full recognition of risk, and lax loan pricing standards were observed during the monetary easing of the late 1980s.[37]

Insurance policies provided a major vehicle for increased financial asset accumulation – a trend that gave an impetus to Japan's insurance companies. But more remarkable was the impact of the land price boom, which increased the value of the personal sector's landholdings from about twice the annual GNP in 1980 to more than 3.5 times by 1989. With value of land rising so steeply, the overall balance sheet position of the personal sector strengthened enormously and this provided much of the stimulus for consumer demand and housing investments.[38]

Japanese crisis or model?

Recently it was suggested that many of Japan's current problems can be traced to its programme of liberalization and several policy mistakes in the 1980s, but they have been exacerbated by uncertainty, prevarication and the institutional features of the Japanese model. Japan came under strong pressure to stimulate domestic demand as its trade surpluses mounted in the late 1970s and early 1980s. Monetary policy was relaxed in 1983 and further relaxed after the yen's appreciation in 1985. A programme of incremental financial deregulation was launched in the early 1980s, starting with large-scale deposits, while interest rates for small individual accounts were still regulated.[39]

Moreover, easy money for large companies and investors set in train a sharp appreciation in asset prices, focusing initially on land, which Japanese banks have traditionally demanded as collateral. In mid-1985 the value of residential land in Tokyo was about half of Japan's GDP; by the end of 1987, it was one and a half times. Starting from similar baseline, the value of stocks listed on the first section of Tokyo's stock exchange grew more slowly but they too overtook the size of Japan's GDP by 1988; Japan had developed an asset bubble.[40]

A shift from indirect to direct corporate finance also preceded the 1985–86 yen appreciation and accelerated after it. The shift was prompted by increased risk-floating, exchange rate strengthening of the anti-monopoly law and financial deregulation. Since the corporate bond market was still regulated in Japan, much of the finance was raised abroad. But rising land and share prices made it very attractive to raise money through new share issues as well, the more so since dividends were not rising in tandem.[41]

As per estimates by Noguchi, companies raised some $600 billion in equity finance between 1985 and 1990. Some of this money was funnelled into capital spending which recorded double digit increases in the late 1980s, but 70 per cent went into financial investment, unrelated to core corporate activities.[42]

Losing business from their major corporate customers, banks turned to small firms and especially property. Japan's financial institutions provided $220 billion in new loans to the property sector between 1985 and 1990 (compared with total outstanding loans of two-thirds of this figure at the end of 1984) and an estimated $75 billion through non-bank financial institutions, notable among which were now infamous housing loan (Jusen) companies.[43]

Of course, there were several pressures on individuals to make investment decisions to jump on the bandwagon, and at the systematic level, a lack of preparedness for risk, partly as a result of the land myth and the legacy of the pre-deregulation risk dispersion mechanism. Excessive capital investment was not the result of state direction, but was exacerbated by 'match thy competitor' competition.

The boom and bust cycle

The financial liberalization process significantly influenced the nature of the late 1980s boom. Finance-sensitive expenditure is by nature more volatile and always tends to rise more strongly during boom periods. But the size and pattern of the differential between the two during the late 1980s appear to be somewhat out of the ordinary. The average annual growth rates over the period from 1985 to 1990 (in real terms) were 10.9 per cent for machinery and equipment investment, 10 per cent for investment in housing and 12 per cent for consumer expenditure on durable goods.[44]

This boom was sustained by low or declining interest rates and a large sustained increase in broad money. This stance reflected the fact that monetary policy during 1987–88 was geared to holding the yen–dollar exchange rate broadly stable in pursuit of the international understanding from the Louvre Accord. Of course, it was suggested that the first best policy for achieving this would have been international fiscal policy coordination (lower US budget deficit). But the policy makers settled on international monetary cooperation as an imperfect substitute.[45]

An important worry for policy makers was that continued rapid appreciation of the yen would be severely deflationary for the Japanese economy. But as it turned out, the deflationary effect of a strong yen was overestimated. As Ueda argued, the monetary policy was too expansionary in the late 1980s. The initial easing of policy was prompted by widely shared worries about the deflationary effect of a strong yen. Once implemented, it proved hard to correct, as political pressures made it difficult for the BOJ to reverse the stance of monetary policy. For this argument, the lack of generalized inflation during this period should be kept in mind, as it suggests that monetary policy was not too loose. Moreover, the experience of other countries also showed that asset prices during deregulation tend to acquire a life of their own that monetary policy, by itself, could not counter without being excessively deflationary.[46]

Looking back, monetary policy should have been tightened much earlier than 1989. There were several reasons why it was not. The international agreement to maintain loose monetary conditions after Black Monday was one factor, but West Germany, also with a buoyant economy, raised its interest rate in 1988. Japanese authorities were under pressure not to follow suit, not just from the USA, but also from domestic manufacturers already struggling to adapt to the yen's appreciation. As a senior MOF official recently suggested, there was a belief that it was now Japan's duty as the world's largest creditor nation to maintain a low interest rate and that Japan's economy was strong enough to do so. [47]

The impact of wider access to finance was magnified by substantial increases in asset prices due to easy credit conditions. This was so obvious from equity prices, as non-financial corporations borrowed funds to purchase equities; they drove up equity prices and rising land prices played a similar role. Banks' reserves also benefited from this boom, as did their ability to issue new equity.

Moreover, Basle capital adequacy rules did something to limit the ultimate damage done by this, by allowing only 45 per cent of unrealized capital gains from equity holdings to be counted as tier-two capital. No doubt, this process mentally clouded the contemporary judgements of whether asset prices were a cause for concern; since it could be argued that an increase in the prices of assets, relative to general price level, was a natural consequence of liberalization, as artificial constraint on borrowing had been removed.[48]

But it was impossible to know how much the relative price of assets had to change and how far speculative excesses were involved. As K. Ohmae recently suggested, towards the end of 1990, the financial and real estate communities of Tokyo whispered the imminent fall of companies as symbolic of the bubble economy of the late 1980s.

The unsustainable rise in equity prices towards the end of the 1980s sharply reduced the cost of equity finance for Japanese firms. This helped them to undertake real investments, with returns lower than in other countries, and to invest heavily in financial assets. Recent studies on the cost of capital in Japan suggested that it was much more than the cost of capital in other industrial countries, as observed in comparison of US and Japanese capital costs.[49]

The intensity of the real estate lending boom and bust cycle was fuelled by a sharp increase in real estate-related lending. As the BIS report observed, bank lending for real estate purposes increased at an annual rate of 19 per cent between 1983 and 1990, before declining sharply in 1991. The comparable rate of expansion in the US and UK was less than 15 per cent a year (1992 Report, p. 117).

Moreover, specialized finance institutions for consumer credit, etc. that were outside the control of the authorities provided the major share of this credit. Since government regulations denied these institutions assets to soften financial markets, they had to borrow from banks, thus increasing banks' real estate exposure.

The banks and other financial institutions that gave loans against real estate at inflated prices, faced in 1991 and 1992 a steep rise in doubtful loans. Concerning the actual size of these loans, several estimates were made by different agencies, but one fact emerged: these doubtful loans were a significant proportion of the average bank's total loans outstanding. While the value of collateral held by banks would limit their losses, the banks and other financial institutions no doubt faced a very heavy adjustment burden during the 1990s. The scale of the problem was likely to stretch Japan's traditional mechanism for rescuing problem banks, and also there was a need to search for alternative solutions; for example, the decision in October 1991 to extend the

Deposit Insurance Corporation's help for the merger of Tohasogu Bank, was the relief action by the insurance system.[50]

The ongoing difficulties of the banks were further compounded by a sharp decline in unrealized projects on their huge securities holidays. During fiscal year 1991, city banks and long-term credit banks' latent profits fell by over ¥14 trillion since the market value of equities dropped significantly. This decline in banks' financial position led, in the first half of 1992, to a decline in bank share prices, even sharper than that in share prices in general. All this also weakened the close bank–corporate customer links.

As Takeda and Turner suggested, these pressures made the banks place greater weight on prudence and profitability and less on growth.[51]

Moreover, securities companies were also hard hit by the stock market slump; their predicament was made worse by the fact that the bursting of the equity market bubble in the early 1990s brought to light a considerable amount of questionable financial practices. These included the compensation of large investors for stock market losses, alleged attempts to manipulate equity prices and the use of window dressing to cover up the losses. These various scandals attracted wide public attention, along with serious consequences. The only hope was that the greater transparency of rules governing securities companies' behaviour and the existence of a special watchdog committee would do much to restore public confidence at home as well as overseas.

3
Deregulation and Liberalization Tribulations – the 1990s

In the late 1980s, Japan was moving to a competitive market-based system of banking and capital markets. The financial institutions were under great pressure to cut costs, increase efficiency and develop new financial products, with a view to compete. Of course, the new environment created new kinds of risks, along with new opportunities and dangers of taking risks, including interest rate risk for assets and liabilities, exchange rate risk and credit risk due to intense competitive pressures on corporations.

While in the second half of 1980s Japan enjoyed above-trend growth and near-zero inflation, these conditions also led to a significant decline in the country risk premium and a marked upward adjustment in growth expectations, which boosted asset price inflation, fuelled by credit expansion. At the same time, Japanese banks were considered among the strongest in the world.

During the late 1980s, the pace of financial liberalization and deregulation accelerated, which spurred price competition and also prompted banks and other depository institutions to take greater risks, including increased lending to the real estate sector as land prices rose. These institutions loosened their audit standards and the MOF took several measures to limit total bank lending to the real estate industry, reducing the banks' asset growth.

The forces leading to the bubble in asset prices started building up much earlier, with the slow-down in the Japanese economy. The government deficit started rising and the share of government bonds rose from 5 per cent of GDP during the 1970s to over 18 per cent during the late 1980s. The growth of the Japanese money supply and the easy availability of funds were the initial spark before the bubble, when Japanese firms were taking advantage of recent deregulation to borrow at low rates in the Eurodollar markets, only to reinvest at higher rates in Japan. This activity put additional upward liquidity in Japanese markets.

Over the decade, from its 1989 peak, the Nikkei share price index fell by more than 50 per cent. Between 1991 and 2000 land prices declined by more than 30 per cent. Recent OECD estimates suggest that the net wealth losses incurred by the economy between 1989 and 1997 due to this asset price collapse amounted to more than two years' wealth of GDP or about $7 trillion, of which more than 50 per cent was directly borne by the households.[1]

As Andre Boltho and Jenny Corbett suggested, this massive loss in wealth must have had serious negative consequences. Companies, whose business investment had risen by about 8.5 per cent during the 1980s, now recorded negative growth of 2 per cent. Households, whose disposable income in the decade rose very slowly, also restricted their spending, so that private consumption which increased by more than 4 per cent perannum in the 1980s, crept up at annual rate of 1.5 per cent in the 1990s. The banking sector found itself saddled with a large amount of non-performing assets and drastically curtailed its lending.[2]

Moreover, prices of Japanese assets, for example land and financial securities, were very high in the late 1980s. Japanese share prices reflected price/earning ratios that were, on the average, four to five times higher than similar ratios in the USA. The Nikkei index of 225 selected stocks soared from an average of 6870.2 in 1980 to 34,042.8 in 1989; over the 1984–89 period, the Nikkei 25 more than tripled.[3]

Non-residents' stockholdings as a percentage of market capitalization slipped from 7.5 per cent in 1985 to 4.2 per cent in 1990, following the stock market crash. The Nikkei average bottomed out at ¥15,790 in August 1992, and the average was around ¥20,000 during 1994–95 and declined further afterwards.[4]

The progressive tightening of monetary policy in the late 1990s and the inevitable unwinding of the borrowing boom produced a steep drop in the growth of the real money supply, culminating in a decline, and bank lending growth weakened appreciably. While this reflected, in part, a switch of deposits into postal savings accounts and bank debentures (not included in M2 + CDs) as well as expectations of imminent interest rate cuts, the underlying deceleration in liquidity growth was very sharp as a dramatic unwinding of the excesses of the 1980s boom occurred.[5]

Serious observers like Kazuo Sato saw the rapid rise in stock prices up to 1989 as an abnormality; in 1991–92, Japanese stock prices experienced their biggest fall. What was responsible for the bubble and its demise? Was it the speculative zeal of the investors or more mundane issues like mismanaged monetary policy or business losses in corporate sectors? For answers here, rigorous analysis of the available evidence for the 1990s is a necessity. Looking back, it can be said that the basic cause of the bubble was not the optimism of the investors, but other more objective factors. While forecasts seem to have played a leading role only at the beginning and end of the bubble period, the major blame must be attributed to the interest rate factor.[6]

Capital deepening in the 1990s

Since the early 1990s the MOF had pursued vigorous liberalization of the bond market, internationalization of the stock and bond markets and introduction of a futures market for bonds and other trades. The private bond market (Shasai) industrial bonds were still lagging behind. The reform programme was based on several measures to broaden the range of bond types on offer by diversifying their maturities and the selling methods. The form in which the yield was offered – fixed rate coupon, floating rate – would differentiate the government bonds and discount bonds also available later.

In the mid-1970s diversification by maturity began and the 5-year discount bonds supplemented the usual 10-year interest-bearing bond issues in 1977, followed by medium-term bonds and very long-term bonds of 15 years upwards in 1983.

As for the secondary government bond market, wide fears about the likely shape of future budget deficits were expressed. Several measures were taken to relax the restrictions on sale by syndicate members of bonds to the general public, and also the authorization of banks' sale of newly issued bonds. For the relaxation of restrictions on syndicate members' sale of government bonds, liberalization started with deficit bonds, then construction bonds and the bonds listed on the stock exchange, and all time restrictions on selling were scrapped in June 1987.

The first detailed sales of newly issued government bonds (*madohan*) by banks were made in April 1983 as per MOF guidelines of March 1982. Other institutions later authorized to engage in retail sale of government bonds include the Zenshinren Bank (1986), post offices (January 1987), agricultural cooperatives (April 1987) and life insurance companies (June 1987).

While banks' dealing in existing public bonds began in June 1984, this restriction was lifted in June 1985. Besides these measures, the growth of the government bond market was also helped by creation of a bond future market in October 1985, and the creation of a financial futures exchange in April 1989 and the adoption of more flexibility in the setting of issue terms.

The incentive to set up futures markets came from recognition of the need to create additional hedging opportunities for security holders, and of the danger that development of the domestic capital market would be adversely affected if Japan did not move to match international competition in the global financial marketplace.[7]

The authorization granted to certain foreign securities companies resident in Japan to act as participants in the bond future markets, alongside member companies of the Tokyo stock exchange, a number of domestic non-member securities companies and other financial institutions licensed to deal in public bonds, was a further testament to the authorities' desire to broaden, deepen and internationalize the domestic bond markets.[8] As for the increased flexibility in issue terms of government bonds, this was made possible by the relaxation of restrictions on resale. It stimulated further demand, thereby broadening and deepening the market.

The success of these measures is obvious from the available data. In fiscal year 1996, of the ¥3190 trillion worth of trade in yen bonds, 95 per cent was accounted for by transactions in government bonds. This compares with 2.3 per cent in fiscal year 1975; moreover, trading in government bond futures during fiscal year 1996 amounted to ¥2517 trillion.[9]

The measures for internationalization of Japanese capital markets consist of those concerning the deregulation of the yen-denominated foreign bond market and Euro-yen bond market, the internationalization of the yen and the authorization of foreign companies to operate in domestic financial markets.

As for the foreign presence in Japan, the rise in foreign stocks, listing the growth in the number of overseas companies with securities dealing licences and admission of foreign companies to the Tokyo stock exchange, are just as important for the growth of the local stock market as was admission of foreigners into trust banking, fund management and investment advisory activities for development of those industries. Further efforts to improve transparency and to eliminate the malpractices and scandals of the late 1980s and early 1990s, through the toughening of insider dealing legislation, would be of some help.

Another positive feature for the deepening of local markets was the ability to engage in stock futures and options trading on the Osaka securities exchange in June 1987. But the segment of the capital market with a less than auspicious track record is the local corporate bond market. With the volume and value of convertible stocks of the issuing company at a stated time in the future and with warrants (providing holders with the right to purchase a given amount of stock at a fixed price at a stated date in the future), bond issues soared during the latter half of the 1980s in line with local stock markets, but the market in straight corporate bonds languished.[10]

Several reasons were suggested for the poor performance of these bonds, for example the inflexibility compared with the Euro-bond market or the domestic convertible debenture market, or the criteria determining the eligibility of issuers of the collateral requirements of terms of issue and of issuing procedures.

Of course, the reform measures began with relaxation of the collateral rule. Initiated in January 1983, the process of deregulation involved relaxation of the criteria determining the eligibility for issues of unsecured domestic bonds. The reform measures of April 1984, October 1985 and February 1987 meant that by the last date, the number of companies eligible to issue unsecured state bonds by public offering increased from 2 in March 1979 to 180.

Under the regime in February 1987, all companies rated AA and above by the rating agency and those rated A with net assets in excess of ¥55 billion could issue unsecured straight corporate debentures by public offering. The companies not satisfying these requirements, but with net assets of at least ¥55 billion, were still eligible to make such issues if they met certain financial requirements (the requirements were tough for firms with net assets of under ¥100 billion).[11]

Moreover, from May 1987, the issuing company was encouraged to solicit competitive bids from a range of securities companies. The improvement in flexibility in issuing conditions secured through this route was complemented by the MOF decision to relax the restrictions on the maturity of issues and to sanction floating rate note (FRN) issues. Hence the traditional range of maturities – 6, 7, 12 and 15 years – was extended to include short-term maturities (4 years and less) and FRN issues were sanctioned, all before the end of 1989.

The private placement (Shibosai) market suffered from restrictions on the size of issue (¥2 billion); the companies that previously issued bonds by public offering were not eligible to make private placement under the no-return rule, the range of purchasers (only 49 institutional investors) could make purchases and for issues of over ¥1 billion, confirmation of investment purposes had to be filed with the head of the securities bureau of the MOF, and on resale the securities bureau had to be informed.[12]

Due to consistent pressure from the corporate sector, this market was reformed in July 1987, by abolishing the no-return rule, raising the limits on individual issues to ¥10 billion and liberalizing the resale of bonds for issues of over ¥2 billion. The only measures to appear before the Big Bang were a sanctioning of five-year issues in April 1993, a relaxation of the eligibility criteria for use of the shelf registration system in fiscal year 1995 and further relaxation of insurance eligibility criteria.

Bursting of the asset price bubble

In 1989, the environment around Kabutocho changed significantly and optimism was snuffed out. This was the end of the world's greatest bull market. All the 22 city, trust and long-term credit banks reported lower pretax profits in 1990 and aggregate net profits of the 12 city banks dropped by 21 per cent. During the year ending March 1991, three long-term credit banks slipped by 3.3 per cent and seven trust banks were the worst sufferers with their profits tumbling by 30 per cent.

Losing business from their corporate customers, the banks turned to small firms and property. Japan's financial institutions provided $220 billion in new loans to the property sector between 1985 and 1990 (compared with total outstanding loans of two-thirds of this amount in 1984) and an estimated $75 billion through non-bank financial institutions and the housing loan companies.

In April 1990, the MOF applied the guidelines limiting total lending to the real estate sector, but lending to 'Jusen' units was exempted. During 1991–92 Jusen lending increased vigorously, and concern over the quality of assets held by these companies was raised as early as 1992. The problem was very serious in 1995, when the MOF did a special study; it was discovered that, out of a total ¥13 trillion, ¥6.5 trillion were unrecoverable. The MOF agreed to dissolve seven housing loan companies and in July 1996, the Jusen Resolution Corporation took over ¥6.4 trillion of unrecoverable loans to these failed companies.

Most of the funding for Jusen companies came from the 21 major banks and agricultural credit cooperatives. The MOF suggested that banks should shoulder more than their pro rata share of the Jusen losses. Banks not related to these institutions were asked to contribute to the loss-sharing scheme by contributing capital or by making below market rate loans to banks that assumed assets of insolvent institutions.[13]

In December 1995, the government proposed a resolution plan for seven insolvent Jusens, but the sharing of the burden was not equitable, and a heavier burden on banks reflected the public perception that the founder banks that had set up Jusen companies were providing personnel to manage operations. Hence it was suggested that the perception of increased risk in Japanese banks in general resulted in a 'Japan premium' in the Eurodollar market – a premium over the London inter-bank interest rate required of Japan's banks. The premium increased further when Daiwa Bank was discovered to have covered up derivative losses of about US$1 billion due to a rogue trader in New York.

By the end of 1995, the major policy issues looming in public view were the Jusen problem, the problem of non-performing bank loans and the risk exposure of a large number of small financial institutions. During 1991–92 two credit rating agencies – Moody's Investors and Standard and Poor – downgraded the ratings for four major trust banks, Mitsubishi Trust, Mitsui Trust, Sumitomo Trust and Yasuda Trust.[14]

As Kazuo Sato recently observed, loose monetary policy was pursued during most of the 1980s, causing a continual decline in interest rates.[15] Several observers attributed the stock market bubble of the 1980s to this monetary policy. Moreover, the high rate of land price inflation in the late 1980s was also attributed to the high rate of money growth. In retrospect, monetary policy should have been tightened much earlier than 1989. There were several reasons why it was not. The international agreement to maintain loose monetary conditions after Black Monday was one factor, but West Germany, also with a booming economy, raised its interest rate in 1988. The Japanese government was under pressure not to follow suit, not just from the USA, but also from domestic manufacturers, already struggling to adapt to the yen's appreciation.[16]

Suggestions were made that the policy delays increased the size of the bubble and later fallout from an index peak of about ¥40,000 in late 1989; share prices dropped 40 per cent in 1990, but held on in 1991 and plunged again in 1992 to just over a third of their peak value. The heady asset price spiral became, over the years, a vicious circle of bad debts and declining asset value. By 1992 nervous voices were raised about the possibility of a China syndrome meltdown. The Nikkei index had broken ¥15,000, dangerously close to the level at which hidden assets that were supposed to cover bad debts would disappear (the level was estimated at somewhere around ¥13,000).

During 1990–91, the growth rate was only about 1 per cent, with multiple quarters of negative growth afterwards for several years. As recent studies highlighted, overall performance during the entire 1990s was very disappointing, with growth slowing down to a rate well below that of the OECD area (see Table 3.1).

By 1995, investor and depositor confidence in the financial system was shaky indeed, and in August 1995, the government had to intervene to stop a run on the largest credit union (Cosmo Credit) and take over the largest thrift bank (Kizu) and a large regional bank (Hyogo, Osaka). All these rescue operations involved significant contributions by public agencies and private institutions; they also depleted the deposit insurance funds and there was wide public opposition to further use of these funds for rescue measures.

Hence the sharp fall in the stock market and land values caused economic downturn and sluggish growth for several years. The sharp decline in household wealth adversely affected consumer expenditure, and excess capacity in several sectors induced business firms to curtail investment, along with a gradual erosion in Japan's full employment record. While open unemployment remains low by European standards (about 6 per cent), in 2003 it crept above US levels for the first time since the war. Also there was a marked decline in the country's public finances. OECD estimates put the 2003 budget deficit at 6 per cent of GDP; more importantly, the level of gross public debt rose well above 130 per cent of output – a worrying development in the light of evolving demographic trends.[17]

As per OECD estimates, taking into account the balance sheets of other public financial and non-financial institutions, the debt ratio would rise to over 170 per cent of GDP.[18] This would be pushed above 200 per cent, if allowance were made for unfunded pension liabilities over the years; even Japan's legendary manufacturing competitiveness has been adversely affected. Companies, whose business investment rose by 9 per cent per annum during the 1980s, now recorded negative growth of 2 per cent. Those households whose disposable income in the decade rose slowly, curtailed their spending; hence private consumption that increased by 4 per cent per annum during the 1980s showed an annual rate of 1.5 per cent during the 1990s.

During the 1980s Japanese banks rapidly extended their operations in other countries – the USA and South-East Asia. On the strength of their appreciating land collateral, the aggregate foreign assets of

Table 3.1 Components of GDP and gross fixed capital formation (billions of yen)

	1985	*1986*	*1987*	*1988*	*1989*	*1990*	*1991*	*1992*	*1993*	*1994*	*1995*
Real GDP	342,950	352,880	367,556	390,325	409,184	429,986	446,315	450,876	452,282	455,197	461,894
Manufacturing	95,718	94,230	98,613	106,506	113,490	121,219	127,598	125,822	120,841	119,986	126,554
Fabricated metals	38,321	39,195	40,953	46,563	51,322	56,470	61,704	59,491	56,996	56,931	62,938
Machinery and equipment gross fixed capital formation	91,322	95,707	104,453	116,428	126,006	136,685	141,163	138,981	136,269	135,243	137,600
Machinery and equipment	27,527	28,282	30,246	35,781	40,142	44,553	46,122	44,213	41,118	39,803	44,440

Note: All data in 1990 prices.
Source: OECD National Accounts Volume 2 (1998b).

Japanese banks in October 1997 were ¥143,800 billion ($1290 billion), while the aggregate assets of Japanese banks in the USA were much larger in absolute terms but were a minor fraction of total bank lending in the US economy. As per the BIS data, out of $276 billion in loans extended by Japanese banks to other Asian countries, one-third was in the five most seriously affected economies of the region.

Recently it was suggested that the overseas exposure of Japanese banks was an important vehicle for transmission of the economic troubles in Japan to the rest of the world. Japan's loans to Asia surged to $265 billion in 1996, helping to finance current account deficits in the run-up to the crisis. Following the baht's fall on 2 July 1997, Japan played an important role in the financial package for Thailand. Moreover, such financial crises will continue to occur in future as well; indeed Japan's current financial deregulation programme that will release some of the $8.5 trillion of individual deposits on to the world markets will virtually ensure that they will. In the early 1990s, it was found that the Japanese banks, when faced with mounting bad loans and a fall in the ratio of capital to risk-weight adjusted assets (CRAR) reduced their foreign lending much more than their loans in the domestic market. This was despite the fact that the principal source of their problems lay in the sharp decline in share and property prices in Japan.[19]

Moreover, between mid-1992 and mid-1995, the yen appreciated in real terms by about 50 per cent and the loss of competitiveness later affected the recovery. It happened again in 1997, when following faster growth in 1996, the MOF sharply tightened fiscal policy. The OECD estimates put the direct restrictive impact of this change at about 2 per cent of GDP.[20] The MOF's efforts to manage the international value of the yen in the late 1980s had a clear policy objective in view of persistent American pressures. Moreover, triggered by bilateral trade imbalances, these pressures were linked to Japan's very high saving rates but Japanese business expected the yen's appreciation to be a lasting result of trade conflicts.

Monetary policy impasse

As Japan enters the new millennium, monetary policy has been at an impasse for years: the BOJ's tight money policy was effective in bursting the asset bubble, followed by prolonged deflationary tendencies, but, by 1994, monetary policy became expansive and base money increased by 5–9 per cent per year. Since this monetary growth was much faster than the sluggish growth in nominal GDP, the velocity of base money declined sharply. Hence this resurgence of strong monetary growth failed to restimulate income growth.

As P.N. Snowden recently observed, increasingly reflecting American monetary policy concerns, with the international overvaluation of the dollar the relative stability of the policy-determined Japanese discount rate led to a declining interest differential in the years to 1985. The Plaza agreement of September involving an understanding that official foreign exchange intervention would seek to drive down the value of the US currency was clearly more successful in securing its objective than was the subsequent Louvre accord to stabilize the dollar at the exchange rate prevailing in early 1987. Some attempt to arrest the slide of the US currency is evident in Japanese short-term rates after 1985, and in relative rate settings during 1987 and 1988.[21]

From 1994, the stimulated effect of the BOJ's strong expansion in base money was ultimately frustrated by a breakdown in the monetary transmission mechanism. From a domestic perspective, Japanese money has three related aspects:

1. *The low interest rate trap*. Starting with short-term interest rates of about 2 per cent in 1994–95, the BOJ reduced the overnight bank lending rate to just 0.5 per cent in 1996 and then announced its famous zero interest rate policy in 1999. With zero interest floors, the BOJ has no further leverage over the economy in this dimension.
2. *The fall in bank lending*. Despite the ultra-low interest rates, commercial bank lending was stagnant, growing less than 1 per cent per year after 1994 and then falling in 1999 and later. But during the 1980s, bank lending had grown much faster than monetary aggregates.
3. *Excess reserve holding by financial institutions*. As interest rates on the inter-bank lending fall to near zero levels and demand by non-banks for credit remains weak and unprofitable, the opportunity cost of commercial banks and *tanshi* (private) brokers holding excess reserves with the BOJ also falls to zero.[22]

Hence suggestions were made that the depth of the Japanese recession is largely a result of macroeconomic policy failure and Japan fell into a liquidity trap where monetary policy is important, since nominal interest rates cannot fall below zero. As argued by Paul Krugman, a liquidity trap arises when the equilibrium real interest rate is negative over a considerable period. Hence even zero nominal rates will be insufficient to bring desired saving and investment into balance and the economy needs rising prices to ensure full employment. In Japan, the problem was a policy failure to adjust monetary policy with a view to generating the necessary inflationary expectations.

A strong case was made against the notion that the weakness of Japan's banking sector, or other structural problems, are important issues in the recent difficulties. The case here depends on the view that there are structural problems and of course, both real and monetary aspects of Japan's difficulties may have similar sources. Declining expectations of future productivity growth in the Japanese economy might have depressed real interest rates, reducing the flexibility of monetary policy.

However, for Krugman it is the expectation of continuing price deflation that keeps real interest rates in positive territory and prevents the needed expansion.[23] For McKinnon and Ohno, it is the expectation that the yen will continually appreciate that inhibits higher spending.[24] However, Krugman observed that monetary policy is ineffective in today's Japan, since the BOJ committed itself to a policy of very low inflation (during 2000–1 inflation was negative); even with zero nominal interest rates, the real rate of interest remains positive. But the population, worried by future demographic projections, has severely reduced its rate of time preference and only a negative interest rate would generate an increase in demand. Recent research showed that declining growth prospects may have depressed Japan's equilibrium real interest rates, but not to the point where it is negative. The countercyclical case for Krugman-style monetary stimulus may be valid. Hence a liquidity trap case should not be seen purely as a monetary phenomenon. To the extent that Japanese real interest rates have been depressed and monetary policy accordingly constrained, declining expectations of future productivity growth are the best plausible culprit for monetary constraint.[25]

The policy recommendation is for the BOJ to convince public opinion that it will follow an irresponsible policy of pursuing a positive rate of inflation for a long period of time; if this policy switch is credible, real interest rates as deflated by future inflationary expectations would turn negative and the economy may revive.

One difficulty with this proposal is how to persuade the BOJ to abandon its mandate for price stability. In mid-2000, when the economy was still stagnating, the BOJ's governor was calling for interest rate increases. Experience so far of policy switches that appeared very credible, showed that these may influence behaviour in financial markets, but have very little impact on the labour market. Hence such threats had to be followed by deeds and the money supply had to be expanded in order to generate the announced inflation. In today's Japan, it is very difficult indeed, as Krugman observed,

> If an economy is truly in a liquidity trap, failure of broad money aggregate to expand is not a sign of insufficiently expansionary monetary policy; the central bank may simply be unable to achieve such an expansion, because of additional days, money is either added to bank reserves or held by the public in place of bank deposits.[26]

The Krugman thesis for Japan is built on the basis of some empirical observations. For some time the economy has been characterized by an output gap, with underutilization of both labour and capital. This may be due to effective demand failure and suggests the need for expansionary monetary policy. With the corporate bank rate, overnight call rate, two-year government bond rate and three-month money market rate approximating 0.68, 0.01, 0.03 and 0.01 per cent respectively during June 2001, the Japanese economy seems to be caught in a Keynesian liquidity trap, where monetary policy is completely ineffective. Moreover, several fiscal stimulus programmes, launched by the government since 1997, have failed to arrest the slide in the Japanese economy.

If this is the case, generating the needed increase in inflationary expectations may require the use of unconventional policy measures, for example buying foreign currency or land; still there is little certainty that demand would pick up. A fall in the real interest rate per se would have some favourable impact on investment.

There is little evidence that interest rates have been an important factor behind the very high investment levels of the past. Present business expectations are heavily influenced by huge overcapacity and poor demand prospects. The upshot is the famous 'liquidity trap' for monetary policy. Not only can short-term interest rates not be cut further to stimulate the private sector, but demand for base money itself has become indeterminate. Hence the national multiplier link from the creation of base money to bank credit creation has been broken.[27]

On the savings side, lower interest rates would depress current disposable income, given the high share of interest-bearing deposits held by Japanese savers. Even negative real interest rates may be insufficient to overcome today's uncertainty and lack of confidence. Even if the

Japanese economy is suffering from demand deficiency with near zero rate of interest, substantial modification of the Keynesian theory and policies is called for.[28]

The only channel of transmission left is through exchange rates. The excess money and large real interest rate differentials vis-à-vis the rest of the world would lower the currency and this could raise both demand for, and prices of, tradable goods and services. But the effect of this may be limited, since Japan, of all the OECD countries, is the least open to the rest of the world. There is little guarantee that getting the expected medium-term rate of inflation in Japan up to 5 per cent through aggressive monetary expansion, going well beyond the already substantial relaxation of the recent past, would stimulate demand to an extent sufficient to overcome the present stagnation and to validate the inflation itself.[29]

Paul Krugman provides microeconomic foundations to the modified Keynesian model in terms of rational behaviour of economic agents; here the following assumptions are crucial:

1. Prices are relatively rigid in the short run, but flexible in the long run. This is a fairly common assumption, suggesting the economy enjoys full employment in the long run.
2. The decisions of consumers and investors are rational and based on current and expected future income and other relevant variables; in his model, Krugman ignores investment and the focus is on utility-maximizing behaviour of the consumer.
3. The central bank is committed to maintain price stability or a fixed rate of inflation.
4. The government expenditure and tax programmes obey the inter-temporal budget constraint.
5. Private economic agents, households and firms are aware of the monetary policy stance and the government's inter-temporal budget constraint.

Under the above assumptions, the economy is likely to be demand-constrained in the short run, but the emergence of a liquidity trap and policy ineffectiveness requires stronger conditions:

1. The current consumption and investment demand must be so insensitive to interest rate variations that even at a zero real rate of interest, aggregate demand falls short of full employment output. To attain full employment, the economy requires a sufficiently high negative real rate of interest.

2. The supply of money in the current period is large enough to push the nominal rate of interest down to zero, but this does not ensure full employment unless the expected weight of inflation is sufficiently high.
3. The insufficiently high-expected rate of inflation is the result of the belief that, as in the past, the central bank will also in the future try to maintain a low rate of inflation, if not price stability.

The monetary policy ineffectiveness premise of the Krugman model seems to fit in with the Japanese experience over the 1998–2003 period. So do the results relating to the impact of fiscal policy. But an increase in government expenditure does not trigger off a multiplier process through an increase in consumption, since the intertemporal budget constraint of households remains unchanged. Of course, the result is the same, irrespective of whether the current increase in government expenditure is financed through taxes, borrowing from the public or printing money.

Hence in order to reduce the output gap through an increase in aggregate demand, the BOJ must try to generate inflationary expectations. But expansion in the money supply may not do the trick, if people believe that there will be a reversal in the central bank's policy stance, once the economy picks up and prices tend to rise.

Krugman suggests that in order to solve the problem, Japan can learn from the experience of other countries, which required their central banks to keep inflation below a pre-assigned rate. Only in this case would the legal stipulation be set on its head. The BOJ should be required to maintain the inflation rate above some targeted level, say 4 per cent per annum, for a period of 10 years.[30]

The McKinnon–Ohno thesis accepts that Japan finds itself in a liquidity trap. But it differs from that of Krugman, since it lays the blame for positive real interest rates not only on the credibility of the BOJ's low inflation policy, but on the expectation of future currency appreciation. It is argued that the past history of US–Japan trade conflicts has set the yen on a relentless upward path and that this trend is incorporated in expectations (the continuing large uncovered interest rate differential between the two countries). The continuing currency appreciation due to foreign pressures lead to falling Japanese tradable prices – a process that is then validated by the central bank's orthodox stance. Hence when monetary policy is caught in a liquidity trap, increased public expenditure is the textbook solution for overcoming a slump, because government expenditure can increase without bidding up the interest rate. But given the state of Japan's public finance and the worries of the populace about their future social security, the fiscal route is not sustainable. From this domestic perspective, it is no wonder that Japanese leaders are discouraged.[31]

'Japan's economy is still fragile, but the Japanese government has run out of policy options; a leading official in the ruling coalition had admitted, it is very difficult to know what to do, to achieve clear economic recovery', said Chikara Sakaguchi, policy chief of the new Komeita Party, a member of the ruling coalition.[32]

Hence the way to achieve such a stabilization of the currency lies in an agreement with the USA to settle on long-term nominal yen–dollar parity. This would require some monetary policy coordination between the two countries. As Boltho and Corbett observed, the major difficulty with this proposal is not dissimilar to that of the Krugman proposal. There one had to persuade central bankers to behave irresponsibly. Here one has to persuade central bankers to coordinate their monetary policies internationally (some would say to behave sensibly).

Given the very patchy and unsatisfactory history of international economic cooperation so far and the opposition of the US authorities to any encroachment on their policy autonomy, the chances of such an agreement being reached seem close to zero at present. It is difficult to see how an end to deflationary expectations on its own will be able to bring forward aggregate demand to anything like the extent needed to overcome the present sluggishness.[33]

Of course, depreciations need not be seen as attempts to export unemployment since, thanks to their favourable domestic multiplier effect, they can substantially raise imports. In case of the USA a 5 per cent depreciation of the dollar might leave the current balance largely unchanged.[34]

But in Japan, with its large trade surplus, the mercantilist effect of a lower currency is likely to be much larger. The Economic Planning Agency world economic model simulations suggest that a similar depreciation would raise real net exports by some 0.4 per cent of GDP over a two-year horizon.[35]

Increasingly reflecting American policy concerns with the international overvaluation of the dollar, the relative stability of the Japanese discount rate led to a declining interest differential in the years to 1985. Some attempts to arrest the slide of the US currency are evident in Japanese short-term rates after 1985 and in relative rate settings during 1987 and 1988.[36]

The implication that Japanese monetary policy in these years was seeking to suppress the continuing rise in the yen is consistent with the more general observation that episodes of increased currency strength have been associated with subsequent monetary relaxation by the BOJ.[37]

In the present context, it is the associated decline in nominal borrowing costs or the lending rate that should be emphasized. As US monetary policy required a counter-inflationary stance between 1987 and 1989, the relative strengthening of the dollar appears to have encouraged the Japanese authorities to lighten monetary conditions.

Investment and stagflation in the 1990s

With macroeconomic policy development conducive to rising capital intensity having characterized the immediately preceding years, the initiation of recession in 1992 also appears to have involved monetary policy influences. The suggestion that financial conditions in Japan were becoming restrictive after 1988 appears to understate the shift in stance as measured by the more comprehensive OECD index of monetary conditions.[38]

Against the background of a subsequent resumption of yen appreciation and of declining interest rates after 1990–91, it is clear that the recession was associated with a sudden decline in the previously elevated level of investment spending. Moreover, as the data in Table 3.2 confirm, the focus of this decline appears to have been narrow. While real GDP records minimal growth between 1991 and 1994, the decline in manufacturing output is especially severe in 1993. Moreover, the subsectors – fabricated metals, machinery and equipment – accounted for about half of the manufacturing reduction. While noting that this coincided with a fall in both export volume and in unit values, the role of declining investment spending is especially clear. The decline in fixed capital formation between 1991 and 1994 is more than accounted for by reduced outlays on machinery and equipment. Also the decline in these series preceded the sharp decline in export revenues in 1993. Rather than triggering a 1980s-style boom in investment spending, falling interest rates and rising yen-induced unit labour costs were to be associated with a recession prolonged by the behaviour of their magnitude during the early 1990s.[39]

Since late 1997, the BOJ had pursued an accommodative policy with a view to enhancing the flow of liquidity in the system. It was so obvious in the balance sheet of the BOJ. Faced with financial turbulence in late

Table 3.2 BOJ interventions through purchase of commercial bills, government bonds and commercial paper

	Exchange rate	*Interest rate (%)*	*Stock price*			*Bank PLR (Y–Y (% change)*	*Money supply (Y–Y (% change)*		*Consumer prices (% change)*		*Producer prices (% change) change)*		*Nominal wages index (Y–Y %*
			Bond yield	*Govern-ment bond yield*	*Banks*		*Narrow*	*Broad*	*3 months*	*Y–Y*	*3 months*	*Y–Y*	
Jan 96	105.60	3.10	2.99	1.63	20,378	2.2	14.8	3.1	–1.2	–0.4	1.0	–0.2	
Feb 96	105.50	3.27	3.20	1.63	20,497	2.2	16.0	2.8	–1.5	–0.2	0.6	–0.1	
Mar 96	106.00	3.24	3.18	1.63	20,437	2.2	16.4	3.0	–0.9	0.1	0.9	0.4	
Apr 96	107.50	3.61	3.25	1.63	21,873	1.6	15.3	3.0	0.4	0.3	0.4	1.3	
May 96	106.60	3.37	3.32	1.63	21,916	1.5	15.6	3.3	2.1	0.3	– 0.1	1.3	
Jun 96	109.00	3.23	3.24	1.63	22,255	1.4	16.6	3.9	2.9		– 0.4	1.4	
Jul 96	109.00	3.30	3.27	1.63	21,379	1.0	13.9	3.6	1.7	0.4	– 0.4	1.4	
Aug 96	108.00	3.16	3.35	1.63	20,861	0.7	14.1	3.9	–0.3	0.2	– 0.1	0.5	
Sep 96	109.25	2.96	2.90	1.63	20,820	0.2	12.0	3.5	–0.7		0.1		
Oct 96	112.60	2.82	2.75	1.63	21,106	–0.5	11.5	3.7	0.3	0.5	0.1	0.3	
Nov 96	112.50	2.70	2.61	1.63	21,127	–0.5	10.9	3.3	1.3	0.5	0.9	0.5	
Dec 96	114.00	2.64	2.49	1.63	20,171	–0.5	10.3	3.2	1.1	0.6	1.7	0.9	
Jan 97	118.50	2.61	2.51	1.63	18,281	–0.1	10.4	3.1		0.6	3.1	1.0	6.6
Feb 97	123.25	2.56	2.40	1.63	18,547	–0.1	10.0	3.0	–0.7	0.6	4.1	1.6	1.8
Mar 97	122.75	2.49	2.36	1.63	18,348	–0.1	9.5	2.7	–0.9	0.5	4.2	1.6	1.5
Apr 97	125.60	2.33	1.99	1.63	18,332	0.0	9.0	3.1	2.0	1.9	6.0	3.2	1.8
May 97	118.00	2.69	2.34	1.63	20,113	–0.1	9.0	3.0	5.4	1.9	5.4	2.7	1.8
Jun 97	113.50	2.54	2.28	1.63	20,520	–0.1	8.6	2.8	8.8	2.2	4.5	1.9	0.9
Jul 97	115.40	2.38	2.11	1.63	20,119	–0.1	8.4	3.0	5.8	1.9	– 0.4	1.8	2.2
Aug 97	118.00	2.34	1.90	1.63	19,101	–0.2	8.5	3.2	2.2	2.1	– 2.4	2.1	1.0

Table 3.2 BOJ interventions through purchase of commercial bills, government bonds and commercial paper – *continued*

	Exchange rate	*Interest rate (%)*	*Stock price*			*Bank PLR (Y–Y (% change)*	*Money supply (Y–Y (% change)*		*Consumer prices (% change)*		*Producer prices (% change)*		*Nominal wages index (Y–Y % change)*
			Bond yield	*Government bond yield*	*Banks*		*Narrow*	*Broad*	*3 months*	*Y–Y*	*3 months*	*Y–Y*	
Sep 97	120.00	2.23	1.78	1.63	18,386	–0.5	8.0	2.8	–0.1	2.4	– 2.4	2.0	1.0
Oct 97	121.00	2.00	1.60	1.63	17,468	–0.4	8.1	2.7	1.6	2.5	– 0.8	1.6	1.4
Nov 97	125.75	1.94	1.52	1.63	15,943	–0.1	9.1	3.2	2.4	2.1	0.0	1.5	0.0
Dec 97	128.95	1.94	1.59	1.63	15,958	0.0	9.3	3.8	1.0	1.8	0.5	1.6	0.7
Jan 98	125.50	1.95	1.68	1.63	15,952	–0.2	9.8	4.3	–1.7	1.8	1.2	0.8	–0.8
Feb 98	125.75	1.95	1.74	1.63	16,766	–0.6	10.8	4.8	–2.6	1.9	0.1	–1.0	–0.1
Mar 98	128.50	1.82	1.61	1.63	16,782	–1.6	8.8	4.5	–1.6	2.2	– 2.9	–1.1	0.6
Apr 98	131.80	1.82	1.55	1.63	15,935	–2.5	8.3	3.5	0.4	0.4	– 5.0	–2.7	–0.7
May 98	135.25	1.60	1.33	1.63	15,476	–2.2	8.0	3.8	2.1	0.5	– 4.0	–1.7	–0.7
Jun 98	139.50	1.50	1.24	1.63	15,131	–2.3	7.7	3.5	2.0	0.1	– 0.9	–0.3	–0.4
Jul 98	140.60	1.68	1.43	1.63	16,392	–2.2	8.3	3.5	0.4	–0.1	1.7	–0.3	–2.5
Aug 98	145.00	1.45	1.24	1.63	15,217	–2.3	8.0	3.9	–2.2	–0.3	2.8	–0.2	–2.4
Sep 98	136.40	1.06	1.08	1.57	14,105	–2.7	7.7	3.9	–2.2	–0.2	0.7	–1.5	–0.7
Oct 98	120.00	0.85	1.07	1.50	13,704	–3.3	8.6	3.9	0.5	0.2	– 3.7	–2.8	–0.1
Nov 98	120.50	0.94	0.96	1.50	14,657		8.4	4.5	3.8	0.8	– 8.7	–3.5	0.1
Dec 98	117.50	1.50	1.28	1.50	14,464		6.2	4.0	4.0	0.6	–10.8	–4.4	–4.2

Notes: 3 months: Average of latest 3 months, compared with previous 3 months. Y–Y: Change over previous years.
Sources: The Economist and Economic Notes by the Japan Development Bank (JDB).

1997, ¥6.5 trillion were injected in December 1997, mainly through 'repo' transactions (in November 1997 Hokkaido Takushoku Bank and Yamaichi Securities collapsed). Between October 1997 and March 1998, outstanding loans of the BOJ to financial institutions increased from ¥0.8 trillion to ¥5 trillion. When the market for commercial paper dried up in times of financial distress, the BOJ extended a helping hand with the result that at the close of the financial year 1997–98, its stock of commercial paper and other bills stood at ¥10.3 trillion compared with average holding of about ¥3 trillion over six months before November 1997.

The suggestion that monetary tightening amplified the ownership-risk constraints on investment spending is consistent with the observation that capital formation in Japan is strongly correlated with the margin between the rate of return on physical assets and long-term interest rates.[40]

During the early phase of 1997–98 and also 1998–99, there was a lull in the market intervention by the BOJ when it allowed its assets to decline; the result was a slower growth in the money supply, some hardening of corporate rates and an appreciation of the yen, but it was not until the last week of June 1998, when the impending bankruptcy of the Long-Term Credit Bank produced adverse effects on the money markets. The BOJ again started injecting substantial liquidity in the system through purchase of commercial bills, government bonds and high quality commercial paper (Table 3.2).

After analysis of several alternative explanations for the Japanese stagnation of the 1990s, T. Bayoumi concluded on econometric grounds that banks' declining lending capacity was the principal cause.[41] But Akihiro Kanaya and David Woo emphasized the role of financial sector liberalization in promoting a bubble economy in the late 1980s and regulatory forbearance as the banks allowed impaired loans to accumulate.[42]

The Japanese stock market peaked at the end of 1989. In April 1990, the MOF began to limit bank lending to the real estate sector in an effort to rein in land prices that began to decline in 1992. As a result banks' asset growth began to level off, declining from ¥508 trillion in 1989 to about ¥491 trillion in 1990. The collapse of asset prices in 1990 caused economic growth to slow, significantly weakening the banks and other institutions. The weakening was manifested in the rapid deterioration of the quality of loans to the real estate industry, erosion of the value of collateral, mounting pressure on bank capital and a decline in debtors' ability to continue servicing.

Of relevance to the intensification of the crisis, as failing financial institutions provoked a credit crunch in 1997, the primacy accorded to monetary policy and exchange rate developments receives support from the Kanaya–Woo study. Moreover, the inaction of the financial liberalization programme in the second half of the 1980s is itself attributed in part to US pressures to weaken the dollar by enhancing the demand for yen-denominated financial assets.[43] Hence with dollar–yen diplomacy clearly in the background, the comparative neglect of exchange rate developments in these studies is striking. From the present perspective, it arises because the link between the yen's secular appreciation and evolving structure, both of the capital stock and of emerging business balance sheet strain, is not acknowledged. The comparative lack of concern with international cost developments may also reflect the general view of the closed nature of the Japanese economy that the present perspective must confront.[44]

As part of the easy money policy, the BOJ has kept the inter-bank overnight loan rate at a record low of 0.25 per cent since September 1998, broadened the scope of 'repurchase' operations by raising the maturity ceiling of eligible commercial papers to one year, established additional channels of credit by promising to refinance half of new loans to banks during the last quarter of 1998 and proposed to purchase the bills issued by financial institutions and collateralized by corporate bonds. Since there was a slow-down in the policy of easy money in December 1998, the BOJ measures did not produce any effect on bank lending, which was declining during 1998–99. The contraction of bank finance in the face of the cheap money policy suggests several difficulties in the transmission mechanism. Of course, the government and the BOJ made a mess of these problems due to delay in policy changes.

As Ryuzo Miyao recently observed, a significant structural shift occurred in the Japanese economic system during 1995 and three important episodes during that year are mentioned:[45]

1. The yen–dollar exchange rate reached a record high level at over ¥80 to the dollar in March 1995. Observing such extraordinary movements in the exchange rates, Japanese firms, both exporting and importing, are presumably forced to strengthen the strategy to hedge the exchange rate risk. It is quite probable that a change in the exchange rate has a lesser impact both negatively and positively on the aggregate economy after 1995. This would seem to be consistent with the observed shift in the effects of exchange rate disturbances;

2. The official discount rates were lowered by the BOJ to a new record low of 0.5 per cent in September 1995. The overnight call rate was also dramatically reduced from 2 to a 0.5 per cent level during 1995. Such a rapid decline in short-term interest rates reaching below 1 per cent may have fundamentally altered the efficacy of monetary policy in Japan. Now that short-term interest rates approach zero bound, less and less room is left for monetary loosening. Raising interest rates is also hard to justify under the recessionary and yen-appreciation environment. Inevitably monetary policy shocks have only a limited impact on the call rate itself and accordingly on the aggregate economy as well. This interpretation seems to fit well with the break in the role of monetary policy in the economy;
3. During 1991–94, there were several failures of small local banks and credit unions. It was in 1995 that there was a public outcry against the depth of these bad loans along with the related problem of the convoy regulatory system managed by the MOF. In August 1995 the largest credit union, Kizu Credit Union, and the largest secondary local bank, Hyogo Bank, failed at the same time. In December 1995 the government announced that it would begin spending public funds to resolve the failed non-bank institutions (Jusens), which incited national outrage. With these events in 1995, the banks presumably strengthened their efforts to reduce bad loans and hence bank lending did not increase despite a very low interest rate policy. The balance sheet problem was also serious on the borrowers' side, which further weakened the credit channel in Japan.

As R. Kato and T. Watanabe argued, the effectiveness of monetary policy was weakened due to the deterioration of the borrowers' balance sheets in Japan.[46]

The fiscal response

The first sign of a change in the government's fiscal measures in view of the continued fall in production and employment came with the announcement in December 1997 of a temporary income tax cut of ¥2 trillion and acceleration of government expenditure proposed for fiscal year 1998. In February 1998, the original budget proposal totalling ¥77.5 trillion was raised by ¥4.5 trillion, in addition to a ¥2 trillion temporary income tax cut announced earlier. The new package included extra expenditure on public works amounting to ¥1.5 trillion. The sum required for the public works programme was proposed to be met by borrowing from the next year's budget. The MOF hoped that the economy would stage a recovery during 1998–99.

As was recently suggested, if demand management policies are almost impotent, the alternative for the MOF may be to wait for recovery.[47] As Dominic Wilson recently suggested, since for various reasons, Japanese demand had declined continuously during the 1990s, it was highly unlikely that changed price expectations either working through lower real interest rates or a more stable exchange rate would be sufficient to revive it.

As for lower spending propensities, the reasons lie on the household side with the future stringency of a lower growth environment and on the corporate side with the excesses of the bubble period. Consumer sentiment was negatively affected by the increasing gloom of official and private projections on longer-run growth. In the early 1990s many forecasters expected medium-term rates of growth of the order of 3–4 per cent per annum but by the end of the 1990s, these projections came down to only 1.5 per cent. Combined with the economy projections about the future burden of an ageing population, these forecasts certainly pushed Japanese households, as argued by Krugman (1998), into adjusting consumption today to offset an increasingly uncertain flow of consumption tomorrow. The real side explanations appear to be compatible with some of the facts of the recent Japanese economy, suggesting that these forces led to a collapse in private spending. Hence the notion that real side developments as well as inflationary targets could help to provide a means of escape from the liquidity trap by raising real interest rates, suggests that structural policy and monetary stimulus should be seen as complementary at least over the long term.

The idea that there are powerful real reasons for sluggish investment and consumption based on revised productivity expectations also matches some of the more detailed evidence from Japan. Recent work at the IMF supports the notion that a significant part of Japan's weakness comes from a stock adjustment in the capital market, following the revision of very optimistic views of future growth. Ramaswami and Rendu find that negative shocks to investment (residential and non-residential) appear to be important contributors to deceleration of output. It is argued that these negative shocks reflected the unwinding in the 1990s of overinvestment that took place in the latter half of the 1980s. This adjustment took place against the background of an unprecedented build-up in capital stock during the bubble period.

What is less well known is that unlike other countries that had an asset price bubble burst, for example Sweden and the UK, Japan did not experience a subsequent collapse in private consumption expenditure. There was a severe decline in business investment from about 20 per cent in 1990 to 16 per cent in 1998, but the share of business investment in GDP in Japan was 11 percentage points higher than in the USA in 1990; moreover, following the slump, the share of business investment in GDP is just 3 percentage points higher than in the USA.[48]

Japan had built up very high levels of debt compared with other industrial countries, but when asset prices collapsed in the 1990s, the expectations on which the debt was initially taken out did not subsequently materialize. While all industrial countries experienced a decline in the share of employment in manufacturing in the 1980s, Japan's decline was not as steep as in the USA or Europe. But beginning in 1994, there was a very sharp decline in Japan's manufacturing sector for various reasons; since there is a strong correlation between the rate of investment and size of manufacturing sector, the drop in investment might be linked to the shrinking manufacturing sector. Since the current rate of private investment in Japan is in the neighbourhood of historic lows, this suggests that the process of capital stock adjustment is more or less complete. Of course, a sharp increase in the capital – output ratio may signal over investment and the issue is whether Japan's capital–output ratio increased in relation to its trend growth.

The real effects of the bubble

Recently it was suggested that the shock to consumers' financial wealth brought about by collapsing stock and land prices was estimated at ¥450 trillion over the 1990–99 period, averaging around ¥75 trillion per year. But there is lot of uncertainty over the strength of wealth effects on consumption in Japan. A while back the EPA estimated that consumption would fall by 4 per cent of any capital loss with a lag of one year.[49] On this basis, the direct effects of the wealth shock would be expected to take around ¥3 trillion a year of annual consumption, a reduction of about one percentage point relative to trend – not far from what actually happened.

A major shift in the MOF's attitude was clear in April 1998 when within a few days of the acceptance of original budget proposals for fiscal year 1998, the government announced two additional packages totalling ¥20.7 trillion to provide a boost to the economy: one was a plan to use ¥4 trillion out of postal funds (outside the budget for investment in the stock market). The second was enlargement of the budget by ¥14.7 trillion ($147 billion) and marked a reversal of the policy of fiscal consolidation in the two earlier budgets. The new measures included allocation of ¥7.7 trillion to public works programmes, expenditure of ¥1.5 trillion on investment in high technology and a ¥4 trillion cut in income tax spread equally over two financial years, 1998 and 1999.

In 1999 Japan's fiscal deficit exceeded 10 per cent of GNP. Moreover, the Japanese government's gross debt rose from 58.2 per cent of GDP in 1991 and the OECD projected it to increase to more than 114 per cent of GDP in 2000 and 120 per cent in 2001.[50] This upward trend is completely out of step with other G7 countries.

Offsetting this fiscal expansion, the yen appreciated sharply in 1994–95, peaking at a highly overvalued 80 to the dollar in April 1995, and depressed both exposed and private domestic investment. But in 1996 when the yen fell and became less overvalued, output growth spurted to 5 per cent and recovery seemed at hand.[51]

In April 1997 hoping that this fiscal pump-priming had worked but concerned with a build-up of out of control debt, the government of the then Prime Minister Ryutaro Hashimoto seized the opportunity to increase general sales tax from 3 to 5 per cent and to close other tax loopholes. This tax increase sent the still sluggish economy into a severe tailspin from mid-1997 through to 1999.

Since July 1998 after the resignation of Hashimoto, new public spending programmes for infrastructure investments have been continually introduced, since Japan has been under persistent pressure from the US Treasury and observers such as Adam Posen to introduce more Keynesian-style fiscal stimuli.[52]

The second stimulus package of ¥24 trillion was announced in November 1998 and its impact would be obvious during 2000–1. Under this package ¥8.1 trillion were to be spent on telecommunications, education, social welfare and urban development projects. The corporate tax rate was lowered from 46 to 40 per cent and the top income tax rate from 65 to 50 per cent. With a view to providing relief to the most vulnerable groups in society, an emergency job creation fund was set up, ¥1 trillion were set aside to subsidize employers who hired middle-aged and older workers and ¥700 billion were allocated to distribution (as gift certificates among households with children and aged relations). Due to the wide credit crunch, ¥6 trillion were earmarked to help firms facing difficulty in borrowing from banks, ¥1.2 trillion allocated to subsidize interest payments on housing loans and financial assistance was promised to Japanese firms operating in the crisis countries of South-East Asia. As a result of these expansionary programmes, the government hoped that during 2000 and 2001, they would involve a change in the structural deficit of 1 per cent of GDP over that in fiscal year 1998.

Since Japan is already in a serious debt trap, observers like McKinnon and Ohno hold that several more years of public sector fiscal stimulus are simply not sustainable.[53] Moreover, taking a more consolidated approach to public sector gross debt by including the deteriorating position of local governments and presuming that fiscal deficits continue as in 1998–2000 on to 2005, Asher and Dugger produce similar results. Assuming 4 per cent interest charge and existing public debt, they calculate that the total public sector debt/GDP ratio will reach over 200 per cent by 2005 – a level never seen in peacetime in any industrial country.[54]

Moreover, Japan has an ageing population and underfunded social security system, the liabilities of which were not counted as part of the gross debt figures shown in Table 3.1. Nor were the huge contingent government liabilities from bad private bank loans counted, now estimated at $1 trillion.[55] The bad loan portfolio of the government itself jeopardized the fiscal investment and loan programme for housing, agriculture, economic development etc. Hence further fiscal expansion measures were indeed too risky.

Of course, with huge liquid savings balances, Japan's households are not currently liquidity constrained in contrast to what a static Keynesian public spending multiplier which supposes that most agents are liquidity constrained, would project. Nevertheless, the ordinary Japanese still worry about the effect of the disarray in public finance on their social security (pensions, medical care) in the longer run in the face of huge public sector deficits and unsustainable debts; current private spending has weakened further and personal saving has increased, as people decide to protect their own social security – a form of Ricardian equivalence.[56]

Policy options in a liquidity trap

Faced with the puzzle of Japan's stagnation during the 1990s in the face of monetary stimulus, Paul Krugman looks at a more serious scenario of a strong liquidity trap. In this case, the real rate of interest in equilibrium is negative. For this, the depressed outlook for future Japanese performance suggested by a declining workforce and rising dependency rates is cited in the scenario; investment opportunities are shrinking but desired savings are rising, forcing the real interest rate into negative territory. Having shown that this situation may be consistent with the attempted inter-temporal optimization, Krugman's conclusion is that a negative real rate must be established to provoke a switch from future to present consumption expenditure; the key problem is the excessive savings, and Krugman's solution would involve a commitment on the part of the BOJ to pursue an announced policy of moderate inflation over the long term. Of course Krugman acknowledges that his proposal would have the same exchange rate consequences as a monetary expansion under more conventional conditions. Hence a depreciation-induced increase in the yen price of final output (relative to Japanese wages) would be expected to shorten production processes, and a practical corollary for these countries is envisaged. There is little doubt that Japan's growth prospects are much less favourable than a simple extrapolation from the past might suggest. The Ministry of Health and Welfare estimated that the Japanese population will shrink at a rate of 0.2 per cent a year between 2000 and 2025. The labour force is projected to fall even faster; recent estimates of annual decline range from 0.25 per cent by the Japanese Ministry of Health and Welfare to 0.7 per cent per annum by the OECD (1997).[57]

Of course, Krugman does not discuss the structural consequences but anticipates the more conventional objection that his proposal would amount to a 'beggar thy neighbour' policy. From his inter-temporal framework, he derives a coefficient defined by this term and after inserting representative values, computes that the concern would be largely misplaced; with traded goods comprising a fixed endowment in his model, the suggested consequences of the policy are strongly counter-intuitive. The effect of the appreciation is to raise output and employment in the non-traded goods sector alone.[58]

A recent CGE modelling study by Noland et al. suggests that the simulated effect of a 30 per cent real depreciation of the yen during a period of aggressive monetary expansion is associated with an 8 per cent fall in the US output of both motor vehicles and machinery. Trade frictions would frustrate bilateral adjustments and alternative responses to the problem of the liquidity trap might be considered.[59]

There are reasons to doubt that equilibrium real interest rates are negative in Japan; both closed and open economy models broadly support the idea that Japan's miserable growth prospects pushed Japanese real interest rates into low positive territory.

However, McKinnon, stressing political economy factors in the yen's secular strengthening against the dollar, argued that this trend became embedded in market expectations. As US interest rates declined with inflation during the 1990s, comparable Japanese rates were forced towards zero; the uncovered interest parity condition effectively imposed a liquidity trap.[60]

Rather than trying to influence inflation expectations, McKinnon suggests a joint commitment by the American and Japanese authorities to influence those concerning the yen–dollar rate with the key assumption that US inflation would be held at low levels; he suggests agreement on a target forward exchange rate. Without trying to enforce that rate, official interventions would seek to prompt the market rate in the appropriate direction, while international interest rate parity conditions would force Japanese rates to rise towards those prevailing in the USA. This nominal increase would not transfer to anticipate real interest rates; the price increases would support a recovery of domestic consumption and investment spending.

While the two prescriptions differ in that one involves an explicit inflation target but the other focuses on the exchange rate, Krugman's suggested inflation target up to 4 per cent per annum is a little more than that likely to be imported by Japan under the McKinnon strategy.[61] In fact the inflation target would involve the maintenance of minimal nominal interest rates, as compared with the imposition of externally determined levels under the exchange rate target. These higher nominal rates could be expected to worsen the position of debt-burdened borrowers and their creditors in the short term.

Hence Summer's weak 'liquidity trap' case that zero-bound nominal interest rates may limit a counter-cyclical response, which requires the real interest rate to be pushed below equilibrium levels, may still be a valid picture of Japan in recent years, even if Krugman's stronger hypothesis is not, to the extent that Japanese real interest rate expectations of future productivity growth appear a more plausible culprit than demographics.

As P.N. Snowden recently suggested, in the perspective of dissolving the debt overhang, an alternative inflation target policy could be seen as having two advantages. Induced currency depreciation would raise export profitability as low interest rates and inflation eroded existing indebtedness. Recognizing these objections, the question arises as to whether financial asset holders would not respond defensively, especially in the novel policy context of a central bank commitment to promote inflation. If nominal interest rates remained lower, a potential depreciation of the yen could be much larger than purchasing power parity (PPP) calculations would suggest.[62]

Moreover, the contrasting advantage of an exchange rate target approach would be that non-sterilized exchange interventions would be required to establish the target, and the purpose and limits of these actions would be clear. As the target became the focus for expectations, the need for interventions would decline. In the present context, Okina's terse comments are most relevant: 'the alternative requirement that the BOJ should promote inflation actively over a period of years, would be more likely to be resisted on institutional grounds'.[63]

4
The Japanese Banking Crisis of the 1990s

Since 1995 several revolutionary changes have been observed in Japanese financial markets, and also the steady decline in the health of its banking system. This decline began with the bursting of the asset bubble, leading to a serious crisis in April 1997, when gross domestic product and industrial output posted their first decline. Moreover, several problems for the banks surfaced in 1992 and a decade-long slump caused considerable disruption in the flow of credit to business firms. Given the very large size of Japanese banks, this crisis had deep implications for the global economy. During the 1980s, the economy posted a growth of 5 per cent on average, as well as the stock and real estate market being in a boom, fuelled by expansive monetary policy and huge lending by the banking sector. The tightening of monetary policy by the BOJ in mid-1989 to slow down overheating was crucial, leading to a slump of stock and real estate prices. In autumn 1989, a falling market for Japanese equities, when the Nikkei 225 index fell from 38,900 in October 1989 to less than 13,000 and the Dow-Jones index boomed from 2400 in 1989 to more than 10,000. Hence Tokyo, by market capitalization in 1989 still the largest stock exchange in the world by ¥385 trillion, fell to rank third behind New York and London.

Moreover, during the decade, the number of foreign companies quoted on the Tokyo stock exchange declined and the total number of companies quoted was unchanged, but the New York stock exchange showed an increase of 45 per cent.

While most of the underlying causes – excessive asset growth in the boom times, weak corporate governance and regulatory forbearance when the system is under stress – are typical of a banking crisis in general, the Japanese banking crisis serves as a warning that such a crisis can befall a robust and sophisticated financial system. The crisis shows that the cost associated with such a crisis can be considerable. Beyond the fiscal cost associated with the restructuring of the banks (about 12 per cent of GDP already allocated by the government), the banking crisis was responsible for stagnation of the Japanese economy in the 1990s.[1]

Several observers suggested that, because of the importance of credit channels in the economy, the weakening of the banks reduced the effectiveness of loose monetary policy. Recently Kanaya and Woo have argued that weak corporate governance and regulatory forbearance stifled any incentive for meaningful restructuring of the banks and their corporate borrowers.[2]

Against the background of a spiral of deflation, the Japanese financial sector began to suffer during early 1990. It is true that the licensed banks extended only 20 per cent of their total loan book to the real estate and construction sectors; about 80 per cent of total loans were secured by real estate collateral. Against all the odds, Japanese banks managed to tackle the increased pressure for disposal of their problem loans.[3]

The bubble economy and after

The Japanese microeconomic environment during the second half of the 1980s recorded above-trend economic growth and near-zero inflation that led to a significant decline in the country-risk premium and upward adjustment in growth expectations and also fuelled rapid credit growth during this period.[4]

In the second half of the 1990s, acceleration in financial liberalization and deregulation, consisting of relaxation of interest rate controls, started with liberalization of term-deposit rates in 1985, as a result of the pressure from the US government and capital market deregulation, lifting of prohibition on short-term Euro-yen loans to domestic borrowers in 1984, gradual removal of restrictions on access to the corporate bond market and creation of the commercial paper market in 1987.

Relaxation of restrictions on permissible activities of previously tightly segregated institutions included the raising of different types of lending ceilings; for example, agricultural, fishery and credit cooperatives saw an increase in their lending ceilings to non-members.

The MOF gave the following rationale for its deregulation programme:

> The financial system forms the base of an economy. In order to maintain Japan's economic vitality as its society ages in the 21st century,

> our citizens' financial assets must be deployed more effectively and funds must be provided to next generation growth industry and in order to fulfill our global responsibility, we must ensure smooth supply of capital to the world. For this, we must utilize the y. 1200 trillion of individual savings ensuring the optimal distribution of resources through financial market.

These developments had several consequences for Japanese depository institutions.[5]

For several years, there was heavy pressure on banks' risk-adjusted interest rate margins as a result of price competition and banks went on expanding riskier sectors of loan portfolios. Recently it was argued that profit margins of Japanese banks, in decline since the early 1980s, were boosted in the late 1980s by a shift towards higher-risk loans.[6]

The focus of banks on market share and the fact that their lending decisions were guided by collateral needs, rather than on cash flow analysis, caused them to loosen credit standards during rising estate prices. In order to speed up credit check procedures for loan approval, many banks transferred the responsibility for loan risk evaluation from their credit investigation bureaux to less independent monitoring bureaux that reported directly to the banks' sales divisions.[7]

While the stock market from time to time showed signs of recovery, real estate prices were still falling in 2003. On recent estimates, this deflation of real estate value over the period 1993–2003 had added to a total loss of 80 per cent in urban areas, which equals roughly three times the Japanese GDP. In contrast to the stock markets, further deterioration of real estate prices did not stop in 1999 and a further decline of 4.9 per cent was observed.[8]

While several companies were restructuring and selling property in order to consolidate, there was also a downturn in housing demand due to a wide recession. As compared to 1990, commercial real estate in Tokyo was available at 28 per cent and in Osaka at 24 per cent of the price at the time.

Even at the time of writing (2003), there seemed no end to the Japanese banking crisis due to the close links with falling real estate prices. Moreover, the quality of loans to the real estate sector declined over the years and the value of collateral eroded, as the decline in the value of banks' equity holdings put heavy pressure on bank capital. Along with the lifting of restrictions on the access of Japanese firms to the domestic and Euro-bond market, there was market acceleration in new bond issues; between 1984 and 1991 the percentage of funds

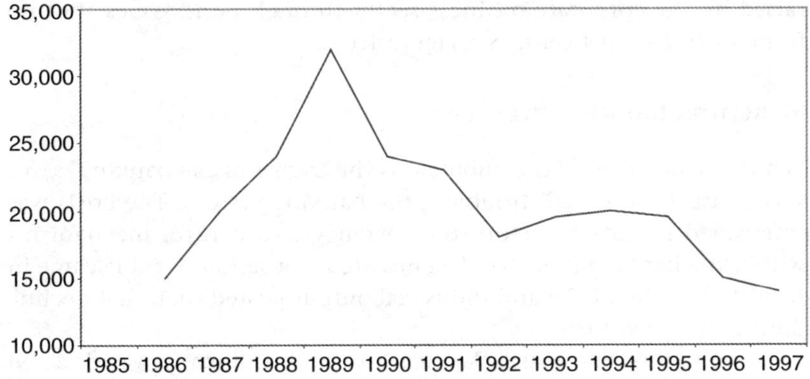

(a)

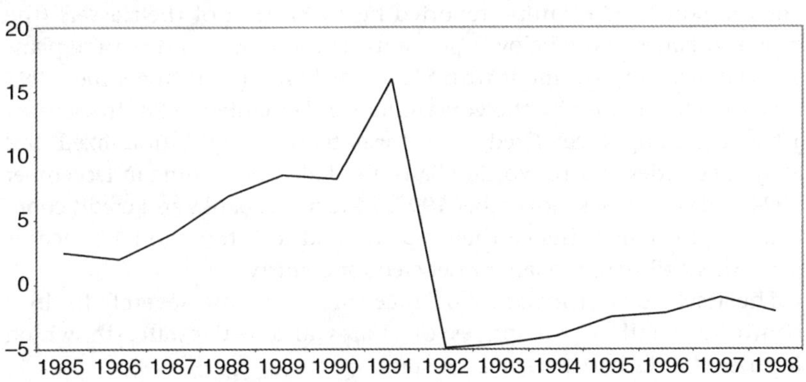

(b)

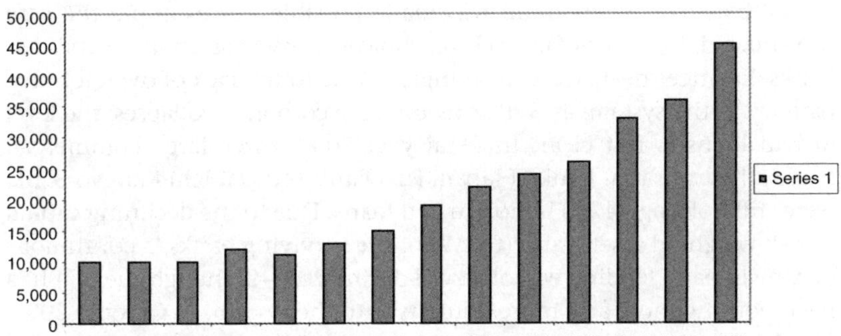

(c)

Figure 4.1 (a) Nikkei 225, Bank of Japan discount rate; (b) growth in residential land prices and (c) outstanding corporate bonds (billion yen)
Sources: (a) and (b) BOJ Research and Statistics Department, Financial and Economic Statistics, Monthly, Tokyo; (c) Federal Reserve Bank of Chicago (1993)

raised by the corporate business sector through bond issues shot up from 3.6 to 24.5 per cent.[9] See Figure 4.1.

Structural banking problems

While the bursting of the bubble was the trigger of the banking crisis, several issues were still troubling the banking system. The crisis was intensified by unsatisfactory transparency and control mechanisms within the banking industry. The first signal of serious trouble came in April 1997, when GDP and industrial output posted their first decline during this downturn.

In April 1999, the Nissan Mutual Insurance Company was declared insolvent and two of the 20 major banks – Hokkaido Takushoku Bank and Nippon Credit Bank – reported heavy erosion of their assets (the capital adequacy ratio below 3 per cent). The announced structural plans showed little improvement with STB going bankrupt in November 1997 and MCB taken over by the government in December 1998. In October 1998, the Long Term Credit Bank was temporarily nationalized and Sanyo Securities and Tokyo City Bank also failed. Beginning in December 1994 and until Black November 1997, 14 regional banks and credit cooperatives also failed. Hence there was no end to international concerns over the stability of the largest net creditor country.

The asset side of the banks' balance sheets was also severely hit by a continuous fall in the prices of shares and real estate, in which Japanese banks had a significant stake.

Against the background of unsatisfactory transparency and control of banks' balance sheets, fraud was made possible, for example the case of Yamaichi. In view of far-reaching choices to assess assets and liabilities, banks' balance sheets were meaningless. Due to the lack of overall transparency in the system, as well as reoccurring corporate collapses, the level of bad loans is not clear. In fiscal year 2000, three large commercial banks, the Industrial Bank of Japan, Fuzi Bank and Dai-Ichi Kangyo Bank, were still holding ¥4700 billion in bad loans. Due to the declining capital to risk-weighted assets ratio (CRAR) of the surviving banks, a continuous decline in bank lending was observed during 2001–2, though the BOJ had been pouring more and more liquidity into the system. In October 2000, the decrease in bank loans on a year-on-year basis was 4.5 per cent and this fall further compounded the ongoing troubles.

In the case of other financial institutions in the economy, growing liquidity problems led to the closure of Yamaichi Securities on 24 November 1997.

Several observers recently suggested that the banking crisis was an obvious result of decade-long financial reform measures undertaken in a half-hearted manner. No doubt systemic collapse of the financial system was recently avoided through prompt action and support from the BOJ. Notwithstanding the fact of a continuous rise in huge bad loans of a really frightening magnitude, as the Financial Supervisory Agency (FSA) reported, by the end of March 2000, the problem loans of the 19 largest banks in Japan amounted to ¥59.5 trillion.

The Japanese financial system was distinguished by a high degree of specialization that was developed during the 1940s to finance wartime industry and in the 1950s to finance economic revival. Several financial institutions were set up, each for a special purpose. In 1971, the Jusens were funded as a union of seven housing loan companies, since the ordinary banks were not able to extend credit to Jusen companies due to the long-term nature of the housing business. The Japanese financial institutions are by law designated to carefully defined areas of activity, and the banks were prohibited from doing business in securities. In this way the government tried to avoid problems emerging in different sectors in the economy. This double demarcation of financial institutions was unique among developed countries and led to 147 licensed banks in Japan operating in highly specialized groups. Even today, the Japanese system is highly overbanked with 842 financial institutions operating in the economy. The old system was not led by market mechanisms but by a system of financial socialism.[10]

Loan loss provisions

Since 1964 banks were allowed to set up tax-deductible general reserve accounts for possible future loan losses. These reserve accounts were meant to cover loans (normal and substandard) and banks were not required to make any additional specific provisions against substandard loans. Banks had the option of setting their general reserves to reflect their average loan loss during any three years, or setting them at a reference level decided by the authorities. Often banks opted to set their general reserves at the reference level (after 1989 the reference level was fixed at 0.3 per cent of total outstanding loans). The ceiling for reserve accounts was fixed at 0.42 per cent of total loans in 1964, but was reduced five times, down to 0.3 per cent by 1989 to reflect the downward trend of historical loan loss.[11]

It is rather surprising that the increase in actual non-performing loans beyond 0.3 per cent of total loans sometime during the 1990s did not cause banks to voluntarily increase their general reserves to take advantage of available tax relief. This would suggest that either banks did not want to transfer their tier-one capital to their tier-two account (when their tier-two capital reached the level of their tier-one capital), or they felt that by raising their reserve accounts, this was a suggestion to the market of expectations of a further increase in non-performing loans. There might have been a coordination problem among the banks, with individual banks not wanting to draw attention to themselves by raising their reserve accounts. If this is true, it raises questions as to why the authorities did not readjust the 0.3 reference level in 1997; the government eliminated the option of using the reference level from the tax regulations.[12]

The banks were very slow to write off loans with little probability of recovery. This was due to a strict tax guideline that allowed write-offs only after a loan loss account had been ascertained in bankruptcy proceedings. In some cases, banks themselves were reluctant to write off loan losses, since the fear was that borrowers might perceive the write-off as a signal that banks had given up on loan recovery.

Strategy of banks

With a view to adjusting to the post-bubble scenario, some banks transferred the responsibility for loan risk evaluation from monitoring bureaux back to credit investigation bureaux. Credit approval procedures thus became tighter and more emphasis was put on borrowers or projected cash-flow analysis, rather than on simple collateral requirements. The collateral value was more closely scrutinized and the

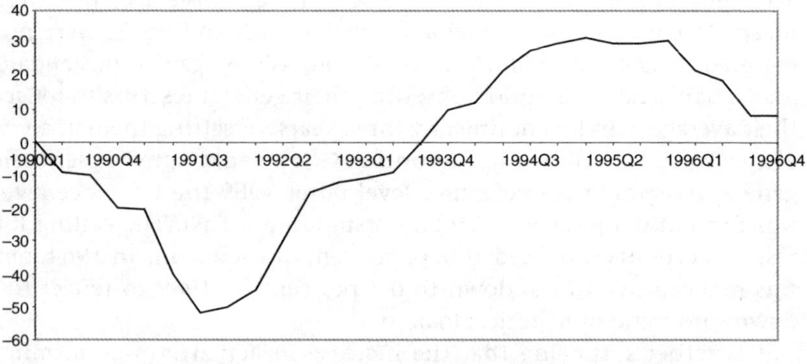

Figure 4.2 Financial institutions' willingness to lend (Tankan Survey)

average loan to collateral ratio for many banks was reduced. This showed that, after the bubble burst, there was significant tightening of credit standards and conditions; as the Tankan Survey showed, the willingness of financial institutions to lend as reported by the firms, declined very considerably during 1990–95 (Figure 4.2).

The main banks and loan restructuring

In the Japanese financial system the main bank is the kingpin; it acts as a quasi-insider monitor of the borrowing firm and as a mediator when borrowers are in trouble.[13]

While during the 1980s, the main bank system worked reasonably well, one advantage was the reduction in monitoring costs in the face of asymmetric information. As Kawai, Hashimoto and Izumida found, firms with main banks pay much lower interest rate premia than do firms without main banks.[14]

The main banks were responsible for identifying problem borrowers before they became insolvent and also for helping them in restructuring their business.[15]

The effectiveness of the main bank system suffered when they were under serious pressure and also because of their reluctance to allow their borrowers to default; the main banks began to exercise forbearance, even when the long-term viability of their borrowers came into question. During the 1990s, Japanese banks widely restructured non-viable loans by reducing interest rates and extending their maturity. But it was not uncommon for banks to capitalize unpaid interest and to open new credit lines in order for borrowers to repay overdue loans. This was possible in the past, because loan classifications and provisioning requirements for restructured loans were weak and banks were able to classify non-performing loans as performing immediately on the restructuring of loans.[16]

Sakura Bank raised ¥200 billion through two convertible preferred stock issues (March 1992 and April 1994), which were converted to common stock on maturity in June 1995 and October 1997. Daiwa Bank issued ¥50 billion of exchangeable bonds in March 1994, which were exchanged into common stock in March 1998. It also raised an additional ¥50 billion through a domestic private placement of convertible preferred stock with 30-year maturity. In 1996 Tokai Bank raised ¥100 billion through a Euro-market issue of $8\frac{1}{2}$-year convertible preference shares.

Banks also used their related companies to clean up their balance sheets. Before December 1998 they were required to consolidate only those subsidiaries and affiliates in which they had more than a 50 and 20 per cent stake respectively. To circumvent consolidation requirements, banks set up related companies, which were neither subsidiaries nor affiliates, and to which they transferred their loans at above market rates.

Increasing the capital base

Banks have two sources of capital – paid-in capital and retained earnings. During the 1980s, several banks raised capital through public offerings with a view to raise their lending in real estate and also to prepare for the based capital accord rules. Even after the bubble burst, banks tried to raise capital in the market to increase their write-offs and provide for huge bad loans. Between 1992 and 1998 only Sakura Bank, Daiwa Bank, Tokai Bank and Mitsubishi Bank were able to raise tier-one capital in the market by issuing debt instruments.

This form of equity issue with delayed conversion was designed to placate Japanese regulators who appeared to believe that ordinary equity issues would at least depress a bank's stock price.[17] Hence it was suggested that these banks had to pay a substantial premium to raise capital in this way, with Tokai Bank security issues underpriced at issue by 13 per cent. But by 1998, due to the sharp decline in bank stocks and downgrading by rating agencies, the banks suspended further moves to raise capital.

The Japanese banks have low net worth; they also hold a large portion of their capital gains in the form of shares (between 8 and 14 per cent) for city and trust banks. Hence a falling market affects the net value of the banks and the quality of their collateral, not least because of shrinking net worth and severe undercapitalization, and a dangerous liquidity crisis was looming over Japan. However, this credit crunch proved to be an unexpected benefit to the underdeveloped investment-banking sector. Issuing asset-backed securities turned out to be a true alternative for those companies that faced credit cuts. This boom resulted in a thriving securitization market.[18]

It was observed that almost all banks issued subordinated debts to compensate for the decline in tier-two capital, caused by the drop in unrealized profits for security holding. Due to the decline in credit ratings, banks began to offer these securities in private offerings to institutional investors, for example insurance companies and the companies in their groups not defined as affiliates. Japanese banks have significant exposure to each others' stock prices through cross-shareholding arrangements, but banks are not allowed to use any subordinated debts issued by them to their affiliates towards their tier-two capital.

The eroding margins

Besides the domestic credit crunch, Japanese banks faced severe losses from Russia, the emerging markets and also the hedge funds, leading to further cuts in loans. Since the banks, over the years, had greatly shrunk their loan books with a view to stabilizing their eroding balance sheets, more and more companies were driven into bankruptcy.

In order to compete with commercial paper and corporate bond markets, the banks expanded their offering of Euro-yen loans to borrowers. Previously these loans were extended only to blue chip firms, with access to international factor markets. Banks began to expand their prime rate offerings to small firms. These moves led to erosion of banks' short-term lending margins (Table 4.1), but the continued decline in interest rates should have benefited banks' lending spreads. Several city banks had a large maturity mismatch between their assets and liabilities, since they are not allowed to issue debentures and until October 1993 were not allowed to offer deposits whose maturity was more than three years (Table 4.2). So their overall interest margins expanded during declines in interest rates.[19]

Table 4.1 Sectoral lending by banks (as percentage of total outstanding loans)

	Manufacturing	*Real estate*	*Construction*	*Individuals*	*SMEs*
1985	26.12	7.71	5.69	9.25	78.50
1986	23.58	9.61	5.52	9.79	74.57
1987	20.46	10.22	5.23	11.29	74.47
1988	19.09	11.14	5.26	12.86	70.46
1989	16.65	11.54	5.40	15.25	68.55
1990	15.74	11.28	5.31	16.27	67.36
1991	15.57	11.60	5.59	16.84	65.84
1992	15.06	12.08	5.94	16.78	66.12
1993	16.04	11.40	6.24	16.09	66.99
1994	15.64	11.69	6.41	15.94	66.48
1995	14.98	11.84	6.42	16.70	65.09
1996	14.56	12.19	6.32	17.32	50.31
1997	14.11	12.49	6.33	17.76	49.89
1998	14.33	10.77	6.47	10.42	59.20

* The numbers do not include Euro-yen loans.
Source: Bank of Japan.

Table 4.2 Interest rate spreads (%)

	*Average time deposit rates, 3–6 months (A)**	*Average new lending rates, short term (B)†*	*Lending spreads, short term (B–A)*	*Average time deposit rates, 2–3 years (D)**	*Average new lending rates, long term (E)†*	*Spreads, long term (E–D)*
1991	5.70	7.73	2.03	6.11	7.59	1.48
1992	3.10	5.65	2.55	4.59	5.89	1.30
1993	1.92	4.35	2.43	2.71	4.66	1.95
1994	1.61	3.53	1.92	2.02	3.91	1.89
1995	0.85	2.70	1.85	1.24	3.08	1.84
1996	0.22	2.03	1.81	0.65	2.50	1.85
1997	0.21	1.91	1.70	0.38	2.27	1.89
1998	0.19	1.88	1.59	0.30	2.21	1.91

* Deposits of less than ¥3 million. The rates exclude regulated interest rates.
† Short-term loans are loans with maturity less than 1 year. Long-term loans are loans with maturity greater than 1 year.
Source: Bank of Japan.

Table 4.3 Maturity structure of loans (as percentage of total loans)

	Within 3 months	*Between 3 months and 1 year*	*Longer than 1 year*	*Others**
1985	21.20	11.80	62.00	6.00
1986	18.70	12.60	61.60	7.10
1987	16.70	18.90	55.70	8.70
1988	16.80	25.50	49.00	9.70
1989	12.60	23.90	53.70	10.80
1990	11.70	19.30	57.40	12.60
1991	11.20	19.00	57.40	13.40
1992	10.70	20.60	56.30	13.40
1993	9.70	21.10	55.90	13.30
1994	9.30	21.50	55.60	13.60
1995	8.80	19.80	58.20	13.20
1996	8.00	19.30	59.00	13.70
1997	8.20	18.60	59.20	14.00

* Others consist mainly of overdraft loans.
Source: Bank of Japan.

With a view to protect their margins, banks began to take on more risk by extending the average maturity of their lending. Between 1990 and 1999, loans with a maturity of more than one year rose from 55 to 67 per cent of total loans, but loans with a maturity of less than three months declined from 12 to 6 per cent (Table 4.3). These changes were due to a shift in bank lending from short-term working capital finance to long-term project finance (shift from loans on bills to loans on deeds, Table 4.4). The lengthening of loan maturity exposed banks to more interest rate risk along with liquidity risk. But the average spreads on long-term lending did not fall.

Under the loans on bills arrangements, banks can always sell their holdings of bills in the secondary markets and also to the BOJ in its 'repo' operations; of course, securitization of loans in deals is not so common in Japan as it is in the USA.

While the Japanese banks have low net worth, they also hold a very large share of their capital base in the form of shares (between 6 and 12 per cent for city and trust banks). Hence a falling market influences the net value of banks and their collateral quality.

With a view to boosting short-term profits, Japanese banks relaxed credit conditions; there was a steady increase in unsecured loans as a percentage of total loans until the mid-1990s. Another piece of

Table 4.4 Bills discounted and loans by type (as percentage of total loans)

	*Bills discounted**	*Loans on bills*†	*Loan on deeds*‡	*Overdrafts*§
1989	6.83	27.56	52.11	13.50
1990	5.89	24.86	54.48	14.77
1991	5.63	23.62	54.52	16.23
1992	4.92	24.07	54.31	16.70
1993	4.75	23.96	54.51	16.78
1994	4.43	23.70	54.43	17.44
1995	4.03	22.48	55.95	17.54
1996	3.80	20.43	57.62	18.15
1997	3.52	19.52	57.90	19.06
1998	2.83	18.43	59.72	19.02

* Bills discounted usually involve commercial bills issued by a third party. Company A receives from company B a promissory note, which company A discounts at a bank. These bills are generally short term, with maturity less than 1 year.
† Loans on bills are backed by bills issued by the borrower. These loans are structured in such a way as to be paid back as the bills mature. The average maturity of this type of loans is less than 1 year. Companies have historically used this type of borrowing arrangements to finance their working capital.
‡ Loans on deeds are loans with a written contract. This type of loan generally carries a maturity between 3 and 5 years. Companies typically use this type of borrowing arrangement to finance medium and longer-term investments.
§ Overdraft loans are loans that carry a commitment by banks to provide loans up to a prespecified ceiling. These loans are also typically used by borrowers to finance short-term liquidity needs.
Source: Bank of Japan.

Table 4.5 Deposit growth of different financial institutions*(%)

	City banks	*Credit cooperatives*	*Postal savings*
1991	–4.84	0.23	14.18
1992	–6.05	2.65	9.31
1993	1.29	3.33	7.90
1994	1.95	4.11	7.66
1995	3.03	–5.4	8.02
1996	0.06	–3.23	5.36
1997	2.86	–3.34	6.96

* Private sector deposits. Includes deposits by other financial institutions.
Source: Bank of Japan.

evidence for relaxed credit conditions is the continued migration of loans from loans on bills to overdrafts.[20] See Table 4.5.

The conditions of loans on bills are more stringent than the overdraft loans that provide borrowers with more flexibility for repayment.

Table 4.6 Security types for bank loans (as percentage of total loans)

	Loans secured by real estate	*Loans secured by stocks and bonds*	*Loans secured by others**	*Loans secured by third-party guarantee*	*Unsecured loans*
1985	21.72	1.96	9.57	26.31	40.44
1986	22.08	2.17	9.87	25.97	39.91
1987	23.19	2.35	9.43	25.61	39.41
1988	23.86	2.62	9.18	26.76	37.59
1989	25.69	2.63	8.31	29.31	34.06
1990	27.22	2.31	8.60	29.93	31.94
1991	28.08	1.91	8.29	30.32	31.41
1992	28.41	1.65	8.11	29.69	32.12
1993	27.93	1.66	8.16	29.93	32.32
1994	26.93	1.52	8.01	30.47	33.08
1995	25.36	1.53	7.90	31.83	33.37
1996	24.08	1.30	7.68	32.86	34.08
1997	23.46	1.38	7.46	34.07	33.63

* Others include deposits.
Source: Bank of Japan.

While the rollover of loans on bills needs to be approved, the roll-over of overdrafts is automatic. As Kanaya and Woo observed, the rise in overdraft loans could be interpreted as an accumulation of disguised non-performing loans.

Recently Woo suggested that until 1995 weakly capitalized banks expanded their lending more rapidly than heavily capitalized banks. This study shows in a series of cross-sectional regressions that bank lending was negatively correlated with bank capital during the early 1990s, in spite of the introduction of the Basle capital standards.

During this period, the American banks, in view of the BIS capital standards, were found to curtail their lending in response (Table 4.6).

Tapping unrealized capital gains

The Japanese banks began to tap unrealized gains on their holding of bonds, stocks and real estate in view of continually shrinking margins and huge bad loans. Several banks realized the hidden capital gains on their real estate holdings by selling their office space, or leasing it back. In several cases, these gains were significant due to the fact that some banks had had these holdings in their possession for many decades. Between 1995 and 1998, the book value of land and property holdings by Japanese banks declined from ¥10 trillion to ¥3 trillion (Table 4.7).

In view of the difference between the book value and market value of banks' real estate holdings, the actual realized gains from liquidation of these holdings were far more than the changes in the book value of these holdings.

While 100 per cent of realized capital gains could be applied to offset pre-tax losses, as against only 45 per cent of unrealized gains, counted in tier-two capital, banks also tapped into unrealized gains on their stock holdings. Due to declining tier-one capital, this method was very popular (see Figure 4.3).

Japanese corporate borrowers and their main banks over the years developed a culture of cross-shareholdings; banks had to repurchase the stocks they sold at market price. By 1997 the banks had almost exhausted the unrealized gains on their securities holdings (Table 4.8).

Table 4.7 Bank holdings of real estate and unrealized gains (in billions of yen)

	Bank holdings of land and buildings	*Unrealized gains on investment securities*	*Unrealized gains on stocks*
1991	5,573	110,703	81,622
1992	7,724	128,968	91,966
1993	8,078	177,671	125,467
1994	7,522	86,526	53,309
1995	10,651	132,976	101,550
1996	9,255	64,436	47,579
1997	8,944	12,420	10,609
1998	3,385	n.a.	n.a.

Sources: Bank Scope, Tokyo; Bank of Japan, *Main Economic Indicators of Japan*, 1999.

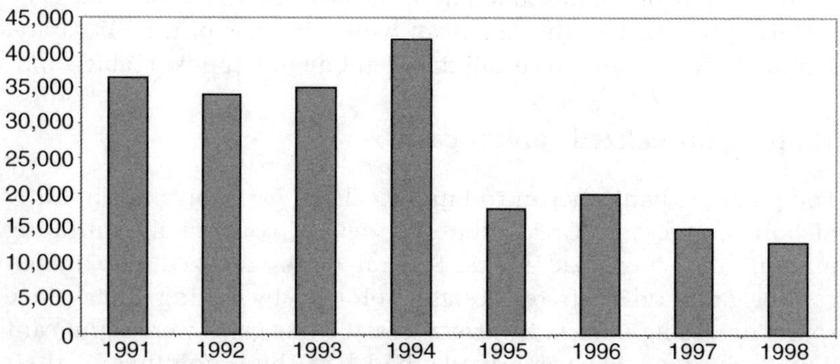

Figure 4.3 Discrepancy between tier-one and tier-two capital (billions of yen)

Table 4.8 Aggregated bank income statement (in billions of yen)

	1991	*1992*	*1993*	*1994*	*1995*	*1996*	*1997*	*1998**
Net interest revenue	14,618	19,189	18,456	19,539	19,523	19,080	17,408	10,562
Other operational income	4,649	4,648	6,269	5,670	6,853	5,272	6,740	3,386
Overheads	13,193	15,332	15,593	16,654	14,474	14,744	14,888	10,526
Loan loss provision	1,650	3,897	9,163	12,544	23,342	11,532	25,809	21,202
Others	982	6	3,163	5,610	6,534	2,160	6,243	7,790
Profits before tax	5,410	4,616	3,131	1,619	–4,905	236	–10,304	–9,990
Tax	3,045	2,780	1,618	1,347	442	597	–619	–2,515
Net income	2,367	1,835	1,515	271	–5,346	–360	–9,683	–7,474
Dividend paid	750	864	875	892	710	675	687	343

* 1998 data are preliminary.
Source: Bank Scope.

The ratio of bank stock holdings to their core capital was about 300 per cent for long-term credit banks and about 200 per cent for city banks. The NIKKO research centre observed that in January 1997 a further decline in the Nikkei average to the 13,000 and 18,000 range could have wiped out the unrealized capital gains of 20 major banks (Figure 4.3).

Corporate governance of Japanese banks

Recently Fukao suggested that a failure of corporate governance was an important factor in the Japanese banking crisis.[21] The governance system of Japanese banks is largely determined by bank ownership structure; while banks' shares are widely held, a few shareholders account for the majority of total outstanding shares of a bank, for example the 30 largest shareholders of Bank of Tokyo Mitsubishi accounted for more than 40 per cent of its outstanding shares in March 1999.

But Kanaya and Woo suggested that the bank ownership structure gave rise to a poor corporate governance system in which shareholders have little control. Mutual life insurers have very little sway over the banks due to the limitations of their own corporate governance. This is related to the fact that the mutual company's policyholders are the nominal owners of the life insurers and may total tens of thousands.

As for the borrower shareholders of the banks, the fact that bank credit has remained, for most of them, the principal source of funding weakens their position as shareholders. This is, of course, the case when these borrower shareholders are themselves in trouble (see Table 4.9).

The Japanese non-financial companies finance about 65 per cent of their liabilities and equity through borrowing as against 13 per cent in the USA in 2000.

The lack of incentive for shareholders to exercise corporate governance power also applies to the employer shareholders of the banks. The interdependence between corporate management and employees often results in the employees siding with the management. But individual investors are generally small. In the case of Tokyo Mitsubishi Bank's total outstanding shares, the individual shareholders account for less than 10 per cent.[22]

Hence it is very rare for the silent majorities to vote against decisions of the management. The composition of the board of directors is also responsible for poor bank governance. Board members are typically promoted from the rank of employees and do not see their role

Table 4.9 Comparison of credit growth of domestic and foreign banks in Japan (in millions of yen and %)*

	Credits by domestic banks	*Credit growth of domestic banks*	*Credits by foreign banks in Japan*	*Credit growth of foreign banks in Japan*
1990	4,243,430	–	–	–
1991	4,458,893	5.08	121,462	–
1992	4,603,939	3.25	106,827	–12.05
1993	4,726,330	2.66	97,340	–8.88
1994	4,748,158	0.46	76,640	–21.27
1995	4,776,618	0.60	76,064	–0.75
1996	4,827,009	1.05	87,185	14.62
1997	4,823,121	–0.08	101,275	16.16
1998	4,779,785	–0.9	107,444	6.09

* End-fiscal year data.
Source: Bank of Japan.

as representing shareholders' interests. For the Japanese banks, it is rare to appoint external directors other than from those companies with which they have long-term business relationships.

Kanaya and Woo observed two harmful effects of weak corporate governance:

1. Bank management is not under pressure to maximize profitability; the focus is on market share and on providing state employment and service for clients. As one bank chairman said, 'our purpose is to serve clients and Japanese industry. There must be profits but profit must be reasonable. If we make too much profit, we are eating the profits of our clients.'[23]

   The average yield on the working assets of Japan's banks, together with their returns on assets (ROA) and returns on equity (ROE), during the 1990s were among the lowest in the industrial countries. Weak profitability means bank loans go bad; banks did not have enough retained earnings to deal with them and also they have problems raising new capital in the market when their capital declines *pari passu* with write-offs and provisioning.
2. The absence of checks and balances means that bank management lacks the incentives for restructuring and will postpone dealing with problems during their tenure. This is one of the reasons why bank management failed to take a proactive stance with regard to dealing with mounting non-performing

loans, resulting in an unnecessary protraction of the crisis. Since internal and external audits are weak, bank management actually tried to conceal their problems; for example, the executives of the Long-Term Credit Bank and Nippon Credit Bank are currently facing trial for fraudulent accounting and false disclosure about losses from bad loans.

The convoy system in the Japanese model

In the late 1990s, with the bubble collapse slowly developing into a full-blown crisis, government policies were widely criticized due to the threat to the global economy. Questions were asked whether all this is related to the Japanese model.

Indecision on the part of the government was also related to issues over how the blame for these continuing bad loans should be apportioned.[24] Perhaps this is the flip side of Japanese capitalism: profit distribution, under bureaucratic guidance incorporating social distribution and stability objectives, as opposed to profit maximization, through market competition, based on clear and legally enforceable rules.[25]

Of course several banks were 'in the same boat', and several large institutions, benefiting from the convoy system (moving the strong along with the weak institutions together), in good times, were to make sacrifices in bad times. This strategy weakens the ability to exercise their shareholder rights. All this is systemic in Japan, but it should not be equated with 'crony' capitalism. This type of ownership structure suggests that bank management can count on the support of majority of their shareholders and also has little trouble in proxy solicitations or at the shareholders' meetings.

But whether the scandals that reached the core financial institutions as well as government officials and also complicated the clean-up process, are also systemic, or are mainly the result of bubble excesses, depends on how the system is defined. Several measures were simply ill-timed for the unlucky ones and led to further serious problems, for example the Toyo Credit rescue in 1992.

The crisis was not limited to the financial sector. Besides the liquidity crisis, banks faced severe losses from the emerging markets, hedge funds and also Russia that led to more restrictions on loans. For several years, Japanese banks had greatly reduced their loan books with a view to stabilizing their declining balance sheets, so more and more companies were driven into bankruptcy.

Moreover, during the bubble boom, construction companies offered guarantees to allow developers to get loans and the government stimulus packages during the 1990s kept them afloat, but plans about public works expenditure drove their share prices down in 1997, followed by rumours about more bankruptcy. A huge public works programme announced in April 1998 gave them some relief.

Looking at the real economy after heavy overinvestment in the late 1980s, a significant cyclical adjustment was to be expected. Also a rise in foreign direct investment during the 1980s and early 1990s, due to the appreciating yen and serious trade frictions with the USA, led several companies to restructure domestic operations towards higher value-added, knowledge-intensive goods, and services. In view of a wide-ranging overhaul in the personnel management system, a heavy decline in manufacturing employment was observed. Similar trends were obvious in the small firm sector and all these developments created a sort of composite recession.[26]

In the new millennium, a sense of depression has been deepened by several social and demographic changes in the economy of workers ageing more rapidly than any other OECD country, along with a declining birth rate. The overall mood in the economy was widely shown in the serial 'Japan 2018' in the Asahi Shimbun by the former bureaucrat Sakaiya. ... By 2018, people should wait until they are 67 for a small pension, the consumption tax rate has increased to 20 per cent, average incomes for workers are taxed at net 40 per cent, real growth is around 0 per cent and the yen is now worth 230 to the dollar.

Since the requirements of urban consumers over the years have become more hi-tech and diverse, they want a more direct say in policy making. Government measures for the governance of a modern industrializing Japan could not satisfy these new demands, because the government could not deliver a successful and growth-promoting economy during the 1990s, due to several scandals related to the bubble excesses and the continuing bad loans and the downturn in the economy. Small investors and depositors were disgusted with all sorts of mismanagement in the banking and financial sector in spite of the boom in discount shopping by small business during the more and more price destructive deflationary trends. This is a sort of protest at the regulatory system in the economy that favours producer interests over those of the consumer.

Hence nothing short of a complete systemic overhaul in the economy will bring about significant changes. Is this the end for the 'Japanese model'?

Prudential regulations and liberalization

In view of growing pressures from abroad for internationalizing the financial system, several deregulation measures were undertaken to increase overall efficiency. Foreign intermediaries were seeking reciprocal rights of access to the Japanese market. Moreover, a high rate of innovations in finance to meet customers' changing needs also created a financial mess, for example a wide range of high-tech derivatives, complex trading technologies, and changes in scale for management of financial services. While highly sophisticated financial products are meant for large corporations, new technologies are also useful in retail financial services as well, for example the ATM, marketing of mutual funds, etc.

At the macro level, the stability of the banking system is under stress due to the exposure of intermediaries to several new risks, changes in market shares of intermediation services by different sectors of financial services and greater variability in profits for individual intermediaries due to growing competition at home as well as abroad, along with deregulation of deposit rates.

At the micro level, risk management is at a premium in spite of the benefits due to diversification, opportunities that offer reduced portfolio risk, along with higher risk-adjusted portfolio returns. As Hugh Patrick recently observed, deregulation took place without the creation of an effective system of prudential regulations to replace postwar systems of regulated interest rates and convoys and constrained competition, which provided safety for the system.[27]

Of course, deregulation generates competition. Banks lost their guaranteed profits, market niches and franchise value of deposit-collecting branches. Banks had to adjust to challenges as well as opportunities of an increasingly risky environment, yet their capital bases were small. This created a situation of moral hazard in which banks took on greater risk in the hope that if they suffered losses, the MOF would bail them out. This was particularly so for the big banks that were really too large to be allowed to fail. Moreover, the increasing use of derivatives in risk management and the growth in off-balance-sheet business causes problems for management, who may fail to grasp fully the risk assumed by virtue of their engagement in such activities. The interest rate and foreign exchange risks are also likely to increase as a result of the interest rate liberalization programme in the former case and the floating of the yen and internationalization of Japanese intermediaries' activity in the latter. The liquidity mix may increase as the funding mix is changed to embrace new borrowing opportunities, and the position risk will also increase as a result of the authorities' willingness to tolerate greater variability in the yield on bonds and other securities.[28]

The policy issues

Since the deregulatory process was gradual, it took a long time for the MOF to realize that it simply could not guarantee all banks against the future.[29] In the mid-1990s, the MOF realized that even depositors might no longer feel completely safe; while depositors were insured up to ¥10 million by the Deposit Insurance Corporation, the insurance fees charged to banks were very low and the DIC reserves miniscule. They could be and in fact soon were depleted by several small banking institution failures.[30]

The MOF should also deal with several new threats and demands in view of the damage from several securities-related scandals, along with the ongoing conflicts of interests resulting from relaxation of controls on the scope of business activity in the economy. These concerns about competitive pressures and equity were obvious in the demands for reciprocity and conversions in the regulation of internationally active intermediaries. The ongoing trend towards globalization of finance has been the overriding factor. Hence the MOF has to deliver cost-effective solutions to issues like the ongoing conflict of interests, increasing concentration and regulatory anomalies in domestic industries.

With a view to guaranteeing basic system safety, the government took several measures; for example, controlled pace of deregulation, expansion of the safety net as an increase in the level of protection given to depositors under DIC arrangements and more powers for the MOF in helping bank mergers, enhanced supervision for financial intermediaries and imposition of tougher capital requirements on banks.

In the summer of 1995, the MOF announced that all deposits would be guaranteed until 31 March 2001, but no specific funds were earmarked to support this pledge in the hope that the announcement would be sufficient to ensure credibility.

Secondly, deposit insurance fees were sharply increased up to US levels. This generated new DIC income and reserves, but the amounts were sufficient only to handle two or three small bank failures. In February 1998, the government enacted its ¥30 trillion bank bail-out package, of which ¥17 trillion were to cover the guarantee on deposits in excess of ¥10 million until 2000, and it seems that a credible safety net for depositors was finally set up. Several inspection procedures have been kept under constant review and since the early 1990s several policy adjustments were made, while more importance was attached to the extent and form of capital enlargement, the management of profitability, risk and liquidity on the assessment of quality of assets and review of management and control systems. The BOJ and MOF made the inspection operations more flexible in view of the emerging new risks in the economy and growing use of derivative instruments. In response to the trend towards globalization of finance, the government sought to develop a liaison with foreign authorities for mutual understanding of each other's policies and also to help the entry and regulation of foreign firms in local markets.

Recently the MOF has been much slower in imposing disclosure, capital strengthening and other prudential regulations. Its supervisory capabilities were hived off in June 1998 to the new Financial Supervisory Agency, directly under the cabinet secretariat. The reluctance of the MOF to move more rapidly in the 1990s to impose a system of prudential regulations was perhaps because it did not fully understand the implications of deregulation. The ongoing deregulation measures undermined the old 'convoy system' and also made the traditional MOF modes of action now rather counter-productive.

Macroeconomic policy mistakes

Recent research underlines the gross policy mismanagement that made banks' bad loan problems more and more serious over the years and it is still hanging on in the new century. Several policy mistakes were observed involving both fiscal and monetary policy instruments, since the BOJ was subservient to, rather than autonomous from, the MOF.

One issue was the timing and degree of commitment when the authorities undertook demand stimulus measures. The other issue was the growing imbalance between the use of fiscal and monetary policy.[31] MOF fiscal policy since early 1980s had aimed at a single-minded pursuit of budget deficit reduction and budget surplus creation, and the burden of compensatory macro-policy fell heavily on monetary policy instruments.

When a long time back in 1986, after a sharp decline in the oil price, the yen appreciated heavily and growth slowed down, the response of the MOF was monetary stimulus. Interest rates were reduced to post-war lows and the money supply was greatly expanded. Of course, this policy led to improved overall growth but this policy package was continued for too long, at least fuelling and also creating the stock and real estate bubbles of 1990. Only in 1989 did the BOJ begin to raise interest rates significantly in several stages in order to control the bubbles, leading to continuing stagnation and overall gloom in the economy.

Moreover, heavy reliance was placed on monetary policy in the mid-1990s and interest rates since 1995 have been at undesirably low levels. All this policy mess, over the years, made it very difficult to stimulate demand; of course very low interest rates helped banks and borrowers and also postponed the resolution of bad loan and corporate bankruptcy problems at a very high cost.

The low interest rate policy has over the years generated a very weak yen; savers as also consumers in the economy were increasingly seeking higher yields in foreign assets. So the real returns on pension funds have been inadequate and all pension programmes are now underfunded. But once interest rates do rise to a more normal level, prices of government bonds and other financial assets will drop, imposing heavy capital losses on the holders.

As Hugh Patrick recently observed, several fiscal stimulus programmes in the mid-1990s were applied; rather too little, too late and also too grudgingly. Moreover, each policy package of tax cuts was presented as temporary, making the stimulus signals so ambiguous. Also the credibility of each fiscal stimulus package was undermined by statements on the real content of the stimulus (the 'real water') and by the focus on public works construction that became so unproductive over the years – roads, railroads and bridges to nowhere. It was not until the supplementary budget of August 1995 that fiscal stimulus was really effective, leading to a good recovery with 3.4 per cent GDP growth in the fiscal year 1996–97.[32]

A major policy blunder was the government decision in late 1996 to shift its top priority policy 180 degrees from sustaining economic recovery to tackling the long-run structural problems of budget deficits. The timing of this measure was far too early to shift the 1997 budget to heavy fiscal restraint from the 1996 budget easing, thus reducing demand generation by more than two percentage points of GDP. Increasing consumption tax by 3.5 per cent, ending ¥2 trillion temporary personal income tax cuts and raising medical care and other user fees did this.

As against hopes of a slight recovery during 1997, the economy declined further and there has been continuing recession during

1998–2003. The GDP growth during these years hovered around only 0.6–1 per cent, against official projections of 2–3 per cent growth in the new millennium.

Moreover, as economic conditions were on the decline in early 1998, the Hashimoto government passed a restrictive 1998 budget, and further in April 1998, a huge supplementary budget of ¥17 trillion, in real demand-generating expenditure and tax cuts; it was passed in June 1998 in an extended Diet meeting.

We find the Japanese economy has been victim of several macro policy mistakes; the MOF banking bureau depended on the restoration of growth to halt and reverse the continuing decline in urban real estate prices with a view to converting marginal bank loans into good loans and also in the hope of relieving the bad loans problem, that was still current in 2003. But on the other hand, the MOF budget and tax bureau continuously brought in budget deficit-reducing measures, which adversely affected the recovery.

In the new millennium, Japan is the largest creditor nation in the world, along with its persistent current account surpluses being invested the world over. Moreover, Japanese banks, insurance companies and other financial firms have vigorously engaged in foreign lending and portfolio investment, hence the increasing foreign exchange risks for these sectors.

As Hugh Patrick observes, as the yen appreciated, the cumulative losses were huge, almost of the same order of magnitude as the domestic bad loan losses. Moreover, the flourishing of a free global capital market (the Euro-market) provided large Japanese creditworthy companies with expensive bond and equity alternatives to loans from Japanese banks. The MOF could not stop this offshore financing process. The ongoing recent deregulation measures under the Big Bang have made it attractive for foreign banks, investment banks, securities companies, mutual funds, insurance companies and asset management companies to compete in the Japanese home market on Japan's hitherto restricted sacrosanct turf.[33]

5
Big Bang Reform Programme and After

In the early 1990s, the failure of government measures to revitalize the economy led to a loss of confidence in these packages. The aftermath of asset inflation revealed several problems in the regulatory framework, and it was suggested that Japanese authorities were committing the same policy mistakes as the US policy makers had done sometime back. Japan's deposit guarantee system remains bimodal, makes little effort to impose discipline on depositors or shareholders and relies on a passive regulatory attitude.

In November 1996, Mr Hashimoto announced plans for profound financial reform. This package of measures was to be implemented in stages by the year 2003, when the blanket guarantee for deposits would end and a new financial supervisory authority created. This really extends beyond the securities-related reforms in London during the mid-1980s; the Financial System Reforms bill, revising 22 laws, followed with long discussions in the Diet and councils and securities and exchange councils (1997).

The reform measures can be divided as follows:

1. Those designed to expand user choice;
2. Those to improve quality of service provision and to promote competition among intermediaries;
3. Those to ensure development of an easy to use market;
4. Those to ensure setting up a fair market; and
5. Those to help preserve financial stability.

The reform package: measures to expand user choice

The first step was taken in April 1998 by deregulating the foreign exchange laws and regulations. With deregulation, Japanese residents can directly open accounts in foreign institutions abroad. Due to foreign competition, financial institutions in Japan became aggressive in pursuing ¥1200 trillion of household savings. The money management funds (MMF) and foreign bonds offering higher yields than yen deposits became very popular. This exodus of savings was partly responsible for the yen's depreciation after April 1998.

In fact this was the beginning of the end of the 'convoy' system that had ruled Japanese financial markets for decades. The Big Bang aimed at making Japanese markets more efficient and internationalized. The market will become more competitive and the users – firms and consumers – will benefit. Also Japanese institutions will become more efficient due to the competitive pressures from foreign institutions.

Recently it was suggested that, after the bubble burst, the Tokyo stock exchange lost more than half of its capitalization since the peak of the bubble (December 1989). There had been a mass exodus of foreign stock listing from the Tokyo Big Bang; trading volumes of Tokyo foreign exchange markets did not grow during the 1990s, but Hong Kong and Singapore were catching up, and the use of the yen in South-East Asia did not grow as was predicted.[1]

Of course, growth of user choice depends on liberalization that allows intermediaries to choose the activities and products to supply. The banks will be allowed to sell securities and investment trust certificates through branches and money management firms, and will help introduce asset management accounts. Both will help the small investment trust industry by broadening the sales channels and also by bringing new customers into securities investments. Once proper safeguards are set up, banks will be able to offer several insurance products; the Securities and Exchange Council argued for private placement of investment trusts to be allowed and also for consideration to be given to introduction of investment company type funds, but the Financial System Research Council was concerned about the possibility of banks using undue influence to promote insurance sales and the risk run by the buyers of insurance products might not be clear. The banks would also become subject to regulations applied under insurance business laws.

The other set of measures here relates to lifting of the ban on derivative transactions. During reforms, several pieces of legislation will be revised, for example the securities in exchange law, the commodity exchange law and the financial futures exchange law. Now use of derivatives is actively encouraged to promote sound risk management, by intermediaries, to improve allocation of risk in the economy and also to raise the international competitiveness of Japan's financial markets.

The trading of options on individual stocks began on 18 July 1997 on both the Tokyo stock exchange and the Osaka securities exchange. Here 33 stocks in total were covered and over-the-counter trading of securities- and commodities-related derivatives followed after some time.

As opposed to the London Big Bang, the Tokyo Big Bang was to be completed in several stages, by 2003. Of course, during the last two years of serious liberalization (2002–4) and global competition some progress was observed in a massive shake-up in the Japanese banking, brokerage and insurance industries.

The Big Bang liberalization focus was on the following objectives:

(a) reduction of MOF power and constitution of an independent supervisory agency;
(b) independence of the BOJ from political influence;
(c) adoption of internationally accepted standards;
(d) desegmentation and consolidation of the banking industry.

Restructuring of the MOF

This was seriously undertaken along with the operating methods of banking supervision, since a lot of arbitrary discretion remained; as a result of these problems, the Financial Supervisory Agency (FSA) was formed which took over supervision from the MOF. The fact remains that bureaucratic connections are still very deep. But the FSA is really serious about restoring the confidence of ordinary investors and announced in May 1999 that its balance sheet audits will be set up in all major Japanese banks.

Independence of the BOJ

The BOJ was under the control of the MOF for several decades. From April 1998, it gained more independence. This was the only central bank worldwide that had to present plans about its future activities to the government. Several keen observers of financial markets are happy with the guidance of the central bank in the new millennium.

Internationally accepted standards

In view of continuing foreign pressure, several decisions for deregulation were taken that conform to international standards. When the Big Bang is completed, brokerage commissions on stock trading and on insurance premiums will be fully liberalized and foreign currency can be freely exchanged.

Desegmentation of the banking industry

One important objective is to abolish various 'firewalls' between banks, securities and insurance businesses and allow these institutions to become more efficient at an international level. Several measures have been launched to raise intermediaries' capabilities to manage risk and the balance sheets with a view to increase the liquidity of loans and other assets. Several measures designed to promote the issue of asset-backed securities (ABS), or securitization, will raise the general efficiency of financial intermediation by helping the functions of initial credit review, credit extension, loan management and risk management. For this, measures being adopted are the preparation of a legal framework for special purpose companies, and the issue of such securities to protect investors' interests against third-party claims, etc.

The Financial System Research Council would like further consideration to be given to promote the securitization of real property collateral, so as to deepen Japan's financial markets and also to help local intermediaries in their disposal of non-performing assets.[2]

The liquidity of money loan certificates will be increased by measures that help the issuance of securities based on money loan trust certificates and thus override the designated asset transfer system.

Another measure planned to raise user choice is the liberalization of cross-border transactions. Moreover, the range of investment and borrowing opportunities open to both companies and individuals will increase significantly once controls on cross-border securities transactions and foreign deposits are liberalized.

The removal of the 'firewalls' between different types of financial institutions will lead to concentration within the industry and more and more mergers and acquisitions in the banking, securities and insurance sector have taken place. These developments will help further reform the financial sector. Holding companies for various financial institutions are also being allowed. Moreover, the institutions preparing to merge will benefit from revised employment laws that make it easy to lay off some staff. Over the next few years in the banking industry, a staff reduction of 15–20 per cent is visualized. In September 1998, there was a merger between the Bank of Tokyo and the Mitsubishi Bank. The alliance between the Industrial Bank of Japan and Nomura Securities in May 1998 and the union of Dai-Ichi Kangyo Bank with Kankaku Securities were also completed.

The measures to promote competition in the Japanese financial system consist of several proposals that will help intermediaries to diversify their operations and funding sources and also allow them more freedom to choose the organizational structure to be adopted. Hence the opportunities for diversification through subsidiaries of all intermediary types will be increased, and securities companies will also have more freedom in their choice of business activities, foreign exchange business will be opened up further to all players, ordinary banks will be allowed to issue corporate bonds, and non-bank financial intermediaries will be allowed to issue corporate bonds and commercial paper and brokerage commission will be fully deregulated.

When the Big Bang is completed, transaction costs will be reduced and those who are using the Tokyo market will benefit from deregulation. Recently it was suggested that the Big Bang should be sequenced so that it would take some time to complete it, but would be carried through to the end. While non-financial institutions in Japan can deal in foreign exchange without banks' intermediation, Japanese investors are not allowed to open accounts with financial institutions in foreign countries. Of course, domestic deregulation was stalled by the vested interests of segmented financial markets. The Big Bang is the final answer to deal with the clash of vested interests.[3]

In Japan, holding companies are prohibited under the Big Bang from setting up financial companies; holding companies will be allowed, so that a single office will control banks, securities firms and insurance companies. Among the changes in foreign exchange in April 1998, the most important is the elimination of exclusive dealing by banks. Now investors are allowed to hold accounts with financial institutions abroad. All these changes have put a lot of pressure on Japanese banks.

The decision to allow the use of holding companies shows the MOF's willingness to revise the anti-monopoly law, but the conflicts of interests still render the universal banking style of Western Europe unacceptable to the MOF. These conflicts of interests will play an important role in shaping the legal framework, allowing for the use of the holding company structure.

While holding companies will be allowed to own a bank with non-bank subsidiaries of the bank being allowed to operate as separate subsidiaries of the holding company, they will not be allowed to own commercial entities. Similar restrictions are to be applied to holding companies owning insurance and securities companies.

A determination to broaden the reforms taking place through subsidiaries is obvious in the proposals for liberalizing controls placed on the business of intermediaries and subsidiaries; under the new reform plan, the remaining restrictions on the scope of banks' securities and trust subsidiaries were lifted in 1999. The banks, securities companies, insurance and trust companies will have complete freedom to enter each others' business by means of area-specific subsidiaries by the year 2003.

But the reform of the rating system used to set non-life premium rates was taken up during December 1998 and phased deregulation of brokerage commissions was completed during 2000.

The political economy aspects

The Big Bang idea was an attempt by the Hashimoto government to pursue structural reforms in domestic and international policy making. Public opinion was against the MOF, as final resolution of the Jusen companies required an injection of ¥685 billion. During the summer of 1996, reform of the BOJ to make it independent from the MOF was undertaken; of course, domestic resistance towards liberalization will be less when a declaration for big deregulation is made internationally, as the US pressure was to keep the Japanese insurance markets under regulation.

The measures to ensure growth of an easy to use market

While financial futures markets had operated at Tokyo International Financial Futures Exchange since 1989, there were several complaints about the limited range of financial futures products available, lack of investor protection in case of failure of financial futures brokers and falling competitiveness of Japanese markets. Several measures are now planned to encourage the growth of new products (for example spread transactions in short-term Japanese yen interest rates futures began in 1998), and also to improve the environment of financial futures transactions to meet international standards and reduce transactions costs.

As for the development of the securities market, the Securities and Exchange Council got most of what it had asked for; now off-exchange trading of listed securities is encouraged; the liquidity of a registered OTC Japanese Security Dealers Automated Quotation (JASDAQ) market is increased, and also securities companies can trade and intermediate in unlisted securities.[4]

Moreover, trading practices in the short-term money market are assessed with a view to enhancing development of the market.

Market capacity will be increased by raising the role of the yen TIBOR (Tokyo inter-bank offered rate) as Japan's effective interest rate indicator, and enlarging the Treasury bill market and reviewing the procedures for insurance of financing bills. Of course, improvements in efficiency will depend on the reviews of the legal framework for several products and market practices about promissory notes on methods used to calculate interest rates in call transactions, and cash collateralized loan transactions in bonds and security will be improved by leasing BOJ-NET (BOJ NETTING) on a real time gross settlement basis by the end of 2003.

Recently it was suggested that the immediate impact on various groups of consumers is not clear. While wealthy individuals will benefit from a wider range of choices in their asset portfolios, small savers and pensioners may suffer from deregulation, as various rates, for example brokerage commission, insurance premiums and bank monthly fees, will be differentiated for different types of customers.[5]

It was feared that the ongoing decline in the financial system may force the BOJ to give more consideration to prudential objectives for policy making and these objectives may conflict with domestic price stability. Of course, the authorities are determined that the introduction of a free market should not be allowed to undermine the soundness of the market.

The Financial Supervisory Agency has a difficult task to implement stringent standards since concerns with prudential policy are always present. The willingness to directly subsidize the banking sector on the basis of systemic risk issues has imposed serious costs on the domestic economy; with the failure of the Hokkaido Takushoku Bank and Yamaichi Securities, no banks or security firms feel safe under market pressures.

Moreover, given the importance of retail operations in the Japanese security markets, it is important to regain the trust of the small investors, by ensuring that they are not disadvantaged vis-à-vis institutional clients. The strengthening of the rules should accommodate higher business ethics, if trust is to be restored.

The deregulation of the foreign exchange market

Of course, deregulation of the exchange market should generate a yen depreciation, since the interest rate in Japan was so much lower than in other countries, but the expected effect on the volatility of the yen/dollar exchange rate is unclear.

During the weeks before the deregulation was launched, market players were of the view that the yen should weaken, as it would be easier for Japanese agents to sell yen for dollars. Also there were rumours of central bank intervention, selling dollars to prevent a dollar appreciation, so that the effects of private market yen sales could be offset by central bank purchases.

On 3 April 1998, Moody's Investor service downgraded, from stable to negative, its outlook for Japanese government obligations. This resulted in the yen–dollar exchange rate dropping to 135 for the first time in six years. In the same week, the BOJ Tankan report revealed that the outlook had turned more negative among Japanese firms.

With the lifting of restrictions on dollar-denominated deposits in foreign countries, the pressures from abroad will force Japanese and foreign institutions in Tokyo to offer better products. This may cause a shift to dollars from the yen and also yen depreciation. The deregulation should simply allow more Japanese firms and households to diversify their portfolios at lower cost.

Takatoshi Ito-Melvin examines tick-by-tick data on the yen/dollar exchange rate for evidence about the spreads. It is observed that Japanese quoted spreads exceed the rest of the markets. This may be due to several reasons. Japanese banks' reputation was seriously damaged when one of the 20 large banks failed in November 1997 and many others have been downgraded. Japanese banks were charged a 'Japan premium' by American and European banks. It is still not clear that the spreads quoted by the Japanese banks converged to those quoted by others following 1 April.

As Kurt Gorger recently suggested, the winners following the Big Bang reforms could be three types of groups:

1. Large city banks that maintained a large network serving private and local corporate customers and offering a wide range of financial products.
2. Large regional banks that maintain a strong local branch network for private customers and small enterprises.
3. Shinkin banks (saving banks) with their roots in the retail market, which have a strong local basis and their activities are aimed at providing easily accessible services for small units and the general public.

The losers after this restructuring could be the following groups:

1. Long-term credit banks, specializing in long-term commercial lending as shown by the collapse of the LTC Bank of Japan.

2. Trust banks, since they do not maintain a branch network. They are restricted to wholesale banking; some of the long-term credit banks and trust banks are expected to merge with banks that maintain a wider network.
3. Small regional banks, for example Hyogo and Taihei-yo Bank, as a result of competition from local, regional and city banks.
4. Credit cooperatives. This sector is around 13 per cent of total loans outstanding in Japan. In 1996, they decided to reduce the number of 3000 rural credit cooperatives to 530 in March 2001.
5. Japan's security firms. Since October 1999, banks' brokerage subsidiaries will have access to the securities business. The foreign financial institutions that gained ground in Japan recently will be able to attract a bigger market share due to the ongoing liberalization.[6]

Japanese banking industry after the Big Bang

When different packages of liberalization measures are due to be implemented in 2003, two separate universal bank holdings could come up:

1. One group is the joint alliance between leading Japanese financial institutions – Industrial Bank of Japan, Dai-Ichi Kangyo Bank and Fuji Bank under the holding 'Mizuho'. These three, ranking among the 15 largest banks in the country, will form, after the proposed marriage, the largest banking group in the world, with assets of about ¥140,000 billion. While DKB and Fuji Bank are additional commercial banks, IBJ is the only institution with experience in investment banking. During the business year 1999–2000, all three banks could get back in the black, after heavy losses suffered recently. Also they are suffering from bad loans. Some observers doubt the usefulness of the alliance, as size alone will not guarantee international competitiveness. Of course, huge investments requirements in the IT sector will be met that may help revitalize the banking sector.
2. The second group is built from the merger of city banks, Sumito and Sakura, completed in June 2001. This merger is really spectacular, since it tears down the walls between the rival Mitsui and Sumitomo groups.

   Recent research suggests that this reorganization in the financial sector is slowly leading to the breakdown of traditional *keiretsu* corporate groups.

As Kazuo Sato observes, the six largest – Mitsui, Mitsubishi, Sumitomo, Fuio, Sanwa and Dai-ichi Kangin – average 4 financial institutions and 26 non-financial corporations, 20 of which are manufacturing, for example heavy industry. The financial institutions are a city bank, a trust bank, a long-life, fire and marine insurance company and a life insurance company. The city bank and life insurance company are of particular importance because they extend loans to the groups of non-financial firms, with the bank serving as the member's main bank. The Fuio group is centred on Fuji Bank and Dai-ichi Kangin on Dai-ichi Kangyo Bank. At one time, the bank names were synonymous with the groups, but as a result of mergers, the Mitsui group bank is called Sakura and Mitsubishi group bank is Bank of Tokyo, Mitsubishi.[7]

Moreover, the increasing financialization of the six groups is also seen in the fact that their share of sales in the non-financial corporate sector stayed at 15 per cent from 1970 to 1990, but fell to 12 per cent in the late 1990s. By contrast, looking just at the banks and insurance companies, the groups' share of total assets rose from 42 per cent in 1970 to 51 per cent in 1980 and 58 per cent in 1990. During the 1990s, the share has fallen somewhat and has been volatile. All this means that by the 1990s, the six groups had transformed themselves from production groups into financial groups. With poor performance of the financial sectors during the 1990s, large business groups have done very poorly.

This poor performance over several years has prompted some action in the form of mergers. In early 2000, all six groups announced mergers involving their main banks or the forming of holding companies that brought their financial institutions together. This reduces the six major groups to four; as regards the banks after the Second World War, holding companies had been part of the *zaibatsu* dissolution, but the 1990–97 revision of the law allows them subject to certain restrictions (Table 5.1).

Hence the *keiretsu* element of the Japanese economy characterized by cross-shareholding and a joint house bank as a coordinator is slowly on the decline in the new millennium. Other emerging banking groups include the alliance of Asahi Bank, Sanwa Bank and Tokai Bank which agreed in autumn 1999 to set up a financial holding company, the merger of Chuo Trust and Banking and Mitsui Trust and Banking into Chuo Mitsui Trust and Banking as of 1 April 2000. Two more large mergers have recently been announced (in June 2000 Sahi Bank pulled out of the planned merger after disputes about management strategy).

A milestone in Japan's reform is the reprivatization of the previously nationalized Long-Term Credit Bank (now called Shinsei Bank) to a consortium of 10 foreign investors, assembled by Ripple Wood (a US equity group). The consortium has names such as Deutsche Bank, GE Capital, ABN Amro, Mellon Bank and other high-grade financial companies. The Nippon Credit Bank (nationalized in 1998) was sold to a consortium of

Table 5.1 Major financial groups in 2001

(a) Mizuho Financial Group
Dai-ichi Kangyo Bank
Fuji Bank
Industrial Bank of Japan (IBJ)
Yasuda Trust and Banking Co. Ltd
(b) Mitsubishi Tokyo Financial Group
Bank of Tokyo Mitsubishi
Mitsubishi Trust and Banking Corporation
Nippon Trust Bank Ltd
(c) Sumitomo Mitsui Banking Corporation
Sumitomo Bank
Sakura Bank
(d) UFJ Group
Sanwa Bank
Tokai Bank
Tokyo Trust and Banking Co.

Notes:
(a) The two banks are merging. With March 2000 assets of US $927 billion, the group would have been the third largest financial institution in the world. Sakura Bank is the result of the 1990 merger of Mitsui Bank and Taiya-Kobe Bank.
(b) Sanwa and Tokai merged in April 2002; UFJ stands for United Financial of Japan. The umbrella company is UFJ Holdings Inc. With March 2000 assets of US$666 billion, the group would have been the fifth largest financial institution in the world.
Source: Hoshi and Kashyap (2001).

Table 5.2 The non-financial corporations entering Japan's banking industry

Corporation	
Ito-Yokado	Bank for individuals specializing in settlement
Sony	Internet banking, which is specializing for individuals: Getting deposits by using the Internet and settlement service for individuals via the Internet
Soft Bank, Tokyo Marine, Oryx (buying Nippon Credit Bank)	Core aim is to support venture corporations
	Loan to venture corporations depending on their intellectual property
	Search and invest in hopeful venture corporations
	Settlement service for electronic commerce trading via the Internet

investors, led by a bank including the insurance group Tokyo Marine and Fire and the leasing group Oryx. As part of the agreement, the government is planning to remove bad assets so that Nippon Credit Bank will be clean at the time of sale; moreover, several new licences have been granted for new entrants from the non-financial industries such as the new Ito Yokado Bank (see Table 5.2).

Macroeconomic effects

As Jenny Corbett recently observed, 'it seems obvious that financial crises matter but in practice, it is not clear that the range of international experience of financial fragility shows the difficulty of categorizing degrees of crisis'.[8] But it is possible to distinguish several phases in the development of the financial crises of the 1980s and 1990s as follows:

1. Collateral values decline relative to loans; this means that banks' risks increase, but there may be no real effects. If the process goes far enough, some borrowers may become technically insolvent in the sense that their liabilities exceed their assets, but since real effects are still small, there is the obvious incentive to wait and see whether asset price recovery sorts the problem out.
2. Asset price declines affect banks' balance sheets, for example via the impact of decline in unrealized capital gains on BIS capital ratios. The banks' need to restore ratios may have an effect on lending behaviour.[9]
3. Non-performing loans increase as a proportion of total loans with interest income losses to the banks. Declines in bank profits may affect lending behaviour, either because of the need to maintain capital ratios or through some other income effect on bank lending (this may be difficult to justify but may be observed in practice).
4. Loan provisions and write-offs increase, with impacts on banks' profits and balance sheets.
5. Corporate failures and banks' write-offs increase to such an extent that banks become insolvent.
6. Bank failures or forced mergers occur with or without public bail-outs. This type of progress of financial crisis might be one way of distinguishing how serious the crises have been in different countries. Lindgren et al. distinguish significant bank problems where banks' balance sheet quality (measured by net worth) is affected by a crisis, where bank failures occur or public bail-outs are necessary.

As Hoshi and Kashyap recently observed, all types of Japanese banks changed the way they funded themselves. One across the board pattern is a reduction in the reliance on demand deposits; almost all of this is attributable to a reduction in corporate checking accounts. While in 1975, corporations held ¥30 billion of demand deposits (32 per cent of total private deposits) at all banks, by 1996 the proportion had declined to 16 per cent (¥63 trillion). This is consistent with the gradual disappearance of banks requiring compensating balances from borrowers.[10]

As emphasized by Shimizu (2000), the long-term credit banks' difficulties were due to this convergence. While they had been mostly dissimilar to start with, they had been most reliant on lending to manufacturers, those most likely to have been maturing long-term loans and most dependent on no-deposit financing.

Of course, the impact of the financial crisis on the real economy is likely to come through its effect on the availability of credit, but it is not easy to distinguish cause and effect when financial crises occur at times of real slow-down. The credit slow-down might be due to demand- or supply-side factors. Of course, the longer the banking sector goes on accumulating bad loans, the more likely it is that there will be real effects.

By the second half of 1999, a major wave of consolidation began. The most remarkable mergers were among the large city banks. The first mega-merger creating the Mizuho Financial Group from Fuji Bank, the Industrial Bank of Japan and Dai-Ichi Kangyo Bank was announced in August with assets of $1.2 trillion (roughly the GDP of France); it would be the largest bank in the world. Shortly afterwards, Sakura and Sumitomo Bank announced their intention to merge to form the Sumitomo-Mitsui Banking Corporation.

The ongoing changes initiated in the banking sector due to Big Bang reforms, proved very significant in expanding fund-raising options available for large firms, since they moved sharply from bank financing to capital market financing. For these firms, the cost of *keiretsu* finance outweighed the benefits. Financial deregulation also started expanding the choices for savers and the range of services offered by banks and other financial institutions, but developments in these areas were much slower than the growth of corporate financing.[11]

Even before the Big Bang, the nature of Japanese corporate governance was changing; large corporations reduced not only their dependence on bank loans, but also the number of board members accepted from the banks. The changed relationship seems to have undermined the ability of banks to monitor customers, and many interventions at troubled banks did not proceed smoothly.

As Jenny Corbett recently observed, at the macro level, the scale of credit crunch that followed the crisis was not extreme. By international comparison, the Japanese system has been marked by a smooth and slow response to development of an extreme asset price cycle. More research is needed to pinpoint areas in which Japanese banks were slow to respond. Provisioning may be one area, but here too, the performance is not as bad as might have been thought. It would be an interesting exercise to examine further whether a slow speed of provisioning could be established and if so, whether it was linked to a conscious decision to preserve smooth profit performance or whether it can be entirely explained by regulatory differences. Japan's experience in 1997, when a number of financial institutions collapsed, suggests that too slow a response to development of significant banking problems can allow a system to fall into a crisis which could have been avoided by prompter action.[12]

Hence looking back, an avoidance of these problems would have required a much earlier liberalization. Had Japan allowed the banks broader powers when bond markets were emerging in the mid-1970s and early 1980s, they might have coped better with the loss of their traditional borrowers.

6
Japanese Banking and Finance in the New Millennium

Introduction

Since the asset price bubble in the early 1990s, the Japanese economy has been stagnant from 1991 to 2004 and the banking sector has also been in trouble; as several observers recently suggested, monetary policy has not been as effective in restoring growth. The government over the years resorted to an expansionary monetary policy along with an expansionary fiscal policy. It is a pity that these standard tools have failed to help the economy. The notion that an important part of the problem is the result of attempts to reallocate resources in the wake of falling expectations of future growth, suggests that lifting expectations of future performance could now play crucial role. If the government could restore faith in Japan's performance, private spending could also be revived; hence structural reforms and rehabilitation of the banking sector have an important role to play.

As Kanaya and Woo suggest, weak corporate governance had several adverse effects. Bank management is not under pressure to maximize profitability. Rather the banks focus on market share and on providing stable employment and services for clients; average yields on banks' working assets, and also the return on assets (ROA) and returns on equity (ROE) during the 1990s, were among the lowest. Weak profitability means that, when loans go bad, banks do not have enough retained earnings to deal with them, and they have problems in raising new capital in the market when their capital declines along with write-offs and provisioning.

Secondly, absence of accountability suggests that bank managements lack incentives for restructuring and postpone dealing with problems. Hence management failed to take a proactive stance with regard to dealing with monitoring non-performing loans. Senior officials in fact tried their best to conceal these problems and several officials are now facing trial for fraudulent accounting, etc.[1]

Hugh Patrick put it rather mildly: deregulation without the creation of an effective system of prudential regulations and supervision to replace the post-war system of regulated interest rates and convoys really constrained competition that provided safety for the system. Banks lost their guaranteed profits, market niches and the franchise value of deposit-collecting branches. Banks had to adjust to the challenges as well as the opportunities of an increasingly risky environment, while their capital bases were small. This created a case of moral hazard, as banks took on greater risk in the hope that if they suffered losses, the MOF would bail them out.[2] Most of the banks failed to take any proper measures to adjust to a new scenario and preferred to wait for stock and property prices to return to their pre-collapse level.[3]

The regulatory weaknesses

Since the deregulatory process was gradual, it took a long time for the MOF to realize that it simply could not, and also should not, guarantee all banks against failure.[4] In the mid-1990s, the MOF realized that even depositors might no longer feel safe, as the flow of deposits from weak to strong banks was not so obvious, because Japanese depositors were hopeful of a full government guarantee; until 1997, the actual guarantee under the deposit insurance scheme was only up to ¥10 million per account. Of course, it would have been in the interest of the government to minimize the potential fiscal cost of bank structuring. To guarantee basic system safety, the government and the MOF took several measures. In the summer of 1995, the MOF announced that all deposits would be guaranteed until 31 March 2001, but no specific funds were earmarked to support this pledge. Moreover, the deposit insurance fees were sharply increased up to the US levels, but this generated new DIC income and reserves, since the amounts were sufficient only to handle two to three small bank failures annually, not more.

Between 1990 and 1995, the government did very little to arrest the decline in the banking system, due to the false hope that the economy would soon turn the corner and a full recovery would buoy up the banks.[5] Of course, spurred by a combination of monetary easing, fiscal stimulus and deregulation measures, economic activity began to recover in late 1995 and in 1996, the economy grew by 5 per cent, the fastest among the group of seven industrial countries. Some boost was also given in early 1997 by anticipation of a hike in the consumption tax rate from 3 to 5 per cent in April that led consumers to bring their purchases forward to avoid additional taxes. Several forecasts were made about growth to restart quickly for a normal cyclical recovery, but the economy failed to recover and in late 1997 continued to fall through 1998–99 as well. This recession left output in the last quarter of 1999 at 4 per cent below its peak in early 1997. This downturn was the worst recession of the post-war period, involving all components of private demand.

To explain this continuing downturn, several triggers were suggested, for example a more than expected drop in household spending. After the April 1997 tax hike, there were the disruptive effects of the failure of a major bank and two large securities firms in 1997, along with tight bank credit, and the advance of a strengthening of bank regulations planned for April 1998. The Asian currency crisis was a further blow to confidence.

Despite a further shift towards stimulative macro-policy, the recession continued further, though short-term interest rates were brought down to almost zero by early 1999 and repeated doses of fiscal stimulus raised the general government fiscal deficits to almost 10 per cent of GDP. The weakness of business investment has in fact been very acute in spite of the government's efforts to reduce the risk of further financial turmoil.

Of course, in early 1999, the economy showed some recovery initiated by a burst of public investment spending, and also an upturn in consumer confidence. But a rapid rise in the yen from its low point in mid-1998 raised wide concerns about the overall impact on the fragile recovery and hence the calls for further easing of monetary policy.

Until 1997, in spite of worsening banking problems, the government hesitated about taking strong action due to fear of a panic. It seems that the regulators exercised forbearance. Kanaya and Woo suggest several recent events in support of their hypothesis – the government had the power to de-license banks and intervened only after the troubled banks became insolvent; for example, the Tokyo metropolitan government in the spring of 1993 knew about the insolvency of Tokyo Kyowa Credit Cooperative and Anzen Cooperative (closed in 1994) after conducting a special joint examination with the MOF.

Banks were allowed to continue to pay dividends, even after it was clear that the retained earnings were needed to strengthen their capital base and to help provide for loan losses. This was due to the belief that suspension of dividend payments would be a signal of

Table 6.1 Aggregated bank income statement (billions of yen)

	1991	*1992*	*1993*	*1994*	*1995*	*1996*	*1997*	*1998**
Net interest revenue	14,618	19,189	18,456	19,539	19,523	19,080	17,408	10,562
Other operational income	4,649	4,648	6,269	5,670	6,853	5,272	6,740	3,386
Overheads	13,193	15,332	15,593	16,654	14,474	14,744	14,888	10,526
Loan loss provision	1,650	3,897	9,163	12,544	23,342	11,532	25,809	21,202
Others	982	6	3,163	5,610	6,534	2,160	6,243	7,790
Profits before tax	5,410	4,616	3,131	1,619	–4,905	236	–10,304	–9,990
Tax	3,045	2,780	1,618	1,347	442	597	–619	–2,515
Net income	2,367	1,835	1,515	271	–5,346	–360	–9,683	–7,474
Dividend paid	750	864	875	892	710	675	687	343

* 1998 data are preliminary.
Source: Bank Scope.

distress and lead to a decline in bank stock. For several years, banks went on paying dividends, even when they recorded negative net profits. As Table 6.1 shows, in 1991 Japanese banks together paid out ¥750 billion in dividends from a combined net profit of ¥2.3 trillion. By 1997, after the banks lost about ¥9 trillion, the dividends paid out were still ¥680 billion.

In Japan, the guidelines issued by the stock exchange require any listed corporation to be delisted if income is negative for three years. In 1995, banks incurred a combined loss of ¥5 trillion, after setting aside ¥23 trillion for provisioning. In 1996, banks tried to avoid reporting losses and also reduced their provisioning by half, with a view to reporting a small profit. Again in 1997, they increased their provisioning; hence for several years, non-performing loans continued to rise in the late 1990s, as well as in 2001.

Loan classification rules were lax as related to international best practice, and it took a very long time for banks as well as the government to recognize the volume of these bad loans in the economy. As J. Levy suggested, when at the end of March 1998 the major banks reported bad loans, based on the more stringent standards introduced, this further raised their disclosed bad loans by 50 per cent compared with the figures that would have been reported under the old system.[6]

The MOF was very slow in imposing disclosure, capital strengthening and other prudential regulations. Its supervisory capabilities appeared so weak that they were hived off in June 1998 to the newly established Financial Supervisory Agency directly under the Cabinet Secretariat. The reluctance of the MOF to move more rapidly in the mid-1990s to impose a system of prudential regulations was probably because it did not fully understand the implications of deregulation. After all, deregulation undermined the old convoy system and made traditional MOF modes of action now seem counter-productive.[7]

The crisis of November 1997

However, the banking system in Japan had been facing serious trouble for several years, and to avoid a systemic crisis, the government pledged public money (¥30 million) in December 1997 to strengthen the Deposit Insurance Corporation and also for the creation of a financial crisis management fund. Depositors' confidence was restored slightly by empowering the DIC to ensure full protection of banks' deposits and most of the credit until March 2001 (but subordinated debts of banks were not fully protected).[8]

In November 1997, the Hokkaido Takushoku Bank, one of the 19 largest banks, and Yamaichi Securities, one of the big four companies, failed. These institutions could not get funding for overnight loans in the call market (inter-bank market), since the market regarded these institutions as too risky to lend to, whereas the government had announced in 1995 that the largest banks would survive and all deposits would be safe.

The market interpreted the failure of two large institutions as a sign that the government had lost its grip on the market. Moreover, the stock prices of several weak financial institutions declined sharply and the 'Japan' premium' shot up to 100 basis points in international financial markets. Of course, the government, after some delay, promised to strengthen the DIC by issuing ¥30 trillion in government bonds to protect deposits from failed institutions and to inject capital into the banks. The government also allowed banks to adopt an accounting method which could hide unrealized capital losses from the securities holding. This was meant to clear the capital adequacy requirements at the end of 1998 as the average stock prices slumped to ¥16,000.

The financial crisis management account is meant to enable the DIC to raise the capital base of banks in order to (1) support the merger of failing banks through purchase of non-performing assets or new capital infusion or their takeover by healthy ones; (2) avert a systemic risk in the economy and also to avoid a financial and liquidity crisis in the region. The plan to provide ¥30 trillion was a response to the panic that followed failure of the Hokkaido Takushoku Bank and Yamaichi Securities: of ¥30 trillion, ¥13 trillion were used to inject capital into solvent but thinly capitalized banks and ¥17 trillion were to be used to protect depositors in failing institutions. In March 1998, the first wave of capital injection of about ¥2 trillion was given to 21 banks (18 large banks and 3 regional banks), but due diligence was less than adequate; it was obvious when the Long-Term Credit Bank was attacked in the market in June and was forced to seek a rescue merger.

The programme of dealing with the financial problems (December 1997) rose beyond short-term crisis management through an injection of liquidity or provision of a safety net to depositors. The major banks availed themselves of this facility and the first round of recapitalization was effected in March 1998 with each bank receiving ¥100 billion. Other steps to overhaul the system were: (1) introduction of self-assessment by banks and the framework of prompt corrective action (PCA) in April 1998; (2) announcement of a scheme to set up an arbitration fund and to change the tax laws to facilitate debt resolution (May

1998). In June 1998 the Financial Supervisory Agency was set up to grant or revoke bank licences and supervise all financial firms.

Cargill, Hutchison and Ito identified several factors for the delay in the regulatory response to the banking troubles – lack of political leadership, existence of competing regulatory authorities and agency problems in administering deposit guarantees. Regulatory forbearance and laxity also served to further weaken the banks, as the moral hazard resulted in the banks going in for a gamble on resurrection. Both the deposits and lending of Tokyo Kyowa Credit Cooperative and Anzen Credit Cooperative doubled between March 1992 and November 1994, but most of the new loans made in this period became non-performing.[9]

New institutional framework

While several changes have been made to the rules about regulation and supervision of banks, and also the operational procedures adopted, serious doubts and concerns about government policies have been expressed by several observers. Because of the resolution policies adopted and government handling with the help of Big Bang measures, Hoshi and Kashyap and Takatoshi Ito have hopes that bad debts will be carefully removed. Even in 2003, these bad loans loomed in high volumes, shaking the confidence of consumers, and scholars such as Hugh Patrick, P.N. Snowden, R. McKinnon and Maximilian J.B. Hall have also recently underlined several problem areas and scope for more effective policies.[10]

In 1997, it was so obvious that even big financial institutions were not too big to fall, and the government declared again and again that no bank would be allowed to do so. Hence because of widespread rumours, depositors continuously withdrew their funds from weak institutions. Until the late 1990s, depositors had no active role in the corporate governance of banks; heavy withdrawals in 1997 forced the government to take serious action on 26 November 1997. The Minister of Finance, Mitsuzuka, said that, regardless of the limited coverage under the deposit insurance system, the government guarantee would be there for the full amount of deposits in yen and in foreign currencies, bank debentures and the trust funds until March 2001.

In February 1998, the Diet passed two rules to amend the Deposit Insurance Law and the Financial Supervisory Agency (FSA) was set up under the Prime Minister, independent of the MOF, in view of public concern at the MOF's involvement in financial scandals. The MOF's

Table 6.2 Capital ratios under the new and old accounting standards for the 19 major banks*

	Capital ratio			Tier 1 capital ratio		
	Mar 97 (%)	*Mar 98 (old standards)* (%)	*Mar 98 (new standards)* (%)	*Mar 97* (%)	*Mar 98 (old standards)* (%)	*Mar 98 (new standards)* (%)
City banks						
Tokyo-Mitsubishi Bank†	9.28	8.20	8.54	4.97	4.27	4.27
Dai-Ichi Kangyo	8.76	7.51	9.09	4.38	3.76	4.63
Sakura	8.93	7.62	9.13	4.46	3.81	4.56
Sumitomo	8.75	8.33	9.23	4.5	4.17	4.76
Fuji	9.23	7.29	9.41	4.8	3.65	4.79
Sanwa	9.11	8.31	9.61	4.55	4.15	4.80
Tokai	9.09	8.82	10.26	4.55	4.41	5.41
Asahi	8.71	7.44	9.39	4.44	3.72	4.69
Daiwa	9.02	n.a.	10.30	4.73	3.56	5.35
Long-term credit banks						
IBJ†	9.04	9.31	9.74	4.83	4.79	4.95
LTCB	9.22	n.a.	10.32	4.61	3.82	5.16
NCB	2.99	n.a.	n.a.	1.5	n.a.	n.a.
Trust banks						
Mitsubishi Trust 2†	9.68	n.a.	10.35	5.15	5.99	5.99
Sumitomo Trust	8.97	n.a.	9.90	5.45	4.22	5.27
Mitsui Trust	9.56	8.66	10.41	5.35	4.33	6.02
Yasuda Trust	9.87	n.a.	13.56	5.73	3.97	7.14
Toyo Trust	10.02	9.29	10.68	5.79	4.64	5.78
Chuo Trust	9.11	n.a.	12.73	4.93	5.03	7.95
Nippon Trust	11.24	n.a.	9.83	10.29	8.21	9.26

* The calculation for the old standards adjusts for the revaluation of real estate holdings (45 per cent of which can be included in tier-two capital under the new standards) as well as the change from the lower of cost or market accounting of unrealized equity. Securities holdings on cost basis accounting from the old standards to the new standards.

† These three banks did not adopt the new accounting methods for unrealized equity securities holdings.

Sources: FitchIBCA, based on published financial statement as of 22 May 1998.

banking and security bureaux were merged to form a new financial planning bureau and the Securities and Exchange Surveillance Council was transferred from the MOF to the FSA.

New laws authorized provision of ¥30 trillion to bail out banks and protect depositors. In March 1998, banks had more problems in meeting capital requirements and applied for a public capital injection (¥100 billion). It was reported that the Bank of Tokyo-Mitsubishi was hesitant about capital injection, but as head of the Tokyo Bankers' Association in 1997, it was the first to announce its affiliation to capital injection and the government provided ¥1.8 trillion (0.5 per cent of GDP). For these banks, as subordinated debts, the government also relaxed accounting rules to help banks strengthen their capital position and allowed banks to count 45 per cent of their revalued real estate holdings towards tier-two capital. The government also allowed banks to change the lower of cost or market accounting to cost basis accounting for equity securities for investment purposes (Table 6.2).

Deposit guarantee

Several changes were made through the deposit insurance reforms of 1998. Japan had for years relied on administrative guidance from the BOJ and MOF, in order to impose regulatory discipline and intervene in financial markets. Japanese regulation had been predicated historically on a no-failure policy and did not rely on deposit insurance rules.

As Takatoshi Ito observes, Japan's deposit guarantee system had until recently not been tested, for several reasons. Japan's macroeconomic environment was conducive to a smooth evolution towards open and competitive markets. Price stability generated only a small gap between regulated and unregulated interest rates and provided few incentives to innovate. The major part of the deposit guarantee is that offered by the DIC for banks and other deposit-taking institutions, other than credit cooperatives, that protects up to ¥10 million per person per bank.[11] An explicit commitment by government to protect all deposits until 2001 was added in 1995.

In February 1998, as part of the emergency package, a financial stabilization law was meant to stabilize the system, and included several innovations:

1. A strengthening of the financial base of the DIC through injection of ¥30 trillion in total (¥7 trillion to meet losses from failure resolution, ¥10 trillion for purchase of assets from failed institutions and

¥13 trillion to finance purchases of preferred stock and subordinated debts).
2. An extension of the power of the Resolution and Collection Bank to allow it to take over financial review of any failed institution.
3. Setting up of an 'examining board' to administer financial assistance available through a financial crisis management account, as per a prescribed set of objective criteria. In October 1998, further reforms were made under financial revitalization legislation, with a view to improving the existing arrangements for resolution of failed financial institutions.

Moreover, the Financial Reconstruction Commission (FRC) was set up in December 1998, under the Prime Minister's Office, and also the Resolution and Collection Corporation (RCC) as a private corporation on the lines of the US Resolution and Trust Corporation to buy banks' bad loans and manage the assets until disposal.

A new account was set up – the financial revitalization account at the DIC with access to public funding of up to ¥18 trillion that could be used for setting up of bridge banks and purchase of assets of the financial institutions. Hence, until end March 2003, the FRC would be able to deal with financial failures through liquidation; over the same period, the RCC could use the resources of the financial revitalization account to purchase bad loans from failed institutions placed under administration.

Another change in the deposit insurance reforms of 1998 was the implementation of the financial function early strengthening laws in October 1998. They were meant to ensure early restoration of financial stability by facilitating swift disposal of bad loans and also creating a new system to recapitalize weak institutions. The DIC financial function early strengthening account was endowed with up to ¥25 trillion of public funds to be used by the RCC to purchase the common or preferred stocks of applicant institutions. This replaced the ¥13 trillion financial crisis management account set up in February 1998.[12]

Through this route ¥8 trillion were injected into 15 major banks in March 1999, with additional sums being injected into 9 regional banks plus the LTC Bank during the following year. This followed the injection of ¥1.8 trillion into 21 banks in March 1998 under the financial stabilization law.[13]

Of course, the deposit insurance reforms of 2000 cemented the reforms of 1998; under this revision to deposit insurance law, the potential size of public sector funds available for financial stabilization was raised from ¥60 trillion to ¥125 trillion for the financial function early strengthening account to recapitalize weak institutions, including the purchase of assets from failed institutions.[14] In July 2000, the Financial Services Agency was set up, following the assumption of the licensing, inspection and supervisory function of the old FSA, and also financial planning, a responsibility earlier undertaken by the Financial Planning Bureau. And it now operates as an external organ of the Cabinet Office.

Further, in June 2001 the new FSA disclosed plans forcing the banks to unwind cross-shareholdings. For this, the Banks' Shareholding Acquisition Corporation was set up to buy shares at market prices from banks unwilling to offload on the open market.

The credit crunch in the economy

For the Japanese banking system, 1997 was a turning point due to increased pressure upon banks to improve their balance sheets, and during the following year a basic shift in the lending behaviour of banks was observed. As David Woo notes, the cross-section correlation between bank lending growth and bank capital which was negative during most of the early 1990s, became positive in 1997, suggesting that weak banks constrained by their capital positions, began to grow less rapidly than better capitalized banks. It was also found that capital weakness tended to constrain bank lending growth more than asset growth, showing that the slow-down in bank lending was not entirely due to funding capacity.[15]

Woo attributes this issue partly to increased failures of distressed financial institutions in 1997, which abated the moral hazard problem by signalling a fundamental shift in the strategy in dealing with these institutions. These changes in strategy, whether prompted by the realization that government resources to rescue the banking system were limited, or by the resolve to introduce discipline into the economy, helped to bring some credibility into the regulatory framework and also led banks to recognize that they would suffer the same fate as banks that had closed, if they did not restore soundness.

Moreover, introduction of prompt corrective action (PCA) in April 1998 (April 1999 for domestic-only operators) under Big Bang reforms for capital ratio requirements as per the American framework has two important elements:

1. Introduction of a self-assessment process that places on the banks the responsibility for valuing their assets on a realistic basis according to well-defined guidelines. These procedures require that banks'

own funding and provisioning for loan losses and capital ratios are subject to review by external auditors and to inspections by bank examiners.

2. The specification of the capital ratio thresholds under which regulators can order banks to take remedial action, for example reduction of branches and divisions and liquidation in the case of insolvency. This constitutes an important milestone, since it narrows the scope for regulatory forbearance by placing pressure on the regulators to act when a bank weakens.[16]

In this manner, market discipline can be improved and excess capacity in the economy reduced in view of the Japanese Shadow Financial Regulatory Committee policy.

Moreover, the fact that the capital ratio of poorly capitalized banks had come close to the 8 per cent threshold also led these banks to cut back on their lending. They cut back their lending to blue chip Japanese corporations with which they had maintained close business ties over the years, but lending to them was no longer profitable. The banks arranged for their securities subsidiaries to help these corporations issue corporate bonds. Banks also cut back their loans to overseas corporations with a high credit rating after the yen had started depreciating against the dollar.

As a recent Tankan survey showed, the willingness of financial institutions to lend, as reported by firms, dropped very markedly in 1997. While lending by foreign banks in Japan contracted even more sharply than domestic banks during the first half of the 1990s, foreign lending has accelerated vigorously since 1997, just when Japanese bank lending really began to decline.

Of course, the credit crunch became more serious when banks were under pressure to improve their balance sheets in late 1997; to the extent that significant disintermediation is still occurring, the authorities' capacity to influence investment may be curtailed.

Paul Krugman forcefully argues against the conventional wisdom that the banking sector has been a major contributor to Japan's problems since bank reform is a microeconomic policy; it is the attempts to clean up the banking sector, not the bank problems themselves, that have led to the credit crunch. In normal circumstances with no liquidity trap, any negative macroeconomic effects from the credit crunch could be offset by loose monetary policy.[17]

Krugman held that, if the economy is in a liquidity trap, expanding the monetary base would have little effect on broader aggregates.

Hence, the observation that the central bank has slashed interest rates and pumped up the monetary base, but that the broader money supply has not grown, does not necessarily imply that the fault lies in the banking system. Also it does not imply that disintermediation is not occurring and there is substantial anecdotal evidence that it is. This means that the BOJ is likely to continue to encounter difficulties in stimulating investment through monetary expansion until the bank clean-up is completed.[18]

In view of continuing international pressure, the government announced that taxpayers' money would be used to fund these new measures for credit guarantee schemes, which had been in existence for the past several years. The banks exploited these guarantee schemes since, with a view to calculate the BIS capital ratio, they were allowed to attach a zero-risk weight to government guarantee loans so that they could engage in more risky lending to boost their margins. But the enforcement of capital adequacy standards is not the only way in which a banking clean-up may affect the real economy. The process of recovering bad loans and putting idle assets back in the market, may also put downward pressure on asset prices and depress new investments – a case of asset overhang.[19] Japan's real estate sector is a prime example of this phenomenon with a surplus of prime properties likely to move over to the market as banks retrieve collateral; real estate activity will certainly remain depressed for a long time.

In Japan banks are prevented from owning more than 5 per cent of outstanding shares of any one company (Anti-Monopoly Law Article 11), but there is no ceiling on the total amount of stocks they may own. The market value of shares held by banks in March 1993 was ¥56.4 trillion, as compared with book value of only ¥34.5 trillion.[20]

While government regulations allowed banks to use only 45 per cent of these unrealized gains (about ¥22 trillion) towards their tier-two capital, these accounted for about 25 per cent of total bank capital in the year. By 1999 these government schemes were growing so rapidly that they almost exhausted their funding. Additional funding of ¥20 trillion was offered to the guarantee schemes in late 1998 and a new round of injection of funds was approved in the summer of 1999. In September 1999, one more scheme was announced to support small and medium-sized companies by guaranteeing their corporate bond issues. Moreover, it was also reported that some banks tried to recover their impaired loans from small and medium-sized companies by requesting them to borrow from these government agencies.

Further recapitalization

Besides undercapitalized banks, solvent banks with a capital adequacy ratio (CAR) of 8 per cent or more could ask for public funding through state purchases of preferred shares. Such funding was restricted to three conditions – the solvent bank is taking over a failed institution or the solvent bank is involved in a merger or other reorganization or the solvent bank would be threatened to stop booking new loans suddenly and massively, if public funds were not granted. Undercapitalized banks operating internationally with a CAR over 4 per cent but less than 8 per cent could seek capital injection through state purchases of preferred shares.

For banks with a CAR of less than 4 per cent, but more than 2 per cent operating internationally, capital injection could be made through state purchases of common or preferred shares. Banks heavily undercapitalized with a CAR less than the above numbers, but whose debts did not exceed their assets, could also seek state capital injection. Such banks were only to be considered for government help if their survival was vital for local business.

The Diet doubled the total amount of government funds set aside for helping the banking sector to ¥60 trillion (12 per cent of GDP), of which ¥25 trillion were earmarked for recapitalizing weak banks, ¥18 trillion for dealing with insolvent banks through nationalization and ¥17 trillion for full deposit protection of insolvent banks. For banks whose debts exceed their assets, a legally defined procedure would deal with the failed institutions, for example the LTCB Bank and Nippon Credit Bank.

The increased funding allowed for additional capital injection into banks. By March 1999, application for the second round of government injection by major banks amounted to ¥7.5 trillion, four times as much as the first round of injection in 1998. The modalities of injection were the purchases by the DIC of preferred shares and/or subordinated debts issued by the banks. These new measures allowed the FSA to tighten operations of its supervisory authority, since it was found after onsite examination of major banks during 1999–2000 that the self-assessment of asset quality by the banks was based on very optimistic assumptions. Once the FSA was satisfied that after the second round of public capital injection, the major banks had sufficient capital, they concentrated on the regional banks. In April 1999, the FSA extended the PCA framework to banks without international operations. In September 1999, the FRC decided to approve the application by four regional banks – Ashikaga Bank, Hokuriku Bank, Ryukyu Bank and Hiroshima Sogon Bank – for capital injection, totalling ¥260 billion, after which they met the CAR of 8 per cent.[21]

Concerns and weaknesses of the reform plan

Recently doubts were expressed whether all these measures would bring the desired effects. The government is still very reluctant to reduce excess capacity in these banking sectors through outright liquidation; rather they prefer to use public management (i.e. nationalization and the bridge bank scheme) and help mergers to handle failed institutions, because of their alarm at the pace of credit contraction. In this manner, zombie-like institutions are kept going well beyond their sell-by dates.[22] In the fiscal year 1999, 20 banking institutions failed following 30 cases in fiscal year 1998, leading to ¥6 trillion of financial assistance being provided by the DIC.

It was recently suggested that the major fault in dealing with long-term banking problems is the government's waiver to enforce an increase of the banks' capital base. The injection of public funds is subject to voluntary submission of a management improvement plan that should include improved efficiency of operations, reduction of staff, cost-cutting measures, reduction of bonus and dividends or a reduction of capital at the cost of shareholders.

If a major realistic assessment of banks' net worth was made, with the banks being forced to write off loan losses immediately, the PCA could be used more forcefully to weed out poor management and liquidate weak institutions.[23]

Recently, it was revealed that the effects of two rounds of financial injection to the major banks during 1998–2000 had fallen far behind early expectations. Moreover, to the extent that weak institutions are assisted, dangerous moral hazards are created. Also, by sustaining overcapacity in the banking sector, it slows down the move to long-term equilibrium in the industry, when each bank would make a normal rate of return: one criticism was made that these initial disbursements by the FRC were a device to allow banks to comply with Basle accord minimum risk–asset ratio of 8 per cent at the end of fiscal year 1998 or to revive bank lending and consumer demand in Japan.[24]

The dangers of using deposit insurance to stabilize the banking and financial sectors have been vividly shown in Japan, with the authorities failing to stick to an earlier pledge to remove the blanket coverage given to depositors at the end of March 2001. The official reason suggested for the delay was to allow more time for the FSA to conduct financial inspection of small financial institutions earlier supervised by local government.

Of course, under the revisions made to deposit insurance law in May 2000, deposits are protected until the end of March 2002, with liquid deposits engaging full protection for one more year. So it would not be until at least March 2003 that depositors once again face haircuts beyond ¥10 million (to cover principal and interest) per customer as per bank limit.

The deposit insurance arrangements in Japan still remain vitally flawed because of their failure to embrace the risk-related premium and the co-insurance principle, for example failings which create a moral hazards for managers, shareholders and depositors alike.[25] Another doubt was recently expressed that injections of public money do not guarantee that commercial banks do not trim their lending. The difficult situation in the banking industry that the BOJ's loose monetary policy tried to counteract will, for the time being, overshadow the real economic development of Japan.[26]

The first results of the injection of government funds by the end of March 1999, showed that 15 out of 18 banks received capital injections of ¥7460 billion, of which ¥5560 billion were convertible preferred stocks, ¥600 billion were other preferred and ¥1300 billion were subordinated debts. Also, ¥2150 billion were raised from private funding to stabilize the banking industry that resulted in a total capital injection of ¥9600 billion (Figure 6.1).

The total public funds of ¥9600 billion resulted in significant improvements in bank finances. The capital base, following BIS guidelines, expanded by ¥7000 billion due to a strong stock market. So Japanese banks were able to raise their BIS CAR by the end of October

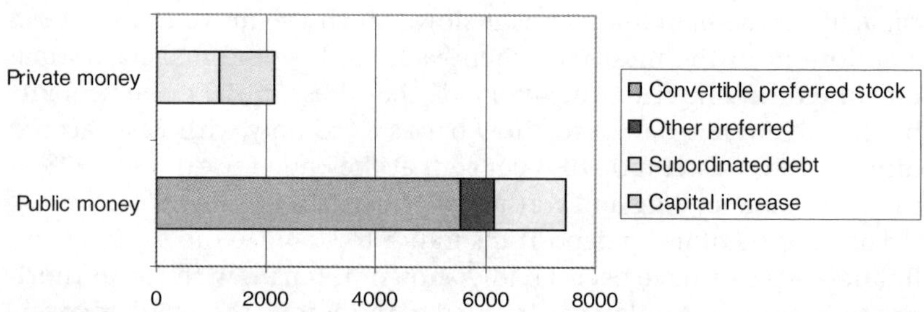

Figure 6.1 Capital increase for 15 banks in fiscal year 1998 (billion yen)

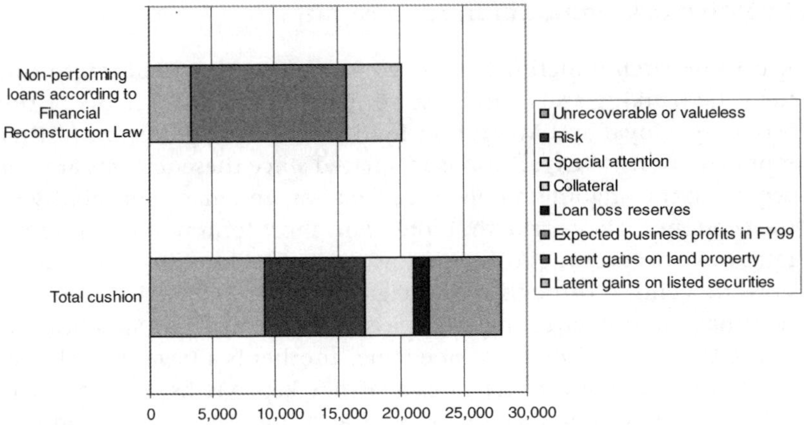

Figure 6.2 Non-performing loans and total cushion of 17 major banks, September 1999 (billion yen)

2000 to 12.3 per cent (in 1990 it was only 8 per cent). By using a total of ¥7000 billion and partly nationalizing all leading banks, Japan made reasonable progress during 2000 and 2001 in stabilizing the banking economy. But the roots of instability in the economy (see Figure 6.2) never really vanished and three problems still trouble the banking sector, even in the new century:

1. In view of the enormous size of banking problems, the whole system is still quite weak. The banks still do not properly fulfil their duty in loan supplies. Moreover, they are facing the difficult task of repayment of their public fund injection within three years.
2. A lot of small and middle-size local and regional banks are in a critical state and not likely to be able to survive; so for these institutions, the forthcoming discontinuation of 100 per cent government protection for bank deposits will be crucial. After the relevant date of implementation, only deposits for ¥10 million will be insured; weak banks are in danger of a run on their deposits.
3. A third area of concern is the life insurance sector in the light of Japan's lasting zero interest rate policy and resulting negative interest margins. Thorough consolidation is to be expected in this industry following massive government aid to Japan's banking system; the same is to be expected for the life insurance industry.[27]

Negative risk premium in interest rates

Recent research underlines the need for several structural reforms to help the banking sector and also to liberalize various sectors of the economy. Goyal and McKinnon hold that this emphasis on further monetary or fiscal expansion is misplaced since these reforms are not central to the ongoing problems of deflation and macro-instability in the economy. They argue that long- and short-term nominal interest rates have been brought to very low levels (the liquidity trap due to pressure coming through the foreign exchanges).[28] While declining nominal interest rates on dollar assets from inflation stabilization in the USA in the 1990s was one issue, another is a negative risk premium in Japanese interest rates that has kept yields on yen assets below those on dollar assets; there is also the fear that the yen will resume appreciating secularly.

As long-term interest rates have been pushed to very low values, short-term interest rates are reduced to zero; Japan is in a liquidity trap, where the BOJ has not been able to halt deflation in spite of boosting the monetary base for several years. It is also suggested that besides the impotence of monetary policy at a zero lower bound of nominal interest rates, compression of lending interest rates towards zero has squeezed bank profit margins.[29] This compression made new bank lending hardly profitable, and hence it was almost impossible for Japanese banks, by themselves, to slowly write off old bad loans out of current earnings. In several countries the spread between deposit rates and lending rates has been raised, so that banks could gradually recover loan losses over time. But in Japan, the compressed spreads have hindered the banks, saddled with sizeable non-performing loans, from earning profits that could be used to restore their capital. It also explains the slump in 'new' bank credit to Japan's private sector.[30]

As Krugman argues, if the economy is in a liquidity trap, expanding the monetary base will have little effect on broader aggregates.[31] Moreover, the formal models such as those of Krugman and Svensson do not show how the BOJ would be able to reinflate the economy (or depreciate the exchange rate) when short-term interest rates are trapped at zero.

Dominic Wilson recently suggested that the enforcement of capital adequacy standards is not the only way in which a banking clean-up may affect the real economy. The process of recovering bad loans and putting idle assets back onto the market may also put downward pressure on asset prices and depress new investment – a case of asset overhang.[32]

Japan's real estate sector is a prime example of this phenomenon. With a surplus of empty property likely to move onto the market as banks retrieve their collateral, real estate activity will almost certainly remain depressed for a longer period. While there has been no trend in appreciation of the yen since the mid-1990s, the absence of such a trend may be rationalized as a result of a strong US economy and a strong dollar policy, where American mercantile pressure has been muted, or as a consequence of a stagnant real Japanese economy relative to a robust US economy in a standard growth model as in Yoshikawa (1990).

Being a creditor nation, Japan has a large negative risk premium that has become more negative, as it continued to run large surpluses during the 1990s and built up foreign currency claims on the rest of the world. A significant portion of these claims was in foreign currency which led to a more negative risk premium in the late 1990s. The foreign currency claims on the rest of the world were small in the 1980s and domestic growth rates were high. The risk premium was small and the interest differential between dollar and yen assets was explained by expectations of a yen appreciation. Since the early 1990s, as Japanese growth slowed and pressure for yen appreciation eased, the interest differential was accounted for mainly by a negative risk premium.

Table 6.3 shows the rise in net foreign assets for 1980 to 2000, as reported in *International Financial Statistics* (IMF, 2002); the breakdown between official reserves and the private sector's net foreign asset holdings is also shown. The table shows a large increase in Japan's net foreign asset position in the late 1980s and the 1990s. At the end of 2000, the total net foreign asset position stood at $1.2 trillion, which is over 20 per cent of GDP or 6 per cent of total assets. A large portion of this position is held by the private sector, though accumulation of official reserves played a large role during the late 1990s.

Table 6.3 shows the officially reported stock of net foreign assets. The unofficial estimates of the stock position (by cumulating current account surpluses) suggest numbers that are about 1.5 times as large as the official data.

Table 6.4 shows different estimates of Japan's cumulative current account surplus; the second column repeats the official net asset position from Table 6.3. The third column shows the cumulative current account position from Lane and Milesi Ferretti (2001). Both columns show numbers much higher than the official estimates. The final column cumulates the balance on goods and services (the balance on income is excluded) using a 6 per cent yield on assets. The 6 per cent

Table 6.3 Japan's net foreign asset position (billions of US dollars)

Year	*Total net foreign assets*	*Private sector net position*	*Official reserves*
1980	12.52	–13.20	25.72
1985	130.38	103.15	27.23
1990	329.36	249.65	79.71
1995	817.60	632.42	184.82
1997	958.73	737.62	220.81
1998	1153.64	937.26	215.83
1999	829.12	540.10	287.66
2000	1157.93	796.82	36.99

Source: *International Financial Statistics*, IMF (March 2002).

Table 6.4 Alternative estimates of Japan's net foreign asset position (billions US$)

Year	*Official estimate (IMF, 2002)*	*Lane and Milesi-Ferretti (2001)*	*Goyal (2001)*	
			Cumulative current account surplus	*Capital accumulation (6% interest rate)*
1980	12.52	16.29	12.52	12.52
1985	130.38	101.49	138.43	135.54
1990	329.36	445.96	511.39	506.99
1995	817.60	1030.48	1099.86	1127.81
1997	958.73	1336.66	1277.93	1337.25
2000	1157.93		1653.18	1817.08

Note: Column 4 (Cumulative current account surplus) sums the balance on goods, services and income. Column 5 (capital accumulation) computes stocks from flow data (the balance on goods and services only) as follows: Stocks (t) = $(1+i)$ Stock (t–1) + Flow (t).

yield comes from Figure 6.2, where return on long-term user bonds was at least 6 per cent until the late 1990s. These estimates suggest that the stock of net foreign assets and the external exposure of Japanese financial institutions are very large.

The share of net foreign assets data in foreign currencies is difficult to ascertain. Some data are available through the BOJ's locational international banking statistics that report balance sheet positions of banks and non-banks vis-à-vis non-residents in any currency. It is shown in Table 6.4.

Moreover, corresponding to the increase of Japan's net foreign asset position in Tables 6.3 and 6.4, there was an increase in net assets vis-à-vis foreigners, throughout the 1990s – a significant portion of these net assets is in foreign currency. While non-banks hold the vast majority of net foreign assets and net foreign currency assets, about 70–80 per cent of their net foreign asset positions is in foreign currency. Banks borrowed heavily in the short term from abroad in the 1990s. This is shown in their net liquidity position in 1990. After making large foreign exchange losses, they unwound much of their net short-term exposure, while accumulating long-term foreign currency assets.

The balance sheet data do not show the proportion of loans to foreigners or to multinational corporations for the purpose of foreign direct investment (FDI). Even if external FDI is shown in yen, the investment is subject to foreign exchange risk, if the proceeds of investment or the success of investment is linked to the dollar. The key variable for the foreign exchange risk premium is the share of net foreign exchange assets to performing or healthy domestic assets.

If a large share of total domestic assets is at risk of becoming non-performing, as is the case in Japan, then net foreign exchange assets become a larger share of performing assets and suggest a more negative foreign exchange risk premium. As non-performing loans have ballooned recently, net foreign exchange assets of about 8 per cent of total assets became a larger share of performing assets. Hence, the story is: as Japan has run current account surpluses through the 1990s and has accumulated net foreign assets, the negative risk premium has become more negative. This more negative risk premium has maintained the interest differential between yen assets and dollar assets even in the absence of a trend of yen appreciation.[33]

The role of structural measures

Of course, adoption of an exchange rate target approach involves huge budgeting support to help resolution of the financial sector problems; other structural implications are also involved. The assistance of the yen's appreciation suggests that recovery on the demand side would have to be generated internally. As a recent study by Oishi and Towe suggests, the potential output gains to be realized from structural reforms could be substantial.[34] When Japan is compared with other industrial countries, very wide variations in sectoral labour activity measures are observed.[35]

But Adam Posen suggested that the short-term consequences of reform policies generally include increased unemployment and cannot form part of any immediate strategy for recovery. As against this view, the Japanese IT and telecommunications sector showed significant dynamism in view of buoyant domestic demand. Hence, to promote investment in more sheltered domestic sectors, a phased introduction of market reforms could be associated with a temporary investment of tax credit. This type of incentive is more likely to stimulate the commitment to investment spending in several activities, leading to several desirable structural changes. So if high aggregate saving is to continue in Japan, a really firm exchange rate commitment would surely support sustained outflows that the limits to domestic investment opportunities would still require.[36]

In recent research studies, it is implicitly assumed that problems faced on a continuing basis for more than a decade are mainly cyclical, and the solution lies in providing a sufficient boost to aggregate demand. Of course, a strong case is made that structural problems lie at the heart of the Japanese problem and unless they are carefully tackled, proactive monetary policies alone cannot deliver the goods, and orthodox measures of raising demand will prove counter-productive. Hence the problem really is a very long-term one, and as a result of ongoing inefficiency in the system will be for years to come.

Looking back, we find even when the BOJ expanded its assets with a view to get over the financial mess, the net injection of reserve money into the system was quite modest. Of the ¥30 billion increase in the balance sheet of the BOJ between January 1998 and March 2000, as much as ¥18 trillion was raised through the sale of BOJ bills (these sales imply an equal withdrawal of high-power money from the system). Moreover, the absorption of government paper by the BOJ has been quite modest for years and so the most useful instrument of monetary policy (variations in high-power money) was hardly used to counter the ongoing slide in the economy.

Recently, it was suggested that the size of the Japanese crisis is particularly large and the extent of moral hazards as a cause of it was particularly great.[37] For years during the boom period, financial institutions were encouraged to undertake more risky lending and the moral hazard issue was a very serious one in Japan.[38]

Moreover, international organizations observed several monetary policy barriers in explaining the Japanese case.[39] When the asset bubble burst, several factors compounded the emerging complications in the economy. Regulatory structures, tax treatment of bad loan provisions and BIS capital norms, all affected banks' response to deal with emerging problems.

Since Japan ran current account surpluses through the 1990s and accumulated net foreign assets, the negative risk premium also became more negative. This has maintained the interest differential between yen assets and dollar assets even in the absence of a trend in yen appreciation. While US nominal interest rates declined due to inflation stabilization in the USA, Japanese long rates have been compressed to very low values. Hence the short rates have been compressed to zero (the case of a liquidity trap) where the BOJ could not halt deflation and reinflate the economy.[40]

While the interest margin on lending shows a slight decline during the 1990s, this decline was more than matched by a decline in general and administrative costs. Moreover, the costs associated with the disposal of non-performing loans increased dramatically in the late 1990s and the export profitability suffered.

As McKinnon recently suggested, the accounting of interest income in Japan is flawed. While Japanese banks have disposed of a large number of non-performing loans, new and larger amounts of bad loans keep appearing on their books. This shows that banks could not do a proper risk assessment of their loan portfolios and did not make sufficient allowance for future loan losses. It is just possible that banks may be evergreening these bad loans and capitalizing interest payments, which they have not received. So their net interest income is overstated and the reported ex-post net margin does not decline.

This means that Japanese banks are not earning adequate profit to cover loan losses even after deregulation of interest rates. Japanese banks could not generate substantially large profit margins. In fact, yields on newly issued commercial paper have been very low since the mid-1990s. They fell from around 2.5 per cent before 1995 to 0.5 per cent since 1996, suggesting that issues of this paper can access credit cheaply and need not pay higher interest rates to banks. Hence the suggestion that low lending spirits are a key element of problems faced by the Japanese banks.

In view of data difficulties, it is almost impossible to judge whether the decline in quality of loans and increased riskiness of Japanese bank lending were particularly severe by international standards. Recent analysis by Jenny Corbett suggests that the share of lending in the real estate sector does not appear to have been high by international standards.[41]

On the deposit side, household savings increased during the 1990s. In 1989, 45 per cent of these savings were held in domestically licensed banks and 32 per cent in the postal saving system. The rest were mostly in financial institutions for agriculture, forestry, fisheries and institutions for small business. By the late 1990s, the share of savings in domestically licensed banks had fallen marginally to 40 per cent but increased to 36 per cent in the postal saving system. But on the deposit side, there has not been much change. On the lending side, there has been a significant increase in the share of loans by government financial institutions, as Fukao recently noted. But this change is not large and there does not appear to be much evidence of undercutting of private lending rates by government financial institutions. The evidence of government financial institutions offering low rates and increased lending to the private sector does not contradict the above case of low rates coming from pressures in the foreign exchange market and government institutions acting in the domestic market to offset some of the decline in lending by commercial banks.[42]

Problem loans, provisioning and write-offs in the new millennium

The ongoing debt problem of the Japanese banks since the early 1990s is related to several complex factors, for example the continuing weakness of the Japanese stock market and domestic property markets, excess capacity in the banking and financial sectors due to supervisory forbearance and also no-failure policies, and also the low profitability of the banking sector and continuing deflation in the economy. While banks have many incentives to hide the extent of bad loans, the definitions of non-performing loans also change over time.

By official estimates, the share of non-performing loans is 7 per cent.[43] While Japanese banks were not required to disclose information systematically on their asset quality, following recommendations by a public committee, banks were required to make public details of their asset quality from March 1993 in a format suggested by the Federation of Bankers' Association. For major banks (city banks, test banks, long-term credit banks), minimum disclosure was of the gross amount of lending to bankrupt firms and lending on which interest payments were more than six months overdue. The public committee did not ask for immediate disclosure of lending on which interest had been reduced or waived, and doubtful loans of non-bank financial institutions were not disclosed.

With ex-ante profit margins being about 1.7 per cent and given a spread of 1.7 per cent, it will take over 56 years to cover loan losses. This assumes no new defaults and no infusion of funds. If there is a continuing risk of default, then this is an underestimate and it will take longer to cover the losses in the past 10 years; there is also little change in the total deposit base of domestically licensed banks. There has been public infusion of funds but these have been few and in times of crisis only.[44]

From March 1996, banks began to report bad loans on a broader basis. This included loans to companies receiving financial support in forms other than loan rate reductions. The latter category formed about 21 per cent (¥3.7 billion of the total reported bad loans of 21 major banks of ¥18 billion in September 1996). In early 1998, the MOF widened the official definition of bad loans to include loans overdue by three to six months and to bad loans with interest rates above the official discount rate (ODR), but below commerical rates as part of restructuring loans. On this basis, bad loans for major banks in March 1999 rose to ¥29 trillion.

In Japan, three definitions of bad loans are popular. One is a risk management loan published by each bank on its financial statement as of March 2000; bad loans on this definition totalled over ¥30 trillion or 6 per cent of GDP. The second definition is based on the classification of loans the FSA uses for analysis. The banks classify as per their perception of collectivity. On this definition, the amount of bad loans as of March 2000 is ¥63 trillion or 13 per cent of GDP.

Since March 1999, each bank is required to publish the data laid down by the Financial Reconstruction Act. On this definition, bad loans of Japanese banks were about ¥33 million or 6.5 per cent of GDP in March 2000. But unofficial estimates of the share of bad loans are as high as 20 per cent. For such high loan losses, it would take over 100 years to recover losses at a spread of 2 per cent. For a spread lower than 1.9 per cent banks are running at a loss, since the spreads required for Japanese banks to make profits and cover losses are much larger than they have been able to generate.

Recently it was observed that between fiscal years 1992 and 2000 the banking industry has incurred ¥72 trillion of losses on its disposal of bad debts, including direct write-offs of ¥30 trillion and transfer to allowances for loan losses of ¥36 trillion, yet Japanese banking still faces a huge burden. The latest official figures show that, for the deposit-taking sector as a whole, bad loans (risk management loans) plus restructured loans amounted to ¥43.5 trillion at the end of March 2001. This compares to the figure of ¥35 trillion recorded at the end of March 1998 when reasonable disclosure standards were first introduced.[45]

Hence, low lending spreads are a key component of the problems in Japan. A spread of over 3 per cent which the US banks have been able to generate, suggests that with a 6 per cent initial non-performing loan and smaller lending spreads, Japanese banks face a very difficult time to cover losses. What the impact is on bank lending if banks are unable to break even is an important question.

On the deposit side, household savings increased throughout the 1990s. In 1990, 40 per cent of these savings were held in domestically licensed banks, but rose to 36 per cent in the postal savings system. On the deposit side, there has not been much change, but on the lending side, there has been an increase in the share of loans by government financial institutions. But this change is not large and there is not much evidence of undercutting of private lending rates by government institutions.

As for the true scale of Japan's deposit-taking sectors and current bad debt problem, the available evidence suggests that the upper and lower boundaries lay between ¥43 trillion and ¥145 billion respectively (assuming a correct coverage ratio was applied at the end of March 2001). Without an accurate estimate of the migration of loans from good to bad, it is not possible to provide an accurate estimate of the upper bad debt boundary. Recently it was feared that both the FSA estimate of collateral coverage and the assumed rate of migration of loans from category 2 to category 3 will prove widely optimistic, as the FSA admitted in July 2001 that major banks had underestimated such loans by up to 30 per cent.

In early 2003, the banking sector still had a massive bad loan problem even after substantial write-offs (by over ¥30 trillion). As the 1990s ended, the level of loan loss allowances at just over ¥12 trillion was less than half the amount of bad loans by any of the three definitions. As Hoshi and Kashyap observed, the rate at which banks will continue to have to devote earnings to provision against bad loans, depends on the rate and degree of economic recovery.[46]

In early 2002, the Japanese government announced plans to force banks to write off existing bad debts within two years and any new bad debts within three years. With a clean-up deadline in danger of slipping to 2007, even this target does not seem realistic. While the FSA insists that ¥15 trillion are still potentially available for the financial function, the early strengthening account will only be used to recapitalize the banking system in the event of a systemic crisis, and Mizuko holdings maintain that the new preference shares will be used by major banks to raise new capital, should current FSA inspections of loan books suggest further provisions are called for. Others fear that the risk of contagion will be heightened if any preference shares issued are simply absorbed by affiliated companies or life insurance companies.

What may be of more interest in bank behaviour is the level of provisioning before and during the crisis. To some extent it is determined by national registration and tax treatment.[47] But there is an element of discretion by bank managers. Moreover, interests of different shareholders in banks will be different with regard to provisioning. Managers' and owners' incentives will depend on the extent of safety nets. If risks are low, and safety nets are high, there is likely to be low provisioning. Depositors have an interest in higher levels of provisioning, since it may reduce the chance of bank collapse. Moreover, the level of discretionary provisioning might be informative about the government structure in banks.[48]

After the trap

Hence national monetary policies must support any long-run exchange rate target, but once the expectation of an ever-higher yen was successfully quashed, almost all the monetary adjustment would be in Japan. With little or no change in the Federal Reserve policy of stabilizing the American price level, the independent anchor would be necessary or desirable. Since the purpose of long-term stabilization of the exchange rate is to end deflationary pressures, that is where the main monetary adjustment would take place.

Once the foreign exchange value of the yen and the future Japanese price level is securely anchored, whether the BOJ should tighten or ease domestic monetary policies is not clear. The possibly sharp increase in nominal interest rates would tend to reduce the demand for base money. If this effect dominates, the BOJ would need to reduce the monetary base quickly in order to prevent capital outflows and a sharp depreciation of the yen below its agreed dollar benchmark.[49]

During 1999, a lively debate began whether the BOJ was stimulating sufficiently. Several observers regarded the BOJ policy as not sufficiently stimulative, as shown by the price deflation in the late 1990s.

The debate highlighted the importance of preventing deflation as well as inflation. Concerns were also raised about the ability of the BOJ to maintain its new independence in the context of changes in Japan's political institutions.

The BOJ, while removing itself from the MOF's influence, may become more dependent on politicians. In Japan political institutions are changing, since politicians increasingly realized that they will be punished for poor economic performance. A reduced national consensus for economic growth and a more politically active household sector are generating fractionalized political institutions willing to use monetary policy to enhance political power. The BOJ could become more sensitive to political influences, especially since the Cabinet, with the consent of the Diet, selects six of the nine members of the revised and enhanced monetary policy board.

A number of observers have suggested that further institutional change is required that would help the BOJ in preventing deflation as well as inflation and in remaining politically independent. Specifically, the BOJ should adopt an explicit inflation target. Explicit inflation targeting would have prevented the policy mistakes of 1998 and 1999, and would go a considerable way to ensuring that monetary policy does not become an instrument of political manipulation to maintain and enhance political power.[50]

7
The Internationalization of the Yen in the New Millennium

As Japan expanded trade and investment with East Asian countries due to the rapid appreciation of the yen after the Plaza accord in 1985, yen-invoiced trade increased sharply in Japan's trade with South-East Asian countries and shot up further during the 1990s. This trend put Japan into the centre of gravity of regional development, and Japanese influence in the region has increased over the years. But the yen-invoiced ratio of trade declined considerably from 1994 in Japan's exports to East Asia, and the US dollar was still used more than the yen even in March 2003.

It is widely believed that market forces have pulled the region closer and a yen block is slowly emerging.[1] Our focus now is on the issue of what happens if there were a yen block.[2] Of course, implications of the use of the yen in international transactions are mixed despite Japan's emergence as the world's largest creditor country. Its capital outflows have not significantly facilitated the yen's internationalization because capital flows have been primarily denominated in currencies other than the yen. The available evidence shows that the share of international trade transactions denominated in yen is much smaller than currencies of other large industrial countries. While the use of the yen as a regional currency showed increasing trends in Asia during the 1990s, a yen zone still does not appear to be emerging.

International currency use

The use of a currency in the world system is more complex than a national currency. While money is determined by government fiat in the domestic context, the choice of currency to be used for international transactions is the result of market-determined processes. Several factors are necessary for a currency to be used internationally:

1. There needs to be confidence in the value of a currency and in the issuing nation's inflation performance;
2. The country should have a deep open and broad domestic financial market. Active short-term (Treasury bill and commercial paper) markets contribute to international demand for currencies, reflecting central banks' and other investors' preferences for liquid and safe financial investments;
3. The larger a nation's share in world exports and greater the extent to which those exports are dominated in the exporter currency, the greater the demand for that currency by foreigners in order to pay for imports.

Japan's strong economic performance allowed the country to emerge as a world power. Also during the 1980s, Japan recorded lower consumer price inflation at 2.5 per cent per annum than other large industrial nations. Then during the 1980s, Japan's share of world exports rose by 2.5 percentage points, reaching over 9 per cent by the end of the decade, and the direction of Japanese trade moved steadily towards the Asian region paving the way for a large regional use of the yen.

A currency becomes an international reserve, invoicing and settlement currency when there is confidence in the economy and the markets are fair. A national currency could become international money if it 'met various needs of foreign official institutions and foreign private parties more effectively than other financial assets could'[3].

As told by Robert Mundell, history has shown us, as in case of sterling and the US dollar, that the top currency is provided by the dominant power, that is the country who has the largest share of world exports, has a confidently valued currency and has a deep open and broad domestic financial market.[4]

Of course, international dominance of a currency is directly related to its share in the world's exports, the proportion of specialized manufactured products in those exports, the extent to which those exports are denominated in the exporters' currency, demand for that currency by foreign firms in order to pay for their imports and the extent to which dominant powers trade with poor countries.[5]

Besides the share of world exports, there needs to be confidence in the value of a currency and in the political stability of the issuing country, if a currency is to be accepted as a key currency. A relatively low level of inflation and of inflation variability depends on stable government policies. Another factor for the international use of a currency is that a nation should possess financial markets that are sought with a large assortment of financial investments, are deep with developed secondary markets and are free of controls.

It should also have financial institutions which are competitive in offshore financial centres. Well-developed financial markets contribute to the demand for international currencies and facilitate the supply of such agencies. These factors together – pertinent trade patterns, low inflation and deep financial markets – foster the use of a currency for international transactions.

The yen's significance as a reserve currency rose from 4.6 per cent of world official foreign reserves at the end of 1980 to 8.6 per cent in 1991. During the 1990s, mismanagement by government led to low growth in the share of the yen in world official reserves, which dropped to 5 per cent in 2000.[6]

During the 1990s, Japan's share of world exports rose by 2.5 per cent reaching 9.1 per cent in 1990 – a larger increase than any other major industrial country. The yen made little progress towards becoming a international key currency as shown by the international balances (Table 7.1).

Table 7.1 shows two types of transactions – current account transactions (imports and exports) of goods and services and capital account transactions (international sales and transfer of other assets). In the former category, 35 per cent of Japan's export transactions in 1989 were yen-based, up 4.7 per cent from 1980. Yen-based transactions accounted for only 14 per cent of Japan's total import transactions in 1989, up by

Table 7.1 Currency denomination of Japanese foreign trade (% of total)

	1975	*1980*	*1983*	*1986*	*1987*	*1988*	*1989*
Exports							
Japanese yen	17.5	29.4	40.5	35.5	34.7	34.3	34.7
Other	82.5	70.6	59.5	64.5	65.3	65.7	65.3
Of which:							
US dollar	–	–	–	54.2	55.6	53.2	52.4
Imports							
Japanese yen	0.9	2.4	3.0	9.7	11.6	13.3	14.1
Other	99.1	97.6	97.0	90.3	88.4	86.7	85.9
Of which:							
US dollar	–	–	–	83.2	80.5	78.5	77.3

Source: *Annual Report*, International Finance Bureau, Japanese Ministry of Finance, various issues; and data provided by the Japanese Ministry of Finance; Tavlas and Ozeki (1991).

Table 7.2 Yen Invoicing of Japanese trade, 1975–89 (%)

	1975	*1980*	*1983*	*1985*	*1986*	*1987*	*1988*	*1989*
1. Yen-denominated exports	17.5	29.4	40.5	35.5	35.5	34.7	34.3	34.7
2. Yen-denominated imports	0.9	2.4	3.0	7.3	9.7	11.6	13.6	14.1

Source: Ministry of Finance, Kokusai Kinyu kyokunenpo, *Annual Report of the International Finance Bureau* (Tokyo, various issues). Das(1993).

Table 7.3 Comparison of the world's foreign exchange markets (US$ billion, %)

	*Foreign exchange daily average volume**				
	Tokyo	*London*	*New York*	*Singapore*	*Hong Kong*
1989 Q4	111	184	115	55	19
1992 Q4	120 (8)	290 (58)	167 (45)	74 (35)	60 (33)
1995 Q4	161 (34)	464 (160)	244 (46)	105 (42)	90 (50)
1998 Q4	149 (–8)	637 (37)	351 (44)	139 (32)	79 (–12)

* Total of spot, outright forward and foreign exchange swaps; number in brackets is growth rate compared with previous year.
Source: BIS (1998).

12 per cent from 1980. Obviously, the proportion of yen-denominated trade is still small, since in 1980, 98 per cent of US exports and 85 per cent of its import transactions were in dollars (Table 7.2).

Of course, it is controversial whether Japan needs the condition of convertibility of its current and capital accounts. Japan experienced high inflation variability in the early 1980s, but the inflation performance established credibility for its monetary policy from the mid-1980s onwards.[7]

The May 1984 yen–dollar agreement laid down several liberalization measures that helped facilitate yen-invoiced trade over the years, but as the experience of the 1990s shows, yen-invoiced trade is quite low compared to its own currency-invoiced trade of other industrial countries, partly because various liberalization measures did not fully achieve the establishment of well-developed money and capital markets in Japan (Table 7.3).

The yen as international money

There are still several constraints on yen transactions in domestic capital markets and more so in short-term capital markets; the limited international use of the yen is mainly due to the underdevelopment of yen-denominated money and capital markets. In context of trade-invoice currencies, the type of goods traded should also be considered. A trade-invoice currency is selected as a result of bargaining on dividing currency risks between exporters and importers. Several elements are relevant here, for example exchange rate expectations and variability, tradition, differences in attitude to risk, nature of goods traded, market power and financial convenience.[8]

But Evans considers real factors such as trade structure and competitiveness of goods traded rather than financial factors, for example developed capital markets and financial instruments, as key determinants of international currencies. As McKinnon observed, trade in specialized manufactured products tends to be invoiced in the exporters' currency and trade in primary products tends to be invoiced in a major international currency (McKinnon's hypothesis).

Of course, recent data since the mid-1990s confirm the hypothesis that the yen's use as an international currency is slowly increasing. The proportion of Japan's exports denominated in yen rose from 18 per cent in 1975 to 40 per cent in 1983, but was only 35 per cent in the second half of the 1980s.

But in the case of USA about 96 per cent of US exports are denominated in US dollars, but national currency invoicing of exports by major European countries is in the range of 40–80 per cent (highest proportion in the case of Germany). The share of Japanese imports denominated in yen rose steadily from less than 1 per cent in 1975 to 15 per cent in 1990, whereas in the case of the USA this proportion was 86 per cent at the end of the 1980s.

The yen as a medium of exchange

As for use of the yen in international financial markets, the yen's share of external bank loans rose sharply until 1985, reaching 19 per cent, but afterwards there was some decline. As for external bond issues, the share of the yen rose from less than 6 per cent in the first part of the 1980s to 9 per cent in the second half. The share of the yen in Euro-currency deposits rose from 2 per cent in the early 1980s to 6 per cent in 1989.

The yen as a currency used by official agents

The importance of currencies as international units of account and medium of exchange can be seen from their use as official reserves. In the Asian region, the yen's share of foreign exchange holdings has been higher than at the global level in the late 1980s; 20 per cent of such holdings were in yen but more than 59 per cent was held in US dollars and 15 per cent in Deutschmarks.

Recent history behind yen internationalization

At the May 1998 APEC Finance Ministers' Conference, Finance Minister H. Matsunaga announced 'we will continue to take measures to create the market environment in order to enhance the role of yen as reserve and settlement currency'. The MOF report *The Current State of and Prospects for Financial Liberalization and Yen Internationalization* in May 1984 stated,

> If yen became international currency, Japan would be able to contribute to stable development of world economy and convenience for non-residents will be enhanced. The internationalization of yen would (1) eliminate exchange rate risks and reduce hedging costs in trade (2) improve efficiency of corporate financing (3) strengthening the position of Japanese financial instruments in international transactions (4) build a foundation for Tokyo to become a global financial center.

The current status and prospects report identified specific medium- to long-term programmes for financial liberalization and internationalization of the yen but with some reservations.[9]

The MOF was under heavy external pressure from vested interests to open Tokyo markets. The government opted for a policy that set two paths – aiming for relaxation and liberalization of yen-denominated markets. For the external front, policy was that liberalization would proceed to show yen internationalization but care would be taken to minimize the impact on domestic markets. Of course, internationalization of the yen would have been achieved if obstacles were removed and institutions reformed to create an environment for the yen to become currency of choice.

There are two external yen financial and capital markets: the Euro-yen market and the Tokyo offshore market. The Euro-yen is yen-denominated credits and liabilities, traded outside of Japan, especially yen deposits in London or Hong Kong. The European market was successfully liberalized by the mid-1990s. The government removed restrictions on various financial by-products (mid-term and long-term loans), yen-denominated bonds, commercial paper, CDs and cross-industry restrictions applied beyond country boards in guidelines issued by the MOF.

The Tokyo offshore market was in the programme in the current status report and it was set up in December 1986. Its objective was to bring the Euro-yen market to Tokyo. The JOM was treated as an offshore account separate from general account on the books of financial institutions operating in Japan. Deposits in the account enjoyed several privileges, for example exemptions from withholding taxes, interest rate regulations and reserve requirements. Participants were limited to financial institutions due to strict identification requirements placed on non-residents participating in the transactions.

The size of the JOM shot up to ¥97 trillion (¥63.8 trillion of yen-denominated assets and ¥33.3 trillion of foreign currency-denominated assets) at the end of 1997. It became one of the most prominent offshore markets in the world but its yen assets declined sharply to ¥84 trillion (¥48.7 trillion of yen assets and ¥35.3 trillion of foreign currency assets) by the end of 1998.[10]

Major banks had been meeting clients' requests for spread lending (loans with a Libor-based interest rate plus a certain premium that is the standard lending format in the Euro-market) in the form of impact loans from overseas. This was done in order to maintain a lucrative prime rate structure in domestic lending and involved transferring domestic yen assets to a JOM account before loans were made to domestic customers via the Hong Kong branch. In 1998 in an effort to reduce assets on their balance sheets, Japanese banks dropped this unsound practice causing a drop in the balance of offshore market.[11]

Constraints on yen internationalization

Of course the policy to split the domestic market from the international yen market allowed liberalization of the Euro-yen market to precede that of the domestic market and also sheltered the domestic market from external pressures. The Tokyo market was left behind in the global race to develop state of the art financial technology and by the worldwide tide of financial reform. Problems began to surface slowly – the continuation of the administration policy to protect the financial industry, lack of progress in breaking down inter-industry barriers because of resistance to change, uncontrolled swelling of public financing, slow development of infrastructure for the security settlement system that was hampered by the bond trustee bank system, tax reforms that took little account of international trends and the never-ending argument about short-term government security. Several of these features were part of the practices unique to Japan, but were no more compatible with Japan's status as the second largest economy. During the 1990s the Tokyo market lost its international competitiveness; the securities and mid-term to long-term loan business were lost to American, European or Asian financial centres where markets were less regulated, and the hollowing out of Japanese financial industries ensued.[12]

While the MOF continues to interfere with Japanese institutional investments in foreign bonds, the Tokyo market offers few short-term money market items. The Treasury bill market is not very active and commercial paper is not well developed. Several restrictions on Euro-yen investments remain and trading in the government repurchase market is very complicated indeed.[13]

The MOF believes that reform is essential to develop a financial system that can support the Japanese economy in the new century. Now it is widely realized that the Tokyo market is being left behind and ¥1200 trillion of individual assets must be effectively managed; otherwise this money will flow out of the country. Of course, several reform measures are due to the 'Big Bang' package ongoing in the economy, covering several areas for example products, intermediary services, markets and foreign exchange controls. In the product area, securities derivatives were fully derestricted and banks were allowed to sell investment trust instruments and insurance products.

For intermediary services, a holding companies structure was introduced to group together financial intermediaries. Securities companies were made subject only to registration requirements instead of licensing. In the area of markets, off-exchange trading of securities was allowed. Rules regarding consolidated financial statements, market accounting of financial products and the protection of bona fide users of financial services have been thoroughly reviewed. Cross-border transactions of foreign exchange were fully liberalized and the system of authorized foreign exchange banks was abolished.

Prime Minister Ryutaro Hashimoto initiated the Big Bang reforms and commissioned reports from five councils that were submitted in June 1997. Even now the plan for internationalization of the yen has not moved beyond the approach of natural evolution laid out in the current status and prospects reports. One important hurdle for yen internationalization is the tax system.

The unit of account

Of total world trade, about 5 per cent is denominated in yen, which is below that in US dollars and euros, but also below that in UK pounds. The yen is little used even for Japanese export and import transactions but most of the US trade is in dollars. Of Japan's exports about 35 per cent are denominated in yen and only 20 per cent of imports are in yen. This percentage has been gradually rising. About 50 per cent of exports to South-East Asia and 45 per cent of imports from the euro area are in yen and most of the imports from South-East Asian countries are in dollars (Table 7.4).

Table 7.4 Currency breakdown of Japan's export–import settlements* (%)

	World			*USA*			*EU*			*South-East Asia*†		
	Yen	*US$*	*Others*	*Yen*	*US$*	*Others*	*Yen*	*US$*	*Others*	*Yen*	*US$*	*Others*
Exports												
Sept. 1992	40.1	46.6	13.1	16.6	83.2	0.1	40.3	11.1	48.4	52.3	41.6	5.9
Sept. 1993	39.9	48.4	11.7	16.5	83.3	0.2	41.0	7.5	51.5	52.5	44.3	3.2
Sept. 1994	39.7	48.3	12.0	19.0	80.8	0.2	36.6	9.0	54.4	49.0	47.9	3.1
Mar. 1995	37.6	51.5	10.9	17.5	82.3	0.2	37.2	11.3	51.5	47.2	49.9	2.9
Sept. 1995	36.0	52.5	11.5	17.0	82.9	0.1	34.9	12.2	52.9	44.3	53.4	2.3
Mar. 1996	35.9	53.1	10.9	15.9	83.9	0.2	36.1	12.5	51.3	44.1	53.5	2.3
Sept. 1996	35.2	53.3	11.5	14.5	85.4	0.1	33.3	12.4	54.4	46.3	51.5	2.4
Mar. 1997	35.8	52.8	11.3	16.6	83.2	0.2	34.3	13.4	52.3	45.5	51.7	2.7
Sept. 1997	35.8	52.1	12.1	15.3	84.5	0.2	34.2	12.3	53.5	47.0	50.2	2.7
Mar. 1998	36.0	51.2	12.9	15.7	84.1	0.1	34.9	13.2	51.9	48.4	48.7	2.9
Imports												
Sept. 1992	17.0	74.5	8.5	13.8	86.0	0.2	31.7	17.9	50.4	23.8	73.9	2.3
Sept. 1993	20.9	72.4	6.7	13.8	86.1	0.1	45.0	18.2	36.8	25.7	72.0	2.3
Sept. 1994	19.2	73.9	6.9	13.3	86.4	0.3	38.6	21.9	39.5	23.6	74.2	2.2
Mar. 1995	24.3	68.9	6.8	18.4	80.9	0.7	40.6	20.2	39.2	34.1	64.2	1.7
Sept. 1995	22.7	70.2	7.1	21.5	78.4	0.1	44.8	16.1	39.1	26.2	71.9	1.9
Mar. 1996	20.5	72.2	7.3	17.5	82.7	0.0	40.9	15.3	43.8	23.9	74.1	2.0
Sept. 1996	20.6	72.4	7.0	16.4	83.2	0.4	46.1	12.5	41.4	24.0	73.8	2.2
Mar. 1997	18.9	74.0	7.1	14.2	85.6	0.2	41.3	17.0	41.7	23.3	74.9	1.7
Sept. 1997	22.6	70.8	6.6	22.0	77.8	0.2	49.3	13.1	37.7	25.0	73.0	1.9
Mar. 1998‡	21.3	71.7	6.7	16.6	83.3	0.1	44.0	14.4	41.6	26.8	71.5	1.7

* Monthly data compiled using export–import reports mandated by the Foreign Exchange Law.
† South-East Asia includes 22 nations: ASEAN, the NIEs, Cambodia, India, Pakistan, Sri Lanka, Maldives, Bangladesh, East Timor, Macao, Afghanistan, Nepal and Bhutan.
‡ March 1998 is a flash report.
Source: MITI (1999).

Table 7.5 International bond issues by currencies (US$ bn, %)

	1995 Amount issued		*1996 Amount issued*				*1997 Amount issued*		*1998 Amount outstanding*	
US$ bonds	118.9	33	391.8	46	517.4	51	534.6	49	1791.3	44
Yen bonds	76.5	21	134.9	16	129.8	13	69.2	6	481.1	12
Euro-participating currency bonds	55.5	16	212.2	25	221.3	22	301.4	28	1114.9	28
Others	107.5	30	122.6	14	146.8	14	178.5	17	651.9	16
Total international bonds	357.9	100	861.5	100	1015.3	100	1083.3	100	4039.2	100

Note: Euro-participating currencies: for 1995 the Deutschmark; 1996 the EMU currencies; and Euro-area currencies for 1997 and 1998.
Source: International Banking and Financial Market Developments, BIS, Basle, 1999.

The reasons for the low percentage of yen-denominated trade are: (1) Japan's trade structure and (2) characteristics unique to trading partner regions and trade finance. For years, Japan's trade has been vertical, involving imports of raw materials and re-exports of finished goods. The import share of finished goods (60 per cent even in 2000) remains low in comparison with that of the USA and Europe; over 80 per cent of trade in finished goods is denominated in currencies of exporting industrial countries; while trade in raw materials and energy is mostly in US dollars.[14] 'During 1999 Japan sent 36 p.c. of its exports to Asia and 30 p.c. to North America. A large part of Japanese trade with Asia is exports of spare parts and materials to subsidiaries in Asia' (MITI, 1999).

Until the Asian crisis, regional currencies were mostly linked to the dollar and trading partners paid in dollars to guard against exchange risk. The parent companies in Japan tended to bear the exchange risk because the exports were diverted via third countries and because their local affiliates lacked strength in financial markets.

Store of value

In 1995 the yen made up 8 per cent of world reserves but by the end of 1997 its share fell to 4.9 per cent, returning to the level of the early 1980s (IMF various reports). The yen-denominated bonds excluded 20 per cent of cross-border bonds in use in 1995 but with the financial crises, plummeted to 6 per cent – back to the level of the early 1980s (Table 7.5).

Mid-term to long-term overseas lending by Japanese and foreign financial institutions in Japan amounted to $493 billion at the end of 1997,[15] which was around the same level as yen-denominated international bonds. Despite the fact that loans originated in Japan, the majority (81 per cent) were denominated in US dollars and other foreign currencies; only 19 per cent were in yen. There is no stipulation that Japanese loans to non-residents must be in yen; the predominance of dollar-denominated loans reflects differences of borrowers, since in Asia both public and private borrowers have preferred to transact in US dollars over the years, and as Asian countries start to use the yen instead of US dollars, the imbalance will lessen.

Theory of optimum currency areas

The traditional approach tries to single out a crucial economic characteristic which indicates where the borders between different blocks should be drawn.[16]

As Mundell (1961) argued, a pair or group of countries should fix exchange rates between themselves if labour mobility between them was high; otherwise, a country with high employment should be allowed to devalue its exchange rate in order to maintain competitiveness and contain the unemployment level. Mundell also held that the optimum currency area could not be too small because, when nearly all goods were internationally traded, the lack of a fixed exchange rate would mean that the national price level was unstable in the face of exchange rate variations, thus reducing the usefulness of money and distorting the pattern of consumption, investment and saving. Secondly, proliferation of foreign exchange dealers and transactions would impose a real economic cost, but thin foreign exchange markets are likely to be unstable in character.

McKinnon also argued that an open economy should adopt a regime of fixed exchange rates. The case is made that if the share of non-tradables in GDP is low, that sector will not be able to easily absorb the effects of resource reallocation between itself and traded goods sector that were induced by exchange rate fluctuations. So a small non-traded goods sector would have both its output and its price levels destabilized by variations in the exchange rates and that would be harmful to economic efficiency (1963).

From a microeconomic perspective, the major benefit of a monetary union is to reduce the cost and uncertainty involved in transactions among member countries by stabilizing exchange rates with intra-regional trade in the Asia Pacific region, which has been surging since the 1985 Plaza accord.

In view of the diversity among South Asian countries, it is unlikely that Japan, the Asian NICs, the ASEAN countries and China will form a monetary union soon. The yen bloc should start with the participation of Asian NICs, followed by Malaysia and Thailand when they reach a higher level of development.

Theory of optimal peg

The latest crisis in Asia confirmed the hypothesis suggested by C.H. Quan that the traditional exchange rate policy of pegging to the US dollar is no longer compatible with macroeconomic stability in the Asian countries and they should peg closer to the Japanese yen.[17] By reducing the foreign exchange risk associated with yen-based transactions, such a shift in Asia's exchange rate policy would promote wider use of the yen as a regional currency.

Of course choice of exchange rate regime is never a matter of selecting a theoretical optimum independently of the domestic and international political environment; as Williamson suggested, floating is not an appropriate exchange rate policy for most of the poor countries.[18]

Several criteria are relevant when a poor country decides to which currency to peg its local currency. Choosing a peg aims at minimizing the validity in one or more of the major macroeconomic variables – output, current account, inflation – imposed by movements between third currencies. Different rules have been recommended, but usually they involved pegging to a basket of currencies, whose weights depend on the policy objectives and economic structure of the country under consideration. As Takagi[19] suggests, the decision to adopt a basket peg and determination of optional currency weights in the basket constitutes only the initial step in policy implementation.

The presence of multiple currencies in the basket necessitates the choice of an averaging method, depending on what kind of currency characteristics are deemed desirable, since the exchange rate under a basket peg is dictated by a specific rule and yet changes constantly against the intervention currency. The long-term gain from a rule-governed exchange rate policy tends to outweigh the short-term gain from a more discretionary policy of poor countries.

With their currencies pegged loosely to the dollar, growth in South Asian countries has been highly vulnerable to fluctuations in the yen–dollar rate. Every time the yen appreciates against the dollar, the growth rate of South-East Asian countries picks up, as happened between 1986 and 1988 and also between 1991 and 1995. These were the bubble economy years. A depreciation of the yen against the dollar and the Asian currencies affects growth in the Asian countries through several channels:

1. A depreciation of the yen against the dollar makes Japanese exports less expensive relative to Asian countries and Asian products become less competitive against Japanese goods.
2. A weaker yen reduces import prices in Asian countries since they depend heavily on Japan as a source of capital and intermediate goods.
3. A depreciation of the yen reduces the Asian countries' burden of repaying debts in yen terms.
4. With the cost of production in Japan relative to Asian countries falling, the incentive of Japanese companies to relocate production to Asia is reduced, leading to fall in the inflow of DFI from Japan.

Hence stabilizing the yen–dollar rate is desirable for stability in the regional economy. But the yen–dollar rate is beyond the control of Asian countries; a second-best solution to achieve the same goal is to stabilize their exchange rates against the dollar and against the yen.

One way to compromise is to peg a basket of currencies in which the yen carries significant weight. The higher the weight assigned to the yen, the stronger the synchronization between host country currency and the yen. Other things being equal, higher-income countries such as the Asian NICs are most appropriate candidates for forming a monetary union with Japan.

Should the Asian countries shift from traditional regimes of pegging loosely to the dollar to a new one of pegging closer to the yen, the reduction in foreign exchange risk would favour more extensive use of the yen as a regional currency at the micro-level. More and more Asian importers and exporters would prefer to invoice in yen instead of dollars.

What should be done for Tokyo to become an international financial centre?

The Tokyo market is now a top-level world financial market in terms of number of participants, number of transactions and the value of transactions. Now Tokyo has several essential prerequisites for international use for both the yen and dollar. Its inter-bank market is active with average net outstanding balances of more than ¥10 trillion or about $45 billion, as is its foreign exchange market with a daily turnover of spot, forward and swap transactions of over $2 billion.

While Big Bang reforms aim to put the Japanese market on a par with London and New York by 2003, there is little hope of this goal being achieved due to various compulsions for necessary measures to take care of vested interests. This is possible if confidence is developed in the Japanese currency and the financial market.

Barriers to internationalization of the yen

Since the asset price bubble burst in the early 1990s, there has been growing concern that the erosion of Tokyo's role as an international financial centre may reduce the role of the yen as an international currency. Wider use of the yen in Asia is just what is needed to enhance the sophistication of the Tokyo financial market. Without assigning a key role to the yen, the financial Big Bang could at best turn Tokyo into Japan's Wimbledon where most of the champions are foreign players.

The traditional approach to study yen internationalization identifies barriers restraining wider use of the yen in international transactions.[20] Japanese companies' strategy of invoicing in the currencies of export destinations (pricing to market) to maintain market share, along with the fact that Japanese imports mainly consist of primary goods, has limited the use of the yen in denominating trade.

While long- and short-term government bonds, for example US government securities and German bonds, are main assets held by central banks, the Japanese government bonds make up a substantial part of the yen assets held. The government bond yields serve as a benchmark of market interest rates, since they have a lower risk relative to other bonds and higher liquidity due to large market size.

Japanese government bonds have relatively low liquidity. At the end of 1998 the Japanese bond market was ¥423 trillion, of which government bonds made up ¥280 trillion (short-term securities totalled ¥15 trillion and government guaranteed securities, local government bonds, bank debentures, corporate bonds and foreign bonds denominated in yen made up the remainder).[21]

The size of government bonds outstanding is second only to US government bonds. In the Japanese market, government bonds have the highest liquidity in terms of turnover ratio (turnover volume/bonds outstanding).[22] Of the government bonds, of major markets held by non-residents, Japanese government bonds are the least popular at 10 per cent. Another characteristic is that Japanese government bonds lack a benchmarking role. Market interest rates of US dollar bonds are benchmarked against yields of Treasury bill bonds and serve as the basis of interest rates of other securities to reflect credit risk. The low level of liquidity of government securities, compared with those of other countries, is a serious defect of the Japanese bond market. The financial market department of the BOJ defines high market liquidity as a feature of a market where instruments can be traded in large volume in a short period of time with little price fluctuation. One of the criteria used for market liquidity is the bid ask spread, i.e. the difference between the price government bond dealers offer to one another and the asking price. The bid ask spread of Japanese two- and three-year bonds are by far the largest of those of other developed countries; even for 10-year bonds which are regarded as of high liquidity, Japanese government bonds have second largest spread after French bonds.

This lack of liquidity, despite the high level of public debt, is the most serious shortcoming of the Japanese government bond market and other financial markets.[23] To raise the effectiveness of the yen as an international currency, the MOF announced in December 1998 a policy package as follows:

1. Competitive price auction of financing bills.
2. Abolition of withholding tax on interest income for non-residents and the security transaction tax.
3. Introduction of 30-year government bonds and one-year Treasury bills.

Most of these measures have been slowly implemented in its final report *Internationalization of the Yen* published in April 1999. The council on foreign exchange and other transactions (Advisory group of the MOF) called for further measures to improve the repo market (by promoting transactions based on repurchase agreement, instead of cash collateralized lending and borrowing). With the government bond market introducing five-year government bonds, the settlement system moving to a real time gross settlement system and services offered by the BOJ to its overseas counterpart, various innovative proposals have been implemented step by step.[24]

Reasons for failing market principles

The reasons underlying the low liquidity of government bonds are also dragging the pace of internationalization of the yen; the government policy to protect the financial industry minimized the significance of the credit risk differential until around 1997 and there was little need for government bonds to play a benchmarking role. Moreover, this represented the need for a well-developed secondary market, since a large volume of government securities issued was taken up by the underwriting syndicates or by trust fund bureaux and the bulk of bonds in the market were absorbed by the public sector through the BOJ. When the bubble burst and economy plunged into recession, the system finally broke down. The cause for the low liquidity of the government bond market lies in the fact that it has been divided through institutional problems and the over-presence of the public sector. The market has not been completed and the price mechanism has not functioned efficiently.

While the issue of the withholding tax has been the major factor standing in the way of integration of the government security market, there are differences in the withholding tax on interest income paid by residents. In September 1999, interest income of non-residents was exempted from the withholding tax but for various reasons, some non-residents still pay the tax. The different tax treatment divided government securities into taxable and non-taxable groups, lowering the market liquidity. The securities transaction tax and the exchange tax were removed at the end of March 1999.

There are several problems with all three ways to hold government securities – with two types of settlement systems (the transfer settlement system refers to 63 per cent securities and the registration system represents 36 per cent) and the possession of effective bonds (1 per cent). The government securities held by non-residents, who are exempt from the withholding tax, come under the transfer settlement system. Non-residents are not exempt from the withholding tax when they have some control in the registration system or in the safe. They fund settlement when delivery of the security (DVP) system is materialized. Problems still remain, for example a time lag from contracting to settlement and inability to execute cross-border settlements. Developing a legal framework for paperless transactions is another challenge.

The Foreign Exchange Council recently discussed other institutional issues such as diversifying government securities and improving issuing methods. For reduced market liquidity in the government bond market, excessive presence of the public sector is one reason; on 12 December 1998 government bond prices dropped sharply and the yield on benchmark issues climbed by 0.4 per cent from 1.5 to 1.9 per cent. The yen exchange rate fell from ¥115 to ¥117.5 to the dollar. This fall was caused by the MOF suspension of the Trust Fund Bureau's purchasing of long-term government bonds (the Fund had been buying an average of ¥200 billion worth through the BOJ as of January 1991) and also its decision not to underwrite bonds scheduled to be issued in fiscal year 1999. These institutional problems were partially rectified with the abolition in September 1999 of the coupon tax on government bonds held by non-residents.

While the market predicted a significant decline in the supply and demand of government bonds because of the suspension, on the other hand the bond issue was expected to surge from ¥58 trillion in fiscal year 1998 to ¥71 trillion in fiscal year 1999.[25] This strong market reaction reflects the fact that half the bonds are in the hands of the public sector. At the end of 1997 the government (the Trust Fund Bureau, Postal Life Insurance Service and Ministry of Post and Telecommunications) held government bonds worth ¥ 88 trillion (36 per cent of the total) and the

BOJ held ¥26 trillion (11 per cent of the total). The rest was held by the private sector including non-residents (BOJ report, 1999).

Since the Japanese government and the central bank hold bonds until maturity, the bid ask spread tends to broaden, thus squeezing the secondary market. Moreover, government interventions in the long-term bond market (long-term interest rates) are an anomaly in developed countries. Regular buying operations by the government are nothing but attempts at price maintenance and lead to the conclusion that the price mechanism is not functioning properly in the market.

Of course, the Japanese economy has yet to recover from its longest recession in the post-war period since the bursting of the asset bubble of the early 1990s. If the yen is to play the role of the key currency in Asia, Japan needs to put its own house back in order as soon as possible.

A non-transparent future

For some time, the withholding tax on non-residents has been regarded as the reason why Aaa-rated Euro-yen bonds were below that of government bonds. The yield reversed in the first half of 1999 and the situation occurred again just before the withholding tax was to be eliminated in September. Other factors like the perception by non-residents that the government bond market lacks transparency may be to blame. The excessive role played by the public sector has distorted the price mechanism in the Japanese government bond market, but future prospects for solving this problem do not look bright. The lack of transparency is closely related to future correction of the Fiscal Loan and Investment Programme and postal saving systems.

The Fiscal Loan and Investment Programme (FILP) raises interest-bearing funds from postal savings employees and national pension reserves, postal life insurance and other sources. The Trust Fund Bureau manages most of the FILP funds including postal savings and pension reserves.

According to the 1998 annual report, the system pools public funds and allocates them to public institutions for policy implementation. The fiscal investments have been rising steadily as funds under management of the Trust Fund Bureau shot up from ¥167 trillion at the end of 1985 to ¥436 trillion at the end of 1998. Postal savings, which constitute the bulk of reform, increased from ¥101 trillion to ¥251 trillion over the same period. At the end of March 1999, the Trust Fund Bureau had government bonds amounting to ¥95 trillion (Table 7.6).

Table 7.6 The Trust Fund Bureau: special account balance sheet (100 million yen)

Assets	*March 1998*	*March 1999*	*Liabilities and capital*	*March 1998*	*March 1999*
Cash	4	9	Deposits	4,171,674	4,332,739
Securities	1,078,948	1,111,982	Postal and postal book transfers	2,387,459	2,509,679
Long-term government bonds	815,118	930,258	Savings	59,823	52,910
Short-term government bonds	29,725	16,095	Postal life insurance	1,239,87	1,291,16
government agency bonds	193,752	152,637	Employees' pension funds	7	2
Bank debentures	40,358	12,992			
Loans	3,102,856	3,247,424	National pension funds	99,381	103,810
Loans to general special accounts	830,522	928,851	Other deposits	385,133	375,178
			Reserves and profits	11,195	27,634
Loans to local public entities	585,254	620,132			
Loans to government-related institutions	1,687,080	1,698,441			
Others		958			
Total	8,363,613	8,719,770	Total	7,211,659	7,531,236

Source: MOF (1998).

The FILP is under review and will undergo major change. From 2001 postal savings and pension reserves will no longer be required to be deposited with the Trust Fund Bureau. The plan is for FILP financing to come from FILP agency bonds and FILP bonds. Since FILP funds amount to Japan's GDP and all bear interest, reform of the financing methods will have a major impact on the government bond market and related markets. FILP reform raises questions about the structure of government bond market and the balance of supply and demand.

The postal savings network, armed with sovereign credit and huge Teigaku savings, has grown to be the largest financial institution in the world and looks after about 40 per cent of Japan's personal savings. The money is held by the Trust Fund Bureau, with some portion reloaned to the Ministry of Post and Telecommunications and earmarked for the financial liberalization programme (¥55 trillion at the end of 1998 – half of which is invested in government bonds – MPT, 1999).

The plan to reform the FILP calls for all postal savings (¥250 trillion) to be placed under the management of the postal authority in April 2001. Since most of it will be invested in bonds, there is likely to be major turbulence in the ¥425 trillion government bond and corporate debenture markets. Moreover, a large amount of Teigaku savings (about ¥106 trillion, including interest for 2000 and 2001) was invested under a high interest rate in about 1990 and will mature shortly.

Recently it was suggested that if the financial Big Bang is to transform the Tokyo market into a transparent market, two issues are important:

1. Postal savings are 3.5 times higher than the funds of the largest private financial institution in Japan (Bank of Tokyo Mitsubishi – ¥70 trillion at the end of March 1999). The plan is for the postal system to come under a newly formed postal services public corporation to administer it. Hence due to the size of the fund under management, the investment approach should be compatible with market mechanisms and care should be taken not to overly impact the market by becoming a price leader or a market maker.
2. De facto government subsidies for the postal service (postal savings) were exempted from corporate tax, inhabitants' tax, property tax, deposit insurance premium and reserve requirements in March 1997. The Industrial Fund Committee, a subcommittee of the MITI, estimated the total value of these exemptions to be ¥740 billion (Federation of Bankers' Association, 1991).

The uncertainty as to how FILP reform will impact on the government bond market and confirmation of the continuation of postal saving systems have contributed to raising the risk level and reducing the transparency of the Tokyo market for global investors.

Credibility of the Japanese economy

The Foreign Exchange Council is correct in suggesting that the prerequisites for the yen to be a third force in the current bipolar monetary system are credibility in the Japanese economy and financial system, and a stable yen. The fulfilment of these goals will help Japan contribute to the stability of the world economy.

Moody's Investor Services downgraded Japanese government bonds (both yen- and foreign currency-denominated) by one notch from the highest rating of Aaa to Aa1 in November 1998. Standard and Poor's kept the highest rating of Aaa and this rating remained up to September 2001. Moody's reasons for downgrading were the 'increased long-term uncertainty and risk caused by economic stagnation and weakness in fiscal policies, significant decline in govt's fiscal state and serious weakening of the financial system which was inherently weak to begin with in comparison to other developed countries' (Moody's Nov. 1998 press statement).

The rising level of government debt in particular was seen as incompatible with an Aaa rating and as increasing the risk of exchange rate instability in an environment of liberalized capital. On the other hand, Standard and Poor's decided to maintain its Aaa rating, explaining that Japan is the world's largest creditor with the highest foreign reserves and is capable of overcoming mid- to long-term instability, since the economy consists of diverse and competitive industries. Standard and Poor's do share Moody's concern over the fiscal deterioration.[26]

Japan's fiscal deficit is the highest of all the 25 countries in the OECD. According to the OECD, in 2004 the fiscal deficit as a percentage of GDP was projected to be –9 per cent in Japan, +1.8 per cent in the USA and –2 per cent in Germany (Table 7.7).

In 2004, Japan's fiscal deficit is projected to be –6.5 per cent of GDP and the outstanding public debt is expected to climb to 150 per cent of GDP as compared with 42 per cent for the USA and 61.6 per cent for Germany. Japan's public debt is 1.5 times its GDP and is rated at Aa3 by Moody's and Aaa by Standard and Poor's.

The BIS proposed using these ratings in assessing sovereign lending risk in the circulation of national capital adequacy ratios. Many institutional inventory and central banks do not include assets below certain ratings in their portfolios. The downgrading of Japanese government

Table 7.7 Fiscal balance projections for major OECD countries (% of GDP)

	General fiscal deficits				*Public debt balance*	
	1998	*1999*	*2000*	*2004*	*2000*	*2004*
Japan	–6.0	–8.7	–9.0	–6.4	117.6	148.3
United States	1.7	1.9	1.8	2.5	51.7	42.0
Germany	–2.1	–2.2	–1.9	–1.1	63.0	61.6

Note: The general fiscal deficit is a total of state, local and social security funds.
Source: OECD Economic Outlook; and European Commission, *European Economy* No. 4, 1999, for Germany 1998 and 1999.

bonds is serious since a country's private sector debentures are not generally rated higher than its government bonds.

The Japanese rating needs to be on par with that of the USA, Germany, France and Britain if the yen is to become internationally credible and a first-class vehicle of investments. When will the Japanese government institute the necessary physical restructuring?

Stabilization of the yen exchange rate

Of course, major fluctuations in exchange rates expose trading companies to actual and hidden exchange risk and pose difficult problems for banks dealing in foreign exchange, easily upsetting their capital adequacy ratios.

Exchange rate fluctuations are inherent in international transactions and are not necessarily problematic unless there are successive fluctuations and extreme over- or undervaluation. The Japan Foreign Trade Council (JFTC) plotted the yen–dollar exchange rates since the introduction of floating rate systems and found that between 1983 and 1995, exchange rates fluctuated by over 10 per cent annually (JFTC, 1996).

The yen appreciated 40.5 per cent from 1985 to 1986. More recently the yen appreciated 15 per cent against the dollar in two days between 7 and 9 October 1998. The JFTC recommended internationalization of the yen and monetary system reform to institute an exchange rate target zone. Orthodox economists stress the need for sound macroeconomic management, while others advocate the need for intervention by monetary authorities to secure short-term exchange rate stability.

In the study of extreme yen appreciation or depreciation, it can be seen that the major depreciations occurred during the two oil crises in the early 1980s when interest rates were high in the USA and in 1998, when concern over the Japanese economy and financial system heightened, except for the period when interest rates in the USA were in double digits. There were several problems with the Japanese economy that seemed to have weakened the yen significantly. The yen had been steadily appreciating until the peak of 1995 and declined after 1996 as Japan's stagnation set in. Major appreciation (overshooting) occurred mainly because of problems and policies of the USA during stagflation until 1978 and the dollar confidence crisis that culminated in Black Monday (October 1987) and when US officials talked down the dollar around the time of the Mexican currency crisis.

Sound macroeconomic management to stabilize the exchange rate led to a halt in the yen's decline. This is more important for the future, as past experience shows that this alone cannot prevent misalignment. A comparison of the real effective exchange rate for the Deutschmark and yen indicates much higher variability for the yen: from 1986 to 1998, the variances were 265.0 for the yen and 79.2 for the Deutschmark.

During this period the yen and Deutschmark had completely different monetary regimes; the yen was floating while the Deutschmark was within the European monetary system. The Japanese economy had structural weaknesses such as its reliance on imported energy and food. Because of its dependence on the USA for security, Japan had to support America's exchange rate policies. A case in point was the administrative pressure on institutional investors by the Japanese government to refrain from sales of Treasury bonds to cooperate with the USA in defending the dollar.

Between the Plaza accord in 1985 and the end of 1987, the dollar lost 40 per cent of its value against the yen. Japanese life insurers suffered heavy exchange losses but took little action to replace Treasury bonds with instruments of major currency to diversify their portfolios. During this period the authorities exerted pressure on institutional investors through such means as telephone presentations just before bond auction schedules or at monthly meetings for exchanging information. On 7 September 2000 Moody's downgraded its ratings of Japan's yen-denominated domestic bonds from Aaa 1 to Aaa 2 but the foreign currency ratings remain unchanged at Aaa 1.[27]

The yen in the new millennium

The yen exchange rate will remain unstable as long as the yen remains a solo player and until Japan secures an equal footing with the USA.

The most effective action that Japan could take to stabilize the yen is to build a cooperative grouping involving other countries in South-East Asia and Oceania. Unless Japan takes up this challenge with clear political will and starts with what is feasible, the internationalization of the yen cannot be achieved. A rising yen is the last thing Japan needs. The country's troubles are manifold, including deflation, monetary and fiscal policies that are incapable of boosting demand and a financial system saddled with huge bad debts.

Recently it was suggested that the yen would need to fall by almost 10 per cent to give a boost to manufacturers, even if only for the short term, according to Goldman Sachs. The yen's last big surge occurred during the financial crisis in 1998; since early 2000, the yen had been steadily depreciating until September 11th, when it spiked up by more than 2 per cent against the dollar. This led the MOF and BOJ to intervene in the currency markets. Since September 11th, they have sold more than ¥3 trillion ($25 billion), hoping to keep the yen above 120 to the dollar.

A lot of fuss has been made over the 'unsterilized' character of these interventions, because they signal a new and long overdue willingness to loosen monetary policy. When a central bank wants to move exchange rates, it can buy or sell domestic and foreign bonds on the open market, depending on the direction that it wants its currency to take.

Of course in the long run, the yen's biggest enemy is Japan's worsening price deflation, which in 2003 was running at 1.5 per cent per year. Deflation gives Japan painfully high real interest rates even though nominal rates are, in effect, zero.

A yen for action

Japan urgently needs to rid itself of deflation and get the economy growing faster. It seems the policy makers are running out of tools; the government's huge debt limits the scope for further fiscal reflation. There is little room to cut interest rates, since the BOJ's overnight call rate is only 0.25 per cent. Moreover, the BOJ worries that 'monetizing' the government debt would push up bond yields by creating expectations of higher inflation. But expectations of a bit of inflation – as opposed to continuing deflation – are just what Japan needs right now. A cheaper yen would also boost growth by spurring net exports, while combating deflation by pushing up prices.

Recently observers like Lars Svensson favoured a big depreciation of the yen to push up prices; Japan should first set a target for the level of consumer prices, one that would rise over time to allow for a small positive inflation rate. Hence the yen needs to be pushed to an undervalued level, from which the public would then expect an appreciation of the real exchange rate. With the nominal exchange rate brought down by interventions, this could only come about through a rise in prices, creating expectations of future inflation and so reducing real interest rates.

If expectations about inflation are not significantly altered and policy has to work through a direct impact on consumer prices alone, a huge fall in the yen would be needed, since imports are equivalent to less than 10 per cent of Japan's GDP. The yen would need to fall to 170–180 to the dollar, from 120 in 2003, to lift inflation to 1–2 per cent.

Of course, Koizumi has announced that if Japan's economy deteriorates sharply as a result of his reform measures and budget cuts, he will take 'bold flexible measures'. As Rudi Dornbush recently observed, despite today's hopes, sad to say, Japan is likely to remain a great risk to the world economy. It will take a few years to reach a frightening level of crisis, but Japan seems determined to get there.

8 Conclusions

Whether in the new century the 'Japanese model' is facing extinction, depends on how it is defined, making a distinction between a macro-model and a micro or corporate-level model. The macro-level model concerns governance of the economy, as Johnson's 'developmental state' version (1982) assigned a key role to MITI bureaucrats as general headquarters staff of Japanese capitalism.[1] In recent work, the focus of research has been on Japanese financial institutions, the role of the MOF and policy-based finance.

Japan has already frittered away one decade but why should the next one be any different? Only now have recent events persuaded the Japanese people that without reforms, the situation can only get worse. This new awareness was the force behind Prime Minister Junichiro Koizumi's election in 2001. The problem is that the institutions and practices forged to create the Japanese miracle still rule Japan. The picture in 2003 was of an economy which has gone through a decade and half of slow growth and which will recover only if productivity can be increased with the help of modern technology.

Of course, institutional changes are now also essential. For the persistence of each of these features of the Japanese model, various explanations have been offered, and Aoki stressed the interconnections between various key features – the rank 'hierarchy' characteristics of several parts of the model reinforce each other and create a system in which 'instead of facing perfectly competitive markets for factors of production, the firm is related to other agents – the worker, the investor and the supplier – through long-term relational contracting and agents on both sides of various relationships reciprocate economic benefits on a long-term basis'.[2] So the firm becomes a 'nexus of treaties'. The problem now is that the institutions and practices forged to create the miracle still rule Japan and those obsolete institutions have turned into a political and economic straitjacket.

Recently observers like Horiuchi (2000) have indicted the role of financial structure and the role of banks in encouraging overborrowing and excess investment due to lax corporate governance and interconnected lending.[3] The case rests on a very rapid growth of investment during the bubble years of the 1980s that brought the ratios of gross capital formation to GDP to very high levels. Moreover, there is little doubt that the measured rates of growth of capital productivity during the 1990s were very low; as the OECD argues (2003), there is a serious problem of excess capital 'for Japan and capital-output ratios have only just reached the levels of most European countries'.[4] Japan's capital–labour ratio was only around 70–80 per cent of the US level in the 1990s (Van Ark and Pilat, 1993;[5] Wolff, 2000).[6]

Hence in spite of the alarming size of bad loans at the depth of the banking crisis, it is hard to find unambiguous evidence that the system itself was predisposed to encouraging excessive capital-stock build-up in aggregate. But for most of the 1990s, the size of bad loans was no worse than in other countries which had experienced banking crises (Beason and James, 1999).[7] It is just possible that the nature of bank–firm relationships allowed a poor choice of projects within certain industries (e.g. construction). Of course, various regulatory changes and macroeconomic performance have led to widespread changes in corporate financing patterns for some classes of firms (Hoshi and Kashyap, 1999).[8]

This has, over the years, altered the relationship of banks with their traditional clients and forced them into new areas of business. There may be logical continuation of this trend in new century also, driving corporate financing patterns towards US levels of bank-debt finance, and it is just possible that major shake-outs will reduce the banking infrastructure by about 30 per cent. But Gibson recently argued very forcefully that the corporate governance system is directly responsible for low returns to shareholders' wealth and the Big Bang reforms do not address the specific governance features that are responsible for this.[9] The reforms may increase financial sector efficiency, but will not contribute to economic performance until they directly tackle structures which allow managers to concentrate on objectives other than maximizing shareholder returns.

Of course, the role of bureaucracy has been overemphasized both in policy formation and economic development. In the micro-level model, the focus moves from bureaucrats to corporations as value creators, which have powered Japan's growth. But there is less controversy over the characteristics of the micro-level model; it has been argued that excessive attention has been directed towards large corporations at the expense of small firms. After all, Japan ranks alongside Italy in having the highest proportion of small firms – and employment in them – of any OECD country. In the (large firm centred) micro-level model, interests of shareholders are not given overriding priority. Instead the shareholders are given a virtually fixed return, the bulk of the profit is reinvested and companies pursue market share competition (Whittaker and Kurosawa, 1998).[10]

The catch really is that the obstacles to growth are also pillars of the political system. Collusion, regulation and bank loans to the uncreditworthy all serve as covert safety nets in a country where only half the workforce is covered by unemployment insurance. These practices shore up moribund firms and industries, sustaining millions of unnecessary jobs (Katz, 1998).[11] The 'Japanese model', particularly the micro-level variant, has been condemned to oblivion for as long as it has been recognized. The case now made is that a combination of Japan's financial crisis, increasing foreign participation and the Big Bang will bring about several basic changes in Japan's financial markets. Not only will this change the nature of macroeconomic management, but also, through corporate finance, it will have a major impact on corporate governance, bringing a decisive end to the model.

Japan's crisis is thus a crisis of governance in both government and business; a revival will require a fundamental overhaul of several institutions, though even reformers disagree among themselves as to what constitutes reform. It is true that the deregulation of the 1980s began to slowly change one pillar of corporate finance – the 'main bank' system – through internationalization of fund raising and a shift to direct financing. This reduced the ability of the main banks to act as monitors for other lenders and shareholders, and at the same time, it made it harder for bureaucrats to control corporate behaviour through the banks.

The overall outlook for Japan is not very encouraging. Some observers foresee neither reform nor muddling through, but meltdown. Many warned of bank runs in the spring of 2002 when the government lifted full guarantees on all time deposits at the banks; it never happened.

Of course, it is very difficult to judge the extent to which capital stock and balance sheet adjustments are taking place, but they also seem modest. The rate of suspension of dealings with banks (the usual measure of company failure) has risen by about 20 per cent compared to the beginning of the 1990s and the average size of failed companies' liabilities has also increased, yet liabilities of bankrupt corporations still represent only 2.5 per cent of total corporate sector funding (Boltho and Corbett, 2000).[12]

While the number of companies making restructuring announcements rose sharply in 1999, most of these contained few concrete details and may never be fully implemented (OECD, 1999).[13] For observers like Flath (2000) and Ugawa and Kitasaka (2000)[14] who believe there is a need for major shake-outs and the sweeping away of old practices, this is merely further evidence of the entrenched nature of the system.

Some see Koizumi's rise, recent financial reforms and announcements of corporate restructuring as milestones in an incremental process. But reform will not happen this way; rather the coming decade will see a tumultuous battle between the forces of reform and resistance. If the current institutions were capable of incremental reform, Japan would never have got into such trouble. This shows the triumph of 'immobilist' politics (Stockwin, 1988)[15] and vested interests standing in the way of change, as observed recently by Noguchi (1996) and Lincoln (1998).[16]

A more moderate view as taken by Carlile and Tilton (1998) is that the objectives of deregulation and of the changes so far promoted are distinctly Japanese and differ from those of the other OECD countries. How far they will go will depend on the complex interplay of interests of business, politicians and bureaucrats.[17]

With an accelerating pace of deregulation, accounting and disclosure practices are being reformed; the credit rating agencies are growing in importance as judges of creditworthiness. It is just possible that Japan may move towards global standards in terms of regulations and transparency and also in terms of capital costs. Moreover, 'mutual' shareholding is also weakening; now poor performance of such shares is being weighed against the need for funds for restructuring; the downward trend is significant indeed.

The slow pace of reform in Japan for several years has shown a reluctance to abandon past successful formulae, the complexity of the structural issues involved and a desire to preserve the 'social' dimension of the Japanese model, both at the corporate and macro levels, or a 'third middle way' to reform. Hence Japanese savings will be at least partially bottled up at home, almost certainly condemning the country to a lower level of income than what it could otherwise have achieved.

It is unlikely that Mr Koizumi will get the chance to pursue the five or ten-year programme of reforms necessary to return the Japanese economy to normal growth. Japan's budget needs to shift to debt reduction by some 10 per cent of GDP and that in an economy already in recession. As per the government estimates, the non-performing loans (NPLs) now total $450 billion or 10 per cent of GDP, but keen observers maintain that the real number is closer to 20 per cent. What would be the impact of cleaning up the balance sheets of the Japanese banks?

Recent estimates suggest a 1–2 per cent extra dip in growth rate, with no certainty that higher growth will ever follow. The banks need a new capital injection, this time with more stringent conditions than in the failed efforts of 1999. Japan is in fact witnessing the most restructuring where it is least urgent and the fewest reforms where it is most urgent. Japan cannot gain greater competitiveness without more competition. The sine qua non for successful reform is increasing globalization. If competing imports and foreign firms could reach a critical mass on Japanese soil, the domestic anti-competitive practices would become unsustainable.

Today Japan is like a patient that has abused antibiotics so much that they no longer pack their punch. Tokyo is applying more fiscal and monetary stimulus than ever, yet getting fewer benefits than ever. Japan will never solve its chronic deficiency of demand until it shifts a greater share of national income to the consumer. The question is whether demand stimulus is used as an anaesthetic to support the surgery of radical reforms or as a narcotic to dull the pain.

Notes

1 Japan's Problem in the New Millennium

1 IMF, *World Economic Outlook*, Washington, 2000

2 J.M. Keynes, *General Theory of Employment, Interest and Money*, Macmillan, 1936; also W. Buiter and N. Panigirtzoglou, 'Liquidity Traps: How to Avoid them and How to Escape them,' mimeo, Bank of England, London, 1999

3 OECD, *Economic Survey, Japan*, Paris, 2002

4 Shigeru Otsubo and Masahiko Tsutsumi, 'Is the 'Japan Problem Real? How Problems in Japan's Financial Sector Could Affect Developing Regions', Working Paper, The World Bank, No. 1682, Washington, DC, 1996

5 Kazuo Ogawa et al., 'Borrowing Constraints and Role of Land Assets in Japanese Corporate Investment Decision', *The Economic Analysis*, No. 136, Economic Research Institute, Economic Planning Agency, 1994

6 EPA (1990)

7 OECD, *Economic Survey of Japan 1990–91*, Paris, 1991

8 Shigehisa Kasahara, 'A Rescue Plan for the Post-Bubble Japanese Economy', UNCTAD Discussion Paper, June 1994

9 J. Frieland, 'Out of the Rubble', *Far Eastern Economic Review*, 12 November (1992)

10 B. Emmott, *Japan's Global Reach*, Random House, London, 1992

11 D. Burstein, *Yen: Japan's New Financial Empire and its Threat to America*, Simon and Schuster, New York, 1988

12 OECD, *Economic Survey of Japan, 1990–91*, Paris, 1991

13 P.N. Snowden, 'Prolonged Stagnation, Hesitant Recovery: Japan from an "Austrian" Perspective', *The World Economy*, 2001, p. 256

14 Kazuo Ueda, 'Comment', in Takatoshi Ito and Anne O. Krueger (eds), *Changes in Exchange Rates in Rapidly Developing Countries; Theory, Practice and Policy Issues*, NBER East Asian Seminar on Economics, Vol. VII, Chicago University Press, 1999

15 Norio Sawabe, 'The Basle Accord and Accounting for Investment in Securities', *Shoken Keizai* (Financial Economic Review), No. 189, Sept. 1994

16 OECD, *Economic Survey of Japan*, 1991, p. 75

17 Otsubo and Tsutsumi, op. cit.

18 B. Reading, *Japan, the Coming Collapse*, Weidenfeld, London, 1992

19 Sylvester Eigffinger and Adrian Van Rietel, 'The Japanese Financial System and Monetary Policy: a Descriptive Review', *Japan and the World Economy*, 1992, p. 298

20 Nicholas Sargen and K.L. Schoenholtz, 'Japan's Adjustment Miracle and Its Implications for the Yen', *Japan and the World Economy*, 1990, p. 286

21 Toru Kusukawa, 'The Japanese Economy: the Bubble of the 80's and the Recession of the 90's', *Japan and the World Economy*, 1994

22 Ryuzo Miyao, 'The Role of Monetary Policy in Japan: a Break in the 1990s', *Journal of Japanese and International Economies*, 2000, p. 369. Also K. Okina,

'The Risks of Single-minded Targeting', *Financial Times*, London 10 November and K. Ueda, *Monetary Policy under Balance of Payments Disequilibrium*, Kerai Shimpasha, Tokyo, 1992, for more details. K. Ueda, 'Japanese Monetary Policy, Rates or Discretion, Part II, Bank of Japan', Seventh International Conference, 26–27 October 1995.

23 M. Okabe, *The Conduct and the Transmission Mechanism of Japanese Monetary Policy 1975–1989. A Literature Survey*, BOJ, 1990, p.18

24 Y. Suzuki, 'Policy Targets and Operating Procedures in the 1990s: the Case of Japan', in *Monetary Policy Issues in the 1990s*, Federal Reserve Bank of Kansas City, 1989

25 Eigffinger and van Rietel, op. cit., p. 302

26 D. Batten et al., 'The Instruments and Operating Procedures for Conducting Monetary Policy in the Group of Five Countries', IMF Working Paper 1989/57, 21 July 1989

27 Batten et al., op. cit., p. 30; also Shigeo Nakao, 'The Stock Market in Japan and the Globalization of Japanese Money', *Osaka City University Economic Reviews*, Vol. 28, No. 1, 1993, p. 30

28 Eigffinger and van Rietel, op. cit.

29 S. Royama, 'Monetary Policy under the Evaluation of Open Money Markets in Japan', mimeo, 1990

30 T. Tamura, 'The Bank of Japan Mechanism', presentation to DRI Conference, London, 4–5 March 1991. Also Nakao, op. cit.

31 M.M. Hutchison, 'Monetary Control, Interest Rates and Exchange Rates; the Case of Japan, 1973–1986', Working Paper 145, University of California at Santa Cruz, 1986

32 Kusukawa, op. cit., p. 393

33 *Far Eastern Economic Review*, 1992, p. 137

34 Otsubo and Tsutsumi, op. cit.

35 OECD, *Economic Survey of Japan*, 1993, pp. 37–9

36 Kasahara, op. cit.

37 The number of loans left behind by seven failed housing finance companies was estimated at about 300,000.

38 For more details, see *Economic Survey of Japan*, 1995

39 EPA 'World Economic Model – Fifth Version', Economic Research Institute Discussion Paper 20, Tokyo

40 Otsubo and Tsutsumi, op. cit., p. 10

41 Economic Planning Agency, *State of the Japanese Economy – Review and Issues of the Japanese Economy in 1995*, December 1995.

42 Takatoshi Ito, 'The Causes of Japan's Financial Crisis', *Pacific Economic Papers*, No. 288, AJRC, Canberra, 1999

43 Y. Noguchi, *Economics of Bubble, Nihon Keizai Shimbun*, 1992

44 *Nihon Keizai Shimbun*, 20, Feb.1993

45 C. Leadbeater, 'Tokyo Mounts Silent Rescue Operations,' *Financial Times*, 21 Jan. 1993

46 *Nihon Keizai Shimbun*, 30 March 1993

47 Ibid.

48 Hugh Patrick, 'The Causes of Japan's Financial Crisis', *Pacific Economic Papers*, No. 288, AJRC, Canberra, 1999

49 For estimates of bad loans, see Y. Ohara, 'Japan's Banking: the Darkest Hour before Dawn; the Future is in the Hands of the MOF', Center on

Japanese Economy and Business, Working Paper series 127, Columbia University Business School, New York, 1996. Also Terry Marsh and Jean Michel Paul, 'Japanese Banks' Bad Loans, What Happened', OECD, Paris, 1996, mimeo.

50 Maximillian J.B. Hall, *Financial Reform in Japan*, Elgar, 1998, p. 31
51 *Nihon Keizai Shimbun*, 27 Nov. 1993
52 Hall, op. cit.
53 Ibid.
54 Patrick, op. cit.
55 Brian Waterhouse, *Major Banks, FY 1997 Results*, HBSC Securities, Japan Ltd, Tokyo, June 12, 1998
56 Patrick, op. cit.
57 Hall, op. cit., p. 35
58 Otsubo and Tsutsumi, op. cit., p. 13
59 Joyce Manchester and Warwick J. McKibbin, 'The Macroeconomic Consequences of the Savings and Loan Debacle', *The Review of Economics and Statistics*, Aug. 1994
60 Takatoshi Ito, 'Japan's Financial Reform', *Pacific Economic Papers*, No. 288, Feb. 1999
61 Otsubo and Tsutsumi, op. cit.
62 Ito, op. cit., p. 2.6

2 Japanese Financial Deregulation – the 1980s

1 Hugh Patrick, 'Japan's Financial Reform', *Pacific Economic Papers*, No. 288, Feb. 1999
2 For analysis of the main bank system in the high growth era, see Aoki and Patrick (1994)
3 Craig Freedman, *The End of the Economic Miracle*, Elgar, 1998, p. 10
4 Hall, op. cit., p. 21.
5 Patrick, op. cit.
6 Hall, op. cit., p. 22
7 Sena Eken, *Integration of Domestic and International Financial Markets*, IMF Staff Papers, Sept. 1984
8 Japan Economic Institute, *Capital Market Liberalization in Japan*, Washington, DC, March 1984
9 Allen F.B. Frankel and Paul Morgan, *A Primer on the Japanese Banking System*, International Finance Discussion Papers, Washington, DC, Dec. 1998
10 'Japan's Capital Outflows', *Amex Bank Review*, April 1986
11 Kazuo Sato, *The Transformation of the Japanese Economy*, ME Sharpe, New York, 1996
12 L. Goldberg and G. Hanweek, 'The Growth of the World's 3000 largest Banking Organizations by Country', *Journal of Banking and Finance*, 1997
13 Hall, op. cit., p. 77
14 See JCIF, *Overview of Yen-denominated Foreign Bond Market in Japan*, Japan Centre for International Finance, Tokyo, 1988, p. 82.
15 Hall, op. cit., p. 77
16 Economist Publications, *Japan*, London, 1986. Also M. Hanazawa, *The Tokyo Offshore Market*, Fair Fact Series, Tokyo, 1990

17 Hall, op. cit., p. 79
18 MOF, *Financial Statistics of Japan*, 1991; also H. Okumura, *Japanese Financial Deregulation, Recent Developments and Future Outlook*, Nomura Research Institute, Feb. 1998
19 S. Royama, 'Aspects of Financial Restructuring in Japan', *Japan Review of International Affairs*, 1990, pp. 42–65
20 For details see A. Nakaishi, *The Foreign Exchange Markets*, FAIR Institute, Tokyo, 1991
21 Hall, op. cit., p. 21
22 Ibid., p. 84
23 For details of acceptable collateral, see JCIA (1988, p. 18)
24 Hall, op. cit., p. 93
25 D.S. Batten et al., *The Conduct of Monetary Policy in Major Industrial Countries, Instruments and Procedures*, Occasional Paper 70, IMF, 1990
26 Hall, op. cit., p. 99
27 MOF, *Guide to Japanese Government Bonds*, 1997
28 Hall, op. cit., p. 100
29 S.D. Prowse, 'The Structure of Corporate Ownership in Japan', *The Journal of Finance*, 1990
30 Cargill and Royama (1988)
31 M. Takeda and Philip Turner, *BIS Economic Papers*, Nov. 1992, p. 51
32 Wako Research Institute, Tokyo, 1991
33 Takeda and Turner, op. cit., p. 52
34 Sanwa Bank, 1992
35 S. Wagstyh and Robert Thomson, 'A Crunch on Capital', *Financial Times*, 14 August 1991
36 J.A. Frankel, *Japanese Finance: a Survey*, NBER Working Paper 3156, Nov. 1989
37 BOJ, *Recent Developments in Lending Rates*, Special Paper 206, Sept. 1991
38 See Kazuo Ueda, *Japanese Monetary Policy during 1970–90: Rules or Discretion*, BOJ, Tokyo, 1991
39 D. Hugh Whittaker and Yoshitaka Kurosawa, 'Japan's Crisis: Evolution and Implications', *Cambridge Journal of Economics*, 1998, pp. 761–71.
40 Y. Noguchi, *Economics of the Bubble*, Nihon Keizai Shinbunsha, Tokyo, 1992
41 Y. Kurosawa, 'Corporate Finance in Japan', *Financial Digest*, No. 26, Tokyo, Japan Credit Rating Agency, 1993
42 Noguchi, op. cit.
43 Ibid.
44 Takeda and Turner, op. cit., p. 59
45 See K. Iwata, 'Financial Liberalization and its Impact on the Japanese Economy', *Pacific Economic Papers*, No. 134, ANU, Canberra, April 1986
46 Ian Macfarlane discusses this dilemma as it faced Australian monetary policy, Reserve Bank of Australia, Sydney, 1991
47 Y. Teramura, 'Japan in the 1990s', Cambridge University, 1998, mimeo
48 Takeda and Turner, op. cit., p. 59
49 Richard Mattione, *A Capital Cost Disadvantage for Japan*, J.P. Morgan, Tokyo, 1993. Also James Poterba, 'Comparing the Cost of Capital in the U.S. and Japan. A Survey of Methods', *Federal Reserve Bank of New York Quarterly Review*, winter 1991, pp. 20–32

50 *Nikkei Weekly*, 2 Nov. 1991
51 Takeda and Turner, op. cit., p. 63

3 Deregulation and Liberalization Tribulations – the 1990s

1 OECD, *Economic Survey, Japan*, 2001. Paris, See also P. Richardson et al., *Predicting the Evolution and Effects of the Asian Crisis from the OECD Perspective*, Working Paper 236, Paris
2 A. Boltho and Jenny Corbett, 'The Assessment. Japan's Stagnation – Can Policies Revive the Economy?' *Oxford Review of Economic Policy*, No. 2, 2000, p. 3
3 BOJ, *Economic Statistics Monthly*, Jan. 1991
4 'Internationalization of the Yen', *Tokyo Financial Review*, March 1991
5 Takeda and Turner, op. cit., p. 62
6 Kazuo Sato, 'Bubbles in Japan's Stock Markets; Macro-economic Analysis', *Japanese Economic Studies*, July–August, 1995, p. 52
7 For more details, see Suzuki (1987, p. 140)
8 Hall, op. cit., p. 105
9 MOF, *Guide to Japanese Government Bonds*, Tokyo, 1997
10 Hall, op. cit., p. 106
11 For more details, JCIF, *The Past and Present of Deregulation and Internationalization of Tokyo Money and Capital Market*, Policy Study Series No. 10, Tokyo
12 Hall, op. cit., p. 108
13 Takatoshi Ito, 'The Causes of Japan's Financial Crisis', *Pacific Economic Papers*, No. 288, Feb. 1999
14 *The Financial Times*, 20 Feb. 1991
15 Sato, op. cit., p. 52
16 D. Hugh Whittaker and Yoshitaka Kurosawa, 'Japan's Crisis, Evolution and Implications', *Cambridge Journal of Economics*, 1988, p. 763
17 Boltho and Corbett, op. cit., p. 2
18 OECD, *Economic Survey, Japan*, Paris, 2001
19 J. Peck and E. Rosengren, 'The International Transmission of Financial Shocks. The Case of Japan', *American Economic Review*, September 1997
20 OECD, *Economic Survey, Japan*, 1999
21 P.N. Snowden, 'Prolonged Stagnation, and Hesitant Recovery: Japan from an Austrian Perspective', *The World Economy*, 2001, p. 256
22 Ronald McKinnon and Kenicho Ohno, 'The Foreign Exchange Origins of Japan's Economic Slump and Low Interest Liquidity Trap', *The World Economy*, 2001, p. 286
23 Paul Krugman, 'It's Baaack: Japan's Slump and the Return of the Liquidity Trap', *Brookings Papers on Economic Activity*, 2, 1998, pp. 137–205
24 R. McKinnon and K. Ohno, *Dollar and Yen; Resolving Economic Conflict between the United States and Japan*, MIT Press, 1997, Japanese translation, *Nihon Keizai Shimbun* (1998) and (1999) and 'The Foreign Exchange Origins of Japan's Economic Slump and Low Interest Liquidity Trap', *The World Economy*, 2001, 279–315
25 Dominic Wilson, 'Japan's Slow-down, Monetary versus Real Explanations', *Oxford Review of Economic Policy*, Vol. 16, No. 2, 2000, p. 79

26 Krugman, op. cit., p. 158
27 See N. Kiyotaki and K. West, 'Credit, Business Investment and Output Fluctuations in Japan', *NBER MacroEconomics Annual*, 1996
28 Mihir Rakshit, 'Economic Crisis in Japan', *Analytical and Policy Issues, Money and Finance*, April–June 1999, p. 61
29 Boltho and Corbett, op. cit., p. 8
30 Rakshit, op. cit., p. 64
31 McKinnon and Ohno, op. cit., p. 286
32 *Financial Times*, 5 May 2000, p. 4
33 Boltho and Corbett, op. cit., p. 8
34 Krugman, op. cit., p. 163
35 EPA, *World Economic Model, Fifth Version*, Discussion Paper 22, Tokyo, 1995
36 Snowden, op. cit., p. 256
37 K. Ueda in T. Ito and A.O. Krueger (eds), *Changes in Exchange Rates in Rapidly Developing Countries: Theory, Practice and Policy Issues*, NBER East-Asia Seminar, Vol. VII, Chicago, 1999
38 OECD, *Economic Survey 1996–97*, Paris
39 Snowden, op. cit., p. 260
40 OECD, *Economic Survey, 1999*, Paris
41 T. Bayoumi, *The Morning After: Explaining the Slowdown in Japanese Growth in the 1990s*, IMF Working Paper 1999–13
42 A. Kanaya and D. Woo, *The Japanese Banking Crisis of the 1990s: Sources and Lessons*, IMF Working Paper 2000–7, p. 26
43 Ibid., p. 6
44 Snowden, op. cit., p. 264
45 R. Miyao, 'The Role of Monetary Policy in Japan: a Break in the 1990s', *Journal of Japanese and International Economics*, 2000, p. 380
46 R. Kato and T. Watanabe, 'Asymmetric Effects of Monetary Policy. The Japanese Experience in the 1990s', mimeo, Hitotsubashi University, Kunitachi City, 1999
47 Wilson, op. cit.
48 R. Ramaswami and S. Rendu, 'Business Investment in Japan', *IMF Survey*, 13 Dec. 1999
49 Economic Planning Agency, *Economic Survey of Japan, 1991–92*
50 *OECD Economic Outlook*, Dec. 1999, p. 256
51 McKinnon and Ohno, op. cit., p. 281
52 Adam Posen, *Restoring Japan's Economic Growth*, Institute of International Economics, Washington, DC, 1998
53 McKinnon and Ohno, op. cit., p. 282
54 D.L. Asher and R.H. Dugger, *Could Japan's Financial Mount Fuji Blow Its Top*, MIT–Japan Program 2000, Working Paper Series No. 0001 (May), 2000
55 *New York Times*, 30 July 1998
56 McKinnon and Ohno, op. cit., p. 281
57 Ministry of Health and Welfare, 'On the Basic Viewpoint Regarding the Trend towards Fewer Children' (www.Mhw.go.jp)
58 Snowden, op. cit., p. 267
59 M. Noland et al., *The Global Economic Effects of the Japanese Crisis*, Working Paper, Institute for International Economics, 1998, p. 6
60 R. McKinnon, 'Exchange Rate Coordination for Surmounting the East Asian Currency Crisis', *Journal of International Development*, 1999, pp. 95–106

61 Ibid., p. 103
62 Snowden, op. cit., p. 269
63 K. Okina, 'The Risks of Single-minded Targeting', *Financial Times*, London, 10 Nov. 1999

4 The Japanese Banking Crisis of the 1990s

1 Allan Brunner and Steven Kamin, *Bank Lending and Economic Activity in Japan: Did Financial Factors Contribute to Recent Downturn*, International Finance Discussion Papers, No. 513, 1995. Also T. Motonishi and H. Yoshikawa, 'Causes of Long Stagnation of Japan during the 1990s, Financial or Real', conference, NBER, Tokyo, Oct. 1998
2 David Woo, 'In Search of Credit Crunch; Supply Factors behind the Slowdown in Japan', IMF working paper; Washington, 1999; James Morsink and Tamim Bayoumi, *The Monetary Transmission Mechanism in Japan; Selected Issues*, IMF, Washington, 1999; T. Sekine, 'Financial Investment and Balance Sheet Problems in Japan', IMF Working Paper, 1999
3 A. Kanaya and David Woo, 'The Japanese Banking Crisis of the 1990s; Sources and Lessons, IMF Working Paper 7, 2000
4 Y. Yamaguchi, 'Asset Prices in Monetary Policy, Japan's experience,' speech at a symposium at Federal Reserve Bank of Kansas City, Jackson Hall, Wyoming, 26–28 Aug. 1999
5 T. Hoshi and Anil Kashyap, 'The Japanese Banking Crisis, Where Did It Come From and How Will It End', NBER Working Paper 7250, 1999
6 Terry Marsh and Jean Michel Paul, 'Japanese Banks' Bad Loans, What Happened', OECD, Paris, 1996, mimeo
7 Kanaya and Woo, op. cit.
8 Kurt Gorger, 'Japan's Financial Reform', in Arne Holzhausen (ed.) *Can Japan Globalize? Studies on Japan's Changing Political Economy, in Honor of Sung-jo Park*, Physica-Verlag, New York, 2000, p. 70
9 H. Genay, 'The Ownership Structure of Japanese Financial Institutions', Working Paper, Federal Reserve Bank of Chicago, Chicago, 1993
10 Gorger, op. cit., p. 71
11 Federation of Bankers' Association of Japan, Tokyo, 1990
12 Kanaya and Woo, op. cit.
13 M. Aoki and H. Patrick (1994); also S. Fukuda and S. Hirata (1996), 'Main Bank Relationships and Capital Structure in Japan', *Journal of the Japanese and International Economics*, vol. 10, 250–61
14 M. Kauri et al., 'Japanese Firms in Financial Distress and Main Banks: Analysis of Inter-Rate Premia', *Japan and the World Economy*, No. 2, 1996, pp. 175–94
15 Genay, op. cit.
16 Kanaya and Woo, op. cit., p. 14
17 John Amer and Michael Gibson, 'Regulation and the Cost of Capital in Japan: a Case Study', International Finance Discussion Papers, Board of Governors of the Federal Reserve System, July 1996
18 Gorger, op. cit., p. 70
19 BOJ, Tokyo, *Economic and Financial Statistics*, 1996
20 Kanaya and Woo, op. cit., p. 16

21 M. Fukao, 'Japanese Financial Instability and Weaknesses in the Corporate Governance Structure', *Seoul Journal of Economics*, Seoul, Korea, vol. 11, 1998, pp. 381–422
22 BOJ, *Main Economic Indicators of Japan*, Economic Statistics Division, Research and Statistics Dept., April 1999
23 *Euro Money*, March 1998
24 For example, Bungei Shunju, 1995
25 Hugh Whittaker and Yoshitaka Kurosawa, 'Japan's Crisis: Evolution and Implications', *Cambridge Journal of Economics*, 1998, p. 764
26 Y. Miyazaki, *Japanese Financial Reforms*, Chuo Koron, Tokyo, 1992
27 Hugh Patrick, 'The Causes of Japan's Financial Reform', Pacific Economic Papers No. 288, AJRC, Canberra, 1999
28 Hall, op. cit., p. 215
29 See Stephan Vogel, *Freer Markets, More Rules and Regulatory Reform in Advanced Industrial Countries*, Cornell University Press, 1996
30 Patrick, op. cit.
31 Ibid.
32 See here Thomas Cargill, Michael Hutchison and Takatoshi Ito, 'Preventing Future Banking Crisis in Japan', prepared for the Conference 'Preventing Banking Crises; Analysis and Lessons from Recent Bank Failures', sponsored by the Federal Reserve Bank of Chicago and the World Bank, 11–13 June 1997
33 Patrick, op. cit.

5 Big Bang Reform Programme and After

1 Takatoshi Ito and Michael Melvin, 'Japan's Big Bang and Transformation of Financial Markets'. NBER Working Paper 7247, July 1999
2 Financial System Research Council, *Annual Report*, 1997, pp. 17–18
3 Ito and Melvin, op. cit.
4 Securities and Exchange Council, *Annual Report*, Tokyo, 1997, p. 14
5 Ito and Melvin, op. cit.
6 Kurt Gorger, in Arne Holzhausen (ed.), *Can Japan Globalize, Studies on Japan's Changing Political Economy and the Process of Globalisation*, Physica-Verlag, New York, 2001
7 Kazao Sato, 'From Fast to Last; the Japanese Economy in the 1990s', *Journal of Asian Economies*, 13 (2002), p. 228
8 Carl J. Lindgren et al., 'Financial Sector Crisis and Restructuring Lessons from Asia', IMF Occasional Paper, Washington, 1986; also Jenny Corbett, 'Japan's Banking Crisis in International Perspective', in Masahiko Aoki and Gary R. Saxonhouse (eds), *Japanese Corporate Governance*, Oxford, 2000
9 Ben S. Bernanke and M. Woodford, 'Inflation Forecasts and Monetary Policy', *Journal of Money, Credit and Banking*, 29(1991), pp. 653–84
10 T. Hoshi and A. Kashyap, *Corporate Financing and Governance in Japan*, MIT Press, 2002, p. 256; also R.G. Rajan, 'Why Bank Credit Policies Fluctuate; Theory and Some Evidence', *Quarterly Journal of Economics*, 109(2), (1995), 399–442
11 Hoshi and Kashyap, op. cit.
12 Jenny Corbett, 'Crisis, What Crisis? The Policy Response for Japan's Banking Crisis', in Craig Freedman (ed.), *Why Did Japan Stumble*? Macquarie University Press, Sydney, 1997

6 Japanese Banking and Finance in the New Millennium

1 Kanaya and Woo, op. cit.
2 Hugh Patrick, *The Causes of Japan's Financial Crisis*, AJRC Research Center, Canberra, 1999
3 Mitsuru Taniuchi, 'Recent Developments in Japan's Financial Sector: Bad Loans and Financial Deregulation', *Journal of Asian Economics*, 8(2), 1997
4 Brian Waterhouse, 'Japanese Banking Sector', briefing document, 15 June 1998
5 Y. Nishimura, Causes of the failure of supervision over financial institutions, 1999, Bungeishunju, Bunshun Bunko (in Japanese).
6 J. Levy, *Resolving Japan's Banking System Problems, Japan-selected Issues*, IMF, 1998
7 Patrick, op. cit.
8 See IMF, *Survey*, 15 Sept. 1998.
9 Cargill, Hutchison and Ito, op. cit.
10 Hoshi and Kashyap, op. cit.; Patrick, op. cit.; Ito (1999); also M.J.B. Hall, 'Banking Regulation and Supervision in Japan', LSE Financial Markets Group Paper, May 2002.
11 See MOF, *Outline for Emergency Power to Stabilize the Financial System*, Tokyo, Feb. 1998
12 Hall, op. cit.
13 H. Nakaso, *Recent Banking Sector Reforms in Japan, Economic Policy Review*, Federal Reserve Bank of New York, 1999. Also *DIC Annual Report 1999*, Tokyo, Oct. 2001
14 Hall, op. cit.
15 Woo, op. cit.
16 Ibid.
17 Paul Krugman, 'Its Baaack: Japan's Slump and the Return of the Liquidity Trap', *Brookings Papers on Economic Activity*, 2(2), 1998
18 Dominic Wilson, 'Is Shutting Krugman's Liquidity Trap the Answer to Japan's Problems', *Pacific Economic Papers*, No. 297, Nov. 1999
19 L. Gower and D. Wilson, 'Non-performing Assets and Capital Accumulation'. Working Papers in Economics and Econometrics No. 352, Australian National University, 1998
20 M. Fukao, 'Japanese Financial Instability and Weakness in the Corporate Governance Structure', *Seoul Journal of Economics*, 1998, pp. 31–42
21 Kanaya and Woo, op. cit., p. 31
22 See BIS, 'The Financial Crisis in Japan during the 1990s; How the Bank of Japan Responded and the Lessons Learnt', BIS Papers No. 6, Basle, October 2001
23 Hall, op. cit.
24 DIC of Japan, *Annual Report*, Tokyo, Oct. 2001
25 Hall, op. cit.
26 Gorger, op. cit.
27 Ibid.
28 Rishi Goyal and Ronald McKinnon, 'Japan's Negative Risk Premium in Interest Rates: the Liquidity Trap and Fall in Bank Lending', paper presented at the Symposium: Japan's Lost Decade: Origins, Consequences and Prospects for Recovery, University of Michigan, March 2002

29 M. Shirakawa, 'Monetary Policy under Zero Interest Rate Constraint and Balance Sheet Adjustments', *International Finance*, Vol. 4, 2001.
30 Goyal and McKinnon, op. cit.
31 Krugman, op. cit.
32 Wilson, op. cit.
33 Goyal and McKinnon, op. cit.
34 I. Oishi and C. Towe, *Governance, Deregulation and Economic Performance in Japan, Selected Issues*, IMF Staff Country Report No. 98–113, 146–63, 1998
35 OECD, *Economic Survey, Japan*, 1999
36 Snowden, op. cit.
37 See A. Horiuchi, 'The Big Bang, Idea and Reality', in T. Hoshi and Hugh Patrick (eds), *Crisis and Change in the Japanese Financial System*, Kluwer Academic, 2000, Dordrecht; also Z. Nakajima and H. Taguchi, 'Towards a More Stable Framework; Long-term Alternatives – an Overview of Recent Bank Disruptions World-wide', in K. Sakamoto et al., *Financial Stability in a Changing Environment*, St. Martins Press, New York, 41–99
38 S. Royama, 'Aspects of Financial Restructuring in Contemporary Japan', *Japan Review of International Affairs*, Spring, 1990
39 BIS, *Annual Report*, Basle, 1999; also OECD, *Economic Survey of Japan*, 2000
40 McKinnon and Goyal, op. cit.
41 Jenny Corbett, 'Japan's Banking Crisis in International Perspective', in Masahiko Aoki and Garry R. Saxonhouse (eds), *Finance, Governance and Competitiveness in Japan*, Oxford, 2000, p. 152
42 McKinnon and Goyal, op. cit.
43 See BOJ, *Comparative Economic and Financial Statistics, Japan and other Major Countries*, Bank of Japan, Tokyo, 2002
44 R. McKinnon, 'Optimum World Monetary Arrangements or Dual Currency System', *B.N. Lavoro Quarterly Review*, Vol. 16, 1963
45 Hall, op. cit.
46 T. Hoshi and Anil Kashyap, *Corporate Financing and Governance in Japan*, MIT, 2002
47 See Terry Marsh and Jean Michel Paul, *Japanese Banks' Bad Loans; What* Happened, OECD, Paris, 1996; also V. Beattie et al., *Banks and Bad Debts; Accounting for Loan Loss in International Banking*, Chichester, Wiley, 1995, pp. 41–99
48 Corbett, op. cit., p. 153
49 McKinnon, op. cit.; Cargill (2000)
50 Thomas F. Cargill, in M. Blomstrom, *Japan's New Economy; Continuity and Change in the 21st Century*, OUP, 2001, p. 158

7 The Internationalization of the Yen in the New Millennium

1 For early studies on the yen bloc, see Sachio Kojima, 'Moves towards Internationalization of the Japanese Yen and Japan–Australia Currency Relations', in *Harmonization of Japanese and Australian Economic Policies*, Japan–Australia Project, Report No. 3, June 1975; also Jeffrey Frankel, 'Is Japan Creating a Yen Bloc in East Asia and the Pacific Federal Reserve Bank

of San Francisco', Center for Pacific Basin Monetary and Economic Studies Working Paper, 1992–09

2 Tavlas and Ozeki call it the yen zone; also Kiyoshi Kojima, 'Pacific Currency Area; a New Approach to the International Monetary System', *Hitotsubashi Journal of Economics*, Feb. 1970 and Jeffrey Frankel, 'Dollar', in P. Newman, M. Millgate and J. Eatwell (eds) *The New Palgrave Dictionary of Money and Finance*, Vol. 1, Macmillan Press, New York, 1992. J. Frankel and Shang Wei, 'Yen Bloc or Dollar Bloc? Exchange Rate Policies of East Asian Economies', in Takatoshi Ito and Anne O. Krueger (eds), *Macroeconomic Linkages; Savings, Exchange Rates and Capital Flows*, Chicago University Press, 1994, pp. 295–355

3 Robert Z. Aliber, 'The Evolution of Currency Areas; a Speculation on Monetary History', in Richard N. Cooper, Peter Kenen, de Macedo and van Ypersele, *The International Monetary System under Flexible Exchange Rates, Global, Regional and National*, Ballinger Publishing Co., Cambridge, Mass., 1982

4 Robert Mundell, 'Theory of Optimum Currency Areas', *American Economic Review*, Sept. 1961, p. 663

5 George S. Tavlas, 'On the International Use of Currencies; the Case of the Deutsche Mark', IMF Working Paper 90/3, 1990, and Princeton University series Essays in International Finance, March 1991 (revised version)

6 IMF, Annual reports for several years.

7 G.S. Tavlas and Yuzuru Ozeki, 'The Japanese Yen as an International Currency', IMF Working Paper 91/2, 1991, p. 9.

8 Ronald McKinnon, 'Optimum Currency Areas', *American Economic Review*, 51, November 1961; also M. Kawai, 'Japan's Demand for Long-term External Securities in the 1980s', *Annals of Institute of Social Sciences*, University of Tokyo, 1988, 89–141

9 Tetsuji Murase, 'The Internationalization of the Yen: Essential Issues Overlooked', *Pacific Economic Papers*, AJRC, No. 307, Sept 2000, p. 6

10 Bank of Japan, *Financial and Economic Statistics Monthly*, BOJ, Tokyo, November 1999

11 Murase, op. cit., p. 9

12 Ibid., p. 12

13 Kumiharu Shigehera, *Financial Liberalisation and Monetary Policy*, Fair Fact series, Tokyo, 1990

14 MITI, *Outline of Interim Report of Subcommittee for Long-range Issues of the Industrial Structure Council*, Tokyo, Oct. 1996

15 Foreign Exchange Council, *Annual Report on Japanese Exchange Rates*, 1999

16 See here Edward Tower and Thomas D. Willet, 'The Theory of Optimum Currency Areas and Exchange Rate Flexibility', Princeton Special Papers in International Economics, No. 11, May 1976

17 Chi Hung Kwan, 'A Yen Bloc in Asia; an Integrative Approach', *Journal of Asia-Pacific Economy*, 1996; also 'The Possibility of Forming a Yen Bloc Revisited', *ASEAN Economic Bulletin*, August 2000, p. 219

18 Cf. J. Williamson, 'A Survey of the Literature on the Optimal Peg', *Journal of Development Economics*, Vol. 11, 1982

19 Shinji Takagi, 'A Basket Policy; Operational Issues for Developing Countries', *World Development*, Vol. 16, No. 2, 1988

20 Tavlas and Ozeki, op. cit.

21 BOJ, *Main Economic Indicators of Japan*, Economic Statistics Department, April 1999
22 Murase, op. cit., p. 13
23 Ibid., p. 15
24 Kwan, 'Possibility', p. 230
25 *Nihon Keizai Shinbun*, Dec. 1998
26 Murase, op. cit., p. 16
27 Ibid., p. 19

8 Conclusions

1 C. Johnson, *MITI and Japanese Miracle*, Stanford University Press, Stanford, 1982
2 M. Aoki, 'The Japanese Firm as a System of Attributes; a Survey and Research Agenda', in M. Aoki and Ronald Dore (eds), *The Japanese Firm – the Sources of Competitive Strength*, Oxford University Press, Oxford, 1994
3 A. Horiuchi, 'The Big Bang: Idea and Reality', in T. Hoshi and Hugh Patrick (eds), *Crisis and Change in the Japanese Financial System*, Kluwer Academic, Dordrecht, 2000
4 OECD, *Economic Survey – Japan*, Paris, 2003
5 B. van Ark and D. Pilat, 'Productivity Levels in Germany, Japan and the United States', *Brookings Papers on Economic Activity: Microeconomics*, 1993, 1–48
6 E. Wolff, 'Has Japan Specialized in Wrong Industries?', in M. Blomstrom, B. Gangnes and S.J. LaCroix (eds), *Japan's New Economy: Continuity and Change in the Twenty-first Century*, Oxford University Press, 2000
7 D. Beason and J. James, *The Political Economy of Japanese Financial Markets: Myths versus Reality*, Macmillan Press, London, 1999
8 T. Hoshi and A. Kashyap, 'The Japanese Banking Crisis; Where did it Come from and Where will it End?', in B.S. Bernanke and J. Rotemberg (eds), *NBER Mcroeconomics Annual*, MIT Press, Cambridge, Mass., 1999
9 M. Gibson, 'Big Bang Deregulation and Japanese Corporate Governance', in T. Hoshi and H. Patrick (eds), *Crisis and Change in the Japanese Financial System*, Kluwer Academic, Dordrecht, 2000
10 D. Hugh Whittaker and Y. Kurosawa, 'Japan's Crisis: Evolution and Implications', *Cambridge Journal of Economics*, 22, 1998, 7611–771
11 R. Katz, *Japan, the System that Soured*, M.E. Sharpe, Armonk, NY, 1998
12 Andrea Boltho and Jenny Corbett, 'The Assessment: Japan's Stagnation – Can Policy Revive the Economy?', *Cambridge Journal of Economic Policy*, 16 (2)
13 OECD, *Economic Survey – Japan*, Paris
14 D. Flath, *The Japanese Economy*, Oxford University Press, Oxford, 2000
15 J.A.A. Stockwin, *Dynamic and Immobilist Politics in Japan*, Macmillan, London, 1988
16 Y. Noguchi, 'Leaving the 1940 System and Moving into a New System', *Japanese Economic Studies*, 24(3), 1996, 83–94, and 'The 1940s System: Japan under the Wartime Economy, *American Economic Review*, 88(2), 1998, 83–94. Also Ed. J. Lincoln 'Japan's Financial Problems', *Brookings Papers on Economic Activity*, 2, 1998, 347–85
17 L. Carlile and M. Tilton, *Is Japan Really Changing its Ways? Regulatory Reform and the Japanese Economy*, Brookings Institution, Washington, DC

Bibliography

Abegglen, J.C. and G. Stalk, Jr, *Kaisha, the Japanese Corporation*, Basic Books, 1985

Aggarwal, Raj, 'The Shape of the Post-bubble Japanese Business; Preparing for Growth in new Millennium', *The International Executive*, Jan–Feb, 1996

Aggarwal, R. and A. Hiraki, 'Price/Book Value Ratios and Stock Returns; Evidence of Empirical Regularity on Tokyo Stock Exchange, *Finance Review*, 1992, 589–605

Akhtar, M.A., 'Financial Innovations and their Implications for Monetary Policy: an International Perspective, BIS Economic Papers no. 9, Basle, 1983

Alesina, A., 'Macroeconomics and Politics', in S. Fischer (ed.), *NBER Macroeconomics Annual*, MIT Press, 1988

Ali, M.El Agraa, *Japan's Trade Frictions: Realities or Misconceptions*, Macmillan, London, 1988

Amex Bank Review, 'Japan's Capital Outflows: a Boost to Securitisation', 28 April 1986

Ando, A. and A. Auerbach, 'The Corporate Cost of Capital in Japan and the US: a Comparison', in J. Shoven (ed.), *Government Policy towards Industry in the US and Japan*, Cambridge University Press, 1988

Ando, A. and A. Auerbach, 'The Cost of Capital in Japan: Recent Evidence and Further Results', *Journal of Japanese and International Economies*, 4(4), 1990, pp. 323–50.

Argy, Victor, 'International Financial Liberalization: the Australian and Japanese Experience Compared', *Bank of Japan Monetary and Economic Studies*, Tokyo, May 1987, pp. 105–67

Aron, Paul, *Japanese P/E Multiples: the Tradition Continues*, Japanese Research Report no. 35, Daiwa Securities America Inc.; 23 October 1989

Asako, K., Takatoshi Ito and K. Sakamoto, 'The Rise and Fall of the Deficits in Japan', *Journal of Japanese and International Economies*, 5(4), 1991

Asian Development Bank, *Annual Report* for several years

Balassa, Bela and Marcus Noland, *Japan in the World Economy*, Institute of International Economics, Washington, DC, 1988

Ballon, R.J. and S. Tomita, *The Financial Behavior of Japanese Corporations*, Kodansha International, Tokyo, 1988

Bank of England, 'Developments in International Banking and Capital Markets in 1991', *Bank of England Quarterly Bulletin*, London, May, pp. 190–8

Barro, R.J., 'Are Government Bonds Net Wealth', *Journal of Political Economy*, 82, 1994, pp. 1095–118

Batten, D. et al., 'The Instruments and Operating Procedures for Conducting Monetary Policy in the Group of Five Countries', IMF Working Paper no. 57, 1989

Baumgartner, Ulrich and Guy Meredith, *Saving Behavior and the Asset Price Bubble in Japan, Analytical Studies*, IMF, Washington, April 1995

Beason, D. and J. James, *The Political Economy of Japanese Financial Markets: Myths versus Reality*, Macmillan, London, 1999

Beattie, V. et al., *Banks and Bad Debts: Accounting for Loan Losses in International Banking*, Chichester, Wiley, 1995

Berglof, E. and E. Perotti, 'The Governance Structure of Japanese Financial Keiretsu', *Journal of Financial Economics*, 36(4), 1994, 259–84

Bergsten, C.F. and W.R. Cline, *The US–Japan Economic Problem*, Institute of International Economics, Washington, DC, 1985

Bird, Graham, *Managing Global Money, Essays in International Financial Economics*, Macmillan, London, 1988

BIS, *Central Bank Survey of Foreign Exchange and Derivative Markets in April 1998*, Basle, 1998

BIS *Annual Report*, 2002

BIS, *73rd Annual Report*, Basle, 2003

Blanchard, O.J. 'The Lucas Critique and the Volcker Deflation, *American Economic Review*, 74(2), 1984, 211–15

Blanchard, O. and S. Fischer, *Lectures on Macroeconomics*, MIT Press, Cambridge, 1989

BOJ, 'Stepped up Capital Movements in and out of Japan and their Effects on the Japanese Financial Markets, Research and Statistics dept. Special Paper no. L12, Tokyo, 1984

BOJ, 'Structural Changes in the Long-term Bonds', Research and Statistics dept. Special Paper no. 132, Tokyo, March 1986

BOJ, 'Corporate Management under Continued Economic Expansion', Research and Statistics dept. Special Paper no. 199, Tokyo, March 1991

BOJ, 'Deregulation, Technological Progress and Efficiency of the Banking Industry in Japan', Research and Statistics dept. Special Paper no. 214, Tokyo, spring 1992

BOJ, 'Japanese Banks' Capital Ratio and their Earnings Trend: an ROE Analysis', BOJ Special Paper no. 230, Tokyo

BOJ, 1996, *Monthly Finance Review*, December, Tokyo

BOJ, 'For the Improvement of Functions in the JGB Market', Working paper, 99-J-3, working paper series of the Financial Markets Department, at BOJ Tokyo website

BOJ, *Main Economic Indicators*, Economic Statistics division, Tokyo, Nov. 1999

BOJ, 'Microstructure and Market Liquidity of JGB Market', Working Paper 99-J-1, listed at http://www.or.ip

BOJ, *Monthly Report of Recent Economic and Financial Developments*, April 1999

BOJ, 'Developments in Profits and Balance Sheets of Japanese Banks in Fiscal 2000 and Banks' Management Tasks', *BOJ Quarterly Bulletin*, November 2001

BOJ, 'Vocational International Banking Statistics', http/www.boj.or.jp/en/2002

Boltho, A. and Jenny Corbett, 'The Assessment: Japan's Stagnation – Can Policies Revive the Economy?', *Oxford Review of Economic Policy*, no. 2, 2000

Bonne, Peter, *Perspectives on the High Price of Japanese Land*, Harvard University, 1985

Brainard, William C., John B. Shoven and Laurence Weiss, 'The Financial Valuation of Returns to Capital', *Brookings Papers on Economic Activity*, 2, 1980, pp. 453–502

Brittan, S., 'Asian Model, R.I.P.', *Financial Times*, 4 December 1995

Brown, W., 'Opening the Japanese Financial Markets; What Has Changed; What Will Change?,' in Thomas Pugel and R. Hawkins, *Fragile Interdependence, Issues in US–Japan Trade and Investment*, Lexington Books, 1986

Bryant, Ralph C., *Euro-currency Banking: Alarmist Concerns and Genuine Issues*, OECD Economic Studies no. 1, autumn 1983

Buiter, W.H. and M. Miller, 'The Thatcher Experiment: the First Two Years', *Brookings Papers on Economic Activity*, 2, 1981, 315–79

Burstein, D., *Yen: Japan's New Financial Empire*, Fawcett Columbine, New York

Burton, F.M. and Saelens, 'Direct Investment by Sogo Sosha in Europe', *Journal of World Trade Law*, 1983

Campbell, J.Y. and Y. Hamao, 'Predictable Stock Returns in the US and Japan: a Study of Long-term Capital Market Integration', paper at the Conference, Japan in a Global Economy, Stockholm, 1991

Cargill, Thomas, Michael Hutchison and Takatoshi Ito (eds), 'Preventing Future Banking Crisis in Japan', prepared for Conference 'Preventing Banking Crises: Analysis and Lessons from Recent Banking Crises', sponsored by Federal Reserve Bank of Chicago and the World Bank, Washington, 11–13 June 1997

Cargill, Thomas F. and Shoichi Royama, *The Transition of Finance in Japan and the US*, Hoover Institution Press, California, 1987

Carlile, L. and M. Tilton, *Is Japan Really Changing Its Ways? Regulatory Reform and the Japanese Economy*, Brookings Institution, Washington, 1998

Caves, R.E., 'Japanese Investment in the US: Lessons for the Economic Analysis of Foreign Investment', *The World Economy*, vol. 16, May 1993

Chai, S.P., A.E. Tshoegl and C.M. Yu, 'Banks and the World's Major Financial Centres', *Welt. Archiv.*, vol. 122, 1986

Collyns, Charles V. and T. Bayoumi, *Post-Bubble Blues: How Japan Responded to Asset Price Collapse*, IMF, Washington, 2000

Corbett, Jenny, 'International Perspectives on Financing: Evidence from Japan', *Oxford Review of Economic Policy*, winter 1987, pp. 30–54

Corker, R., 'External Adjustment and the Strong Yen', *IMF Staff Papers*, 36(2), 1989, pp. 464–93

Das, Dilip, *Migration of Financial Resources in Developing Countries*, Macmillan, London, 1986

Das, Dilip, *Yen Appreciation and the World Economy*, Macmillan, 1993

Davis, E.P., 'International Investment of Life Insurance Companies', *European Affairs*, Amsterdam, 1990, pp. 224–59

Deckle, Robert, 'Alternative Estimates of Japanese Saving and Comparisons with the US; Can the Capital Gains be Included in Savings?', *Bank of Japan and Boston University*, Dec. 1990

Deckle, R. and Lawrence Summers, 'Japan's High Saving Rate Reaffirmed', NBER Working Paper no. 3690, 1990

Dicken, Peter, 'The Changing Geography of Japanese FDI in Manufacturing Industry: a Global Perspective', in Jonathan Morris, *Japan and the Global Economy*, Routledge, London, 1990

Dobson, Wendy, *Japan in East Asia*, Institute of South-East Asian Studies, Singapore, 1997

Dohner, Robert and Henry Terrel, 'The Determinants of Growth of Multinational Banking Organizations 192–96, International Finance Discussion Paper no. 326, Federal Reserve Board, Washington, June 1988

Dore, R.F., *Flexible Rigidities, Industrial Policy and Structural Adjustment in the Japanese Economy*, Stanford, 1986

Douglass, Clyde M., *Transnational Capital and Urbanization in Japan*, University of Sydney, 1987

Dunning, J.H., 'Explaining International Direct Investment Position of Countries: towards a Dynamic Approach', *Welt. Archiv.*, vol. 117, 1981, and pp. 30–64

Economist, The, London, 'International Finance Survey', 27 April 1991

Egebo, T. and A.S. Englander, 'Institutional Commitments and Policy Credibility: a Critical Survey and Empirical Evidence from the ERM', *OECD Economic Studies*, 18, 1992, 45–84

Eguchi, T., *The US–Japan Imbalances: Causes and Remedies*, JCIF Policy Study no. 12, Tokyo, 1988

Eijffinger, Sylvester and A. Van Rixtel, 'The Japanese Financial System and Monetary Policy: a Descriptive Review', *Japan and the World Economy*, 1992

Eken, Sena, 'Integration of Domestic and International Financial Markets: the Japanese Experience', *IMF Staff Papers*, Sept, 1984, Washington, pp. 499–548

Emmot, B., *Japan's Global Reach: the Influences, Strategies and Weaknesses of Japan's MNCs*, Random House, London, 1992

Emmot, William, *The Limits to Japanese Power in International Economics and the Financial Markets*, Oxford, 1989

Encarnacion, D.J. and M. Mason, 'Neither MITI nor America: the Political Economy of Capital Liberalization in Japan', *International Organization*, 44, 1990, pp. 25–54

EPA (Economic Planning Agency), *Progress in Liberalization/Internationalization of Finance: Economic Survey of Japan, 1983–84*, Tokyo, 1984

EPA, Government of Japan, White Paper, Tokyo

EPA, *Economic Survey of Japan*, Tokyo, 1990

EPA, *Economic Survey of Japan*, several years

EPA, 'The EPA World Economic Model – Fifth Version', Economic Research Institute Discussion Paper no. 20, Tokyo, 1995

EPA, *State of the Japanese Economy; Review and Issues of the Japanese Economy in 1999*, Dec. 2000

Esho, H., 'From a Latecomer Donor to the Top Donor: How Special Is Japanese ODA', *Journal of International Economic Studies*, March 1994

Euromoney supplement, 'Japan: the Land Where the Money Grows', April 1987

Evans, G., 'Japan Takes Over the IMF', *Euromoney*, September 1988, pp. 98–112

Fazzari, Robert, R. Hubbard and Bruce Petersen, 'Investment and Finance Reconsidered', *Brookings Papers on Economic Activity*, 1, 1988, pp. 141–96

Federation of Bankers' Association, *Annual Report*, Tokyo, 1991

Feldman, R.A. and Sakakibara, 'The Japanese Financial System in Comparative Perspective', *Journal of Comparative Economics*, 1983, pp. 1–24

Feldstein, M. and C. Horioka, 'Domestic Savings and International Capital Flows', *Economic Journal*, 90, 1980, pp. 314–29

Feldstein, Robert, *Japanese Financial Markets, Deficits, Dilemmas and Deregulation*, MIT Press, Cambridge, 1986

Financial Times, 'International Economic Indicators, National Accounts', 13 May 1991

Flath, D. *The Japanese Economy*, Oxford University Press, Oxford, 2000

Fortune, 'The Fortune Global 500', 29 July 1991, pp. 65–108

Frankel, Allen B. and Paul B. Morgan, 'A Primer on the Japanese Banking System', International Finance Discussion Paper no. 419, Washington, December, 1989

Frankel, Jeffrey, *The Yen/Dollar Agreement; Liberalizing Japanese Capital Markets*, Policy Analysis in International Economics no. 9, Institute for International Economics, Washington, 1984

Frankel, J. 'International Capital Flows and Domestic Economic Policies', in M. Feldstein (ed.), *The US in the World Economy*, University of Chicago Press, Chicago, 1988

Frankel, J. 'Japanese Finance: a Survey', in Paul Krugman (ed.), *Trade with Japan: Has the Door Opened Wider*? Chicago, 1991

Frankel, J., 'The Japanese Financial System and the Cost of Capital', in Shinji Takagi, *Japanese Capital Markets*, Blackwell, London, 1993

Frankel, J. and Kenneth Froot, 'Short-term and Long-term Expectations of the Yen/Dollar Exchange Rate: Evidence from Survey Data', NBER Working Paper no. 2216

Freedman, Craig, *The End of the Economic Miracle*, Edward Elgar, 1998

French, Irwin and Tokustu, 'The Cost of Capital to Corporations in Japan and the US', *Journal of Banking and Finance*, II, 1987, pp. 313–27

Fukao, Mitsuhiro, 'Liberalization of Japan's Foreign Exchange Controls and Structural Change in the Balance of Payments', *Bank of Japan, Monetary and Economic Studies*, Tokyo, 1990, pp. 101–65

Fukao, M., 'Japanese Financial Instability and Weaknesses in the Corporate Governance Structure', *Seoul Journal of Economics*, Seoul, 11, 1998, pp. 381–422

Fukao, Mitsuhiro, 'Japan's Lost Decade and Weakness in its Corporate Governance Structure', paper presented at the symposium, Japan's Lost Decade; Origins, Consequences and Prospects for Recovery, at the University of Michigan, March 2002

Fukao, M. and Kunio Okina, 'Internationalization of Financial Markets and Balance of Payments Imbalances: a Japanese Perspective', Carnegie-Rochester Conference Series on Public Policy no. 30, 1989, pp. 167–220

Fukuda, S. and Hirata Shinichi, 'Main Bank Relationships and Capital Structure in Japan', *Journal of Japanese and International Economics*, 10, 1996, 250–61

Fukui, Toshihiko, 'Recent Developments of the Short-term Money Market in Japan and Changes in Monetary Control Techniques and Procedures by the BOJ', Bank of Japan Research and Statistics Department, Special Paper no. 130, Tokyo, Jan. 1986

Funabashi, Y., *Managing the Dollar: from the Plaza to the Louvre*, Institute for International Economics, Washington, 1988, pp. 17–21

Garvey, G.T. and P. Swan, 'The Interaction between Financial and Employment Contracts: a Formal Model of Japanese Corporate Governance', *Journal of Japanese and International Economies*, 6, 1992, 247–74

Genay, H. 'The Ownership Structure of Japanese Financial Institutions', Working Paper, Federal Bank of Chicago, 1993

Genda, Y., 'Job Creation and Destruction in Japan, 1991–1995', *Journal of Japanese and International Economies*, 12, 1998, pp. 1–23

Gerlach, M., 'Keiretsu Organization in the Japanese Economy: Analysis and Trade Implications', in Chalmers Johnson (eds), *Politics and Productivity: the Real Story of Why Japan Works*, Cambridge, Mass., 1989

Gibson, M., *Big Bang Deregulation and Japanese Corporate Governance*, Kluwer Academic, Dordrecht, 2000

Glick, Reuven, 'Interest Rate Linkages in the Pacific Basin', *Federal Reserve Bank of San Francisco Economic Review*, no. 3, 1998, pp. 31–42

Glick, R. and M. Hutchison, 'Financial Liberalization in the Pacific Basin: Implications for Real Interest Rate Linkages', *Journal of Japanese and International Economies*, 4, 1990, pp. 36–48

Glynn, L., 'Japanese Banks Abroad: the Next Push', *Institutional Investor*, May 1990, pp. 94–7

Goldbery, L.G. and G.A. Hanweck, 'The Growth of the World's 3000 Largest Banking Organizations by Country', *Journal of Banking and Finance*, 15, 1991, pp. 207–23

Goodhart, A.E. and George Sutija (eds) *Japanese Financial Growth*, Macmillan, London, 1990

Gore, Charles, 'Development Strategy in East Asian Newly Industrializing Economies: the Experience of Post-war Japan, 1953–73', UNCTAD, Geneva, Discussion Paper no. 1994

Gower, L. and Dominick Wilson, 'Non-performing Assets and Capital Accumulation', ANU Working Papers in Economics and Econometrics no. 352, ANU, Canberra

Goyal V.K. and Takeshi Yamada, 'Asset Price Shocks, Financial Constraints and Investment: Evidence from Japan', Dept of Finance, Hong Kong University of Science and Technology, Clear Water Bay, Kowloon, Hong Kong, June 2001, mimeo

Hall, Maximilian J.B., *Financial Reform in Japan*, Edward Elgar, 1998

Hamada, K., 'On the Long-run Capital Ownership Pattern in the World Economy', *NIRA Research Output*, 1991, pp. 60–77

Hamada, Koichi and Akiyoshi Horiuchi, 'Monetary, Financial Real Effects of Yen Internationalization', in S.W. Arndt and J. David Richardson, *Real-financial Linkages among Open Economies*, MIT Press, Cambridge, 1987

Hardouvelis, G.A., 'Evidence on Stock Market Speculative Bubble: Japan, US and Great Britain', Federal Reserve Bank of New York, Research Paper no. 8810, April 1988

Hayashi, F., 'Tobin's Marginal and Average q: a Neoclassical Interpretation', *Econometrica*, 50, 1982, 213–24

Hayashi, F., *Understanding Savings: Evidence from the US and Japan*, MIT Press, Cambridge, 1997

Healey, Derek, *Japanese Capital Exports and Asian Economic Development*, OECD Development Centre, Paris, 1991

Helou, A. 'Capital Exports from Japan; a General Appraisal', in *World Competition*, Geneva, 1989

Helweg, M. Diana, 'Japan: a Rising Sun?', *Foreign Affairs*, July 2000

Hickok, S., 'Japanese Trade Balance Adjustment to Yen Appreciation', *Federal Reserve Bank of New York Quarterly Review* (Autumn), 14(3), 1989, pp. 33–47

Hirata, M., 'Japanese Corporate Response to the EC Market Unification', *Hitotsubashi Journal of Commerce and Management*, no. 25, 1990, pp. 13–33

Hodder, James, 'Is the Cost of Capital Lower in Japan?', *Journal of the Japanese and International Economies*, 5(1), 1991, pp. 86–100

Hodder, J.E. and Tschoegel, 'Some Aspects of Japanese Corporate Finance', *Journal of Quantitative Financial Analysis*, June 1985

Hori, A., 'The Evolution of Reserve Currency Diversification', BIS Economic Paper no. 18, Basle, December 1986

Horiuchi, A., 'The "Big Bang" Idea and Reality', in T. Hoshi and H. Patrick (eds), *Crisis and Change in the Japanese Financial System*, Kluwer Academic, Dordrecht, 2000

Hoshi, T. and A. Kashyap, 'The Japanese Banking Crisis: Where Did It Come From and Where Will It End?', in B.S. Bernanke and J. Rotemberg (eds), *NBER Macroeconomics Annual*, MIT Press, Cambridge, 1999

Hoshi, Takeo and Anil Kashyap, *Corporate Finance and Governance in Japan: the Road to the Future*, MIT Press, Cambridge and London, 2001

Hutchison, M.M., 'Monetary Control, Interest Rates and Exchange Rates: the Case of Japan, 1973–1986', Working Paper no. 145, University of California at Santa Cruz

Ichimura, S., 'Monetary Policy in Japan', Osaka International University, Working Paper no. 8, 1993

Ichimura, S, 'Monetary Policy in Japan', in M. Frantianni and D. Salvatore, *Monetary Policy in Developed Countries*, Greenwood Press, Connecticut, 1993

Ide, M., *Japanese Corporate Finance and International Competition*, Macmillan, Basingstoke, 1998

Ikeo, K.A., 'Micro-theoretic Analysis of Japanese Financial System', *Kyoto University Economic Review*, 1986

Imai, K. and R. Komiya (eds), *Business Enterprise in Japan: Views of Leading Japanese Economists*, MIT Press, Cambridge, 1994

IMF, *International Financial Statistics*, Washington, DC, 2002

IMF, *World Economic Outlook*, Washington, DC, several years

Ito, Takatoshi, *Japanese Economy*, MIT Press, Cambridge, 1994

Ito, Takatoshi, *On Recent Movements of Japanese Current Accounts and Capital Flows in Macroeconomic Linkage*, Chicago, 1994

Ito, Takatoshi, 'The Causes of Japan's Financial Crisis', *Pacific Economic Papers*, no. 288, Feb. 1999

Itoh, H., 'Japanese Resource Management from the Viewpoint of Incentive Theory', in M. Aoki and R. Dore (eds), *The Japanese Firm – the Sources of Competitive Strength*, Oxford University Press, Oxford, 1994

Iwami, Toru, 'Internationalization of Japanese Banks: the Factors Affecting its Rapid Growth', *Journal of International Economic Studies*, Tokyo, no. 3, 1989

Iwata, K. 'Financial Liberalization and its Impact on the Japanese Economy', *Pacific Economic Papers*, no. 134, ANU, Canberra, April 1986

Iwata, K. 'Tax System and the International Capital Flows between the US and Japan', Working Paper, Tokyo University, Tokyo, 1994

Iyori, H. and A. Uesugi, *The Antimonopoly Laws and Policies of Japan*, Federal and Legal Publications, New York, 1994

Japan Development Bank, *Capital Investment Spending*, Tokyo, March 1989

Japan Development Bank/Japan Economic Research Institute (JDB/JERI), 'Policy-based Finance; the Experience of Postwar Japan', World Bank Discussion Paper no. 221, 1994

Japan Economic Institute, *Capital Market Liberalization in Japan*, JEI Report, Washington, no. 10, March 1984

Japan International Development Organization (JAIDO), Tokyo, 1991

Japan Securities Research Institute, *Securities Market in Japan*, Tokyo, 1990

JCIF (Japan Centre for International Finance), *Evaluation and Strategy of Tokyo Financial and Capital Markets*, Tokyo, 1995

JFTC, *Annual Report*, Tokyo, 1996

Johnson, C., *MITI and the Japanese Miracle*, Stanford University Press, Stanford, 1982

Julius, D., *Foreign Direct Investment; the Neglected Twins of Trade*, The Group of Thirty, New York, 1991

Kahkonen, Juha, 'Japan's Capital Flows' in Ulrich Baumgartner and Guy Meredith (eds), *Savings Behavior and the Asset Price 'Bubble' in Japan*, Occasional Paper 124, IMF, Washington, April, 1985

Kanaya, A. and David Woo, 'The Japanese Banking Crisis of the 1990s: Sources and Lessons', IMF Working Paper no. 7, 2000

Kanda, T., 'Japan's Big Bang: Its Impact on the Legal System and Corporate Governance', in T. Hoshi and H. Patrick (eds), *Crisis and Change in the Japanese Financial System*, Kluwer Academic, Dordrecht, 2000

Kane, E.J., 'Competitive Financial Regulation: an International Perspective', in Richard Portes and A. Swoboda (eds), *Threats to International Financial Stability*, Cambridge University Press, 1987

Kasahara, S., 'A Rescue Plan for the Post-Bubble Japanese Economy, the Establishment of the Cooperative Credit Purchasing Company', UNCTAD Discussion Paper no. 77, Jan. 1994

Kato, R. and T. Watanabe, *Asymmetric Effects of Monetary Policy: the Japanese Experience in the 1990s*, Hitotsubashi University, 1999

Katz, R., *Japan, the System That Soured*, M.E. Sharpe, Armonk, NY

Kawai, Masahiro, 'Japanese Investment in Foreign Securities', University of British Columbia Economics Dept. Discussion Paper no. 37, Vancouver, 1991

Kawai, M., 'East Asia's Currency Upheavals and Financial Crisis', MOF Institute of Fiscal and Monetary Policy Seminar Paper, 1998

Kawai, M. and H. Okumura, *Japan's Portfolio Investment in Foreign Securities*, JCIF Policy Study series no. 9, Tokyo, Jan. 1992

Kester, W, 'Industrial Groups as Systems of Contractual Governance', *Oxford Review of Economic Policy*, 8, 1992

Keynes, J.M., *General Theory of Employment, Interest and Money*, Macmillan, 1936

Khosla, A. and Jurio Teranishi, 'Exchange Rate Pass through in Export Prices, an International Comparison', *Hitotsubashi Journal of Economics*, 30, 1989, pp. 31–48

Kinoshita, T., *The $20 Billion Recycling Plan, a Personal View on the Exim Loan*, Export-Import Bank of Japan, Tokyo, Feb. 1988

Kiyotaki, N. and K. West, 'Credit, Business Investment and Output Fluctuations in Japan', *NBER Macroeconomics Annual*, 1996

Kohama, H. and S. Urata, 'The Impact of the Recent Yen Appreciation on the Japanese Economy', *The Developing Economies*, December 1988

Kojima, Kiyoshi, 'Micro and Macro-economic Models of Direct Foreign Investment: towards a Synthesis', *Hitotsubashi Journal of Economics*, 25(1), June 1984

Koo, Richard C., *High Quality Products But Low Profitability, Why Japanese Investors Are Increasingly Rejecting the Time-honored Formula*, Nomura Research Institute, Tokyo, 1992

Koo, Richard C., 'International Capital Flows in an Open Economy, the Japanese Experience', in Shinji Takagi, *Japanese Capital Markets*, Blackwell, London, 1993

Krugman, P.R., 'Exchange Rate and International Adjustment', New York University Center for Japan–US Business and Economic Studies Working Paper No. 39, September 1987

Krugman, Paul, 'Its baack; Japan's Slump and the Liquidity Trap', *Brookings Papers*, 2, 1998, pp. 137–205
Krugman, P.R. and R.E. Baldwin, 'The Persistence of the US Trade Deficits', *Brookings Papers on Economic Activity*, No. 1, 1987, pp. 1–56
Kurosawa, Y., *Corporate Finance in Japan*, Financial Digest no. 26, Japan Credit Rating Agency, Tokyo, 1993
Kusukawa, Toru, 'The Japanese Economy; the Bubble of the 1980s and the Recession of the 1990s', *Japan and the World Economy*, 1994
Kwan, Ch Hung, *An Optimal Peg for the Asian Currencies and the Implications for a Yen Bloc*, Nomura Research Institute, Tokyo, Feb. 1992
Kyuno, Masao, 'A Glimpse of the Financial Revolution in Japan', *Journal of International Economic Studies*, 3, 1989, pp. 1–24
Lane, Philip and Gian Maria-Ferreti, 'Long-term Capital Movements', *NBER MacroEconomics Annual*, 2001
Lincoln, Edward J., *Japan, Facing Economic Maturity*, The Brookings Institution, Washington, 1994
Lincoln, Edward, J., 'Japan's Financial Problems', *Brookings Papers on Economic Activity*, 2, 1998, 347–85
Mckenzie, Colin and Michael Stutchbury (eds), *Japanese Financial Markets and the Role of the Yen*, Allen and Unwin, Sydney for AJRC, Canberra, 1992
Mackinnon, Neil, 'Japanese Corporate and Financial Strategy in the Single European Market', *European Management Journal*, Oxford, 1990
McKinnon, R.I. and K. Ohno, *Dollar and Yen; Resolving Economic Conflict between the US and Japan*, MIT Press, Cambridge, Mass., 2002
McKinnon, Ronald and Kenichi Ohno, 'The Foreign Exchange Origins of Japan's Economic Slump and Low Interest Liquidity Trap', *The World Economy*, 2001
Macrae, Hamish, 'Japan's Role in the Emerging Global Securities Markets', Occasional Paper no. 17, Group of Thirty, New York, 1985
Manchester, Joyce and J. Warwick, 'The Macroeconomic Consequences of the Savings and Loan Debacle', *The Review of Economics and Statistics*, Aug. 1994
Marsh, Felicity, *Japan's Next Export Success: the Financial Services Industry*, Crawford, London, 1986
Matsukawa, Michiya, 'Japanese Trade Surplus and Capital Outflows', Occasional Paper no. 22, Group of Thirty, New York, 1987
Mattimone, Richard P., 'Are Japanese Investors Taking Their Money Home?', *Contemporary Policy Issues*, 1992
Mattione, Richard, *A Capital Cost Disadvantage for Japan*, J.P. Morgan, Tokyo, 1993
Mattione, R. and Norman Klath, 'Japan as World's Leading Foreign Investor', *World Financial Markets*, Morgan Guarantee Trust Co., November, 1989
Mayer, Colin, 'New Issues in Corporate Finance', *European Economic Review*, 32(5), 1988, pp. 167–89
Misra, S.N. 'Japan's Official Development Assistance to India, an Appraisal', Working Paper E.159/1993, Institute of Economic Growth, Delhi, 1993
Miyao, R., 'The Role of Monetary Policy in Japan: a Break in the 1990s?', *Journal of the Japanese and International Economics*, 2000
Miyazaki, *Japanese Financial Reforms*, Chuo Koron, Tokyo, 1997
MOF, *The Current Status and Prospects on Financial Liberalization and the Internationalization of the Yen*, Tokyo, 11 June 1984

MOF, 'Current Plans for Liberalization and Internationalization of Japanese Financial and Capital Markets', Tokyo, June 1987, *Monthly Finance Review*, no. 180, June 1988
MOF, *The Mechanism and Economic Effects of Asset Price Fluctuations: a Report of the Research Committee*, Institute of Fiscal and Monetary Policy, Tokyo, 1993
MOF, *The Fiscal Investment and Loan Program Report*, the Financial Bureau, Tokyo, 1997
MOF, *Plan for Financial System Reform*, Report of the Financial System Research Council, Tokyo, 17 June 1997
MOF, *Report on Fiscal and Monetary Statistics* (Monthly), Tokyo, MOF Printing Office, 1998
MOF, *Internationalization of the Yen for the 21st Century – Japan's Response to Changes in Global Economic and Financial Environment*, The Council on Foreign Exchange and Other Transactions, Tokyo, 20 April 1999
Morgan Guaranty Trust Co. of New York, *World Financial Markets*, 18 March 1988
MPT, *On the Management of Postal Savings and Postal Life Insurance Funds by the Postal Services Agency*, Interim Report, Study Group on the Management of PS and PLI Funds, Tokyo, 4 June 1999
Mulgan, Aurelia George, 'Japan: a Setting Sun?', *Foreign Affairs*, Washington, July–August, 2000
Mundell, Robert A., 'Theory of Optimum Currency Area', *American Economic Review*, September 1961
Murakami, Y. and Y. Kosai (eds), *Japan in the Global Community; Its Role and Contribution on the Eve of the 21st Century*, Tokyo University, 1986
Murchison, D.C. and E. Solomon, 'The Mis-alignment of the U.S. Dollar and the Japanese Yen, the Problem and Its Solution', Technical Paper no.72, Graduate School of Business, Stanford University, 1983
Murphy, R. Tagart, 'Power without Purpose; the Crisis of Japan's Global Financial Dominance', *Harvard Business Review*, March–April 1989
Nakakita, T., 'The Globalization of Japanese Firms and Its Influence on Japan's Trade with Developing Countries', *The Developing Economies*, December 1988, pp. 306–22
Nester, W.R., *Japan's Growing Power over East Asia and the World Economy: Ends and Means*, Macmillan, 1990
Noguchi, Y. *Economics of the Bubble*, Nihon Keizai Shinbusa, Tokyo, 1996
Noland, M., 'Fiscal Policies and the Japan–US Bilateral Current Account, *Japan and the World Economy*, July 1989
Noland, M. et al., 'The Global Economic Effects of the Japanese Crisis', Working Paper, Institute of International Economics, 1998
Oba, Tamomitsu, 'The Yen Must Play More Important World Role', *Euromoney*, London, October 1984, pp. 63–4
O'Brien, Richard and Sarah Hewin (eds), 'Finance and International Economy', *The Amex Bank Review*, Prize Essays, Oxford, 1991
OECD, *Economic Survey, 1996–97*, Paris
OECD, 'Update of Business Cycles', Paris, 1997, mimeo
OECD, *Economic Survey of Japan*, Paris, 1998
OECD, *Economic Survey of Japan*, Paris, 1999
OECD, *Economic Survey, Japan*, Paris, 2002

Ogawa, Kazuo and Shin-ichi Kitasaka, 'Bank Lending in Japan: Its Determinants and Macroeconomic Implications', Chapter 7 of Takeo Hoshi and Hugh Patrick (eds), *Crisis and Change in the Japanese Financial System*, Kluwer, Boston, 2000

Ogawa, Kazuo et al., *Borrowing Constraints and Role of Land Assets in Japanese Corporate Investment Decisions, an Economic Analysis*, no. 136, Economic Research Institute, Economic Planning Agency, 1994

Ohmae, Kenichi, 'Japan's Bubble Deflates', *International Economic Insights*, Washington, June 1991

Okabe, M., *The Japanese Economy*, Macmillan, London, 1995

Okimoto, D. and Nishi, Y. R and D., 'Organization in Japanese and American Semiconductor Firms', in M. Aoki and R. Dore (eds), *The Japanese Firm: the Sources of Competitive Strength*, Oxford University Press, Oxford, 1994

Okina, K., 'The Risks of Single-minded Targeting', *The Financial Times*, London, 10 November 1999

Okita, S., *Japan in the World Economy of the 1980s*, University of Tokyo Press, Tokyo, 1990

Okuda, M., 'Japanese Two-step Loans: the Japanese Approach to Development Finance', *Hitotsubashi Journal of Economics*, 34, 1993, pp. 67–85

Okumura, H., *Japan's Financial Deregulation: Recent Developments and Future Outlook*, Nomura Research Institute, Feb. 1991

Oman, Charles, *New Forms of International Investment in Developing Countries*, OECD, Paris, 1984

Orr, R.M., 'The Rising Sun; What Makes Japan Give?', *The International Economy*, September 1989, pp. 80–3

Osugi, Kazuhito, 'Japan's Experience of Financial Dergulation since 1984 in an International Perspective', BIS Economic Paper no. 26, Basle, Jan. 1990

Otsubo, S. and M. Tsutsumi, 'Is the Japan Problem Real? How Problems in Japan's Financial Sector Could Affect Developing Regions', Working Paper no. 1682, The World Bank, Washington

Ozawa, T., 'Japan as Largest Financier of Multinationalism', *The Exim Bank, Journal of World Trade Law*, Nov/Dec. 1986

Patrick, Hugh and Rosovsky, *Asia's New Giant, How Japan's Economy Works*, The Brookings Institution, Washington, 1976

Peek, J. and E. Rosengreen, 'The International Transmission of Financial Shocks, the Case of Japan', *American Economic Review*, September 1997

Pilat, D. *The Economics of Rapid Growth: the Experience of Japan and Korea*, Edward Elgar, Aldershot, 1994

Porter, M.E., *The Comparative Advantage of Nations*, Macmillan, London, 1990

Posen, Adam, *Restoring Japan's Economic Growth*, Institute of International Economics, Washington, DC, 1998

Poterba, James, 'Comparing the Cost of Capital in the US and Japan, a Survey of Methods', *Federal Reserve Bank of New York Quarterly Review*, New York, winter 1991

Prowse, Stephen, 'Institutional Investment Patterns and Corporate Financial Behavior in the US and Japan', *Journal of Financial Economics*, 27, 1990

Rakshit, Mihir, 'Economic Crisis in Japan: Analytical and Policy Issues', *Money and Finance*, Kolkata, April–June 1999

Reading, S., *Japan, the Coming Collapse*, Weidenfeld, London, 1992

Reisen, Helmet and Axel Van Trostenburg, 'Should the Asian NICs Peg to the Yen?', *InterEconomics*, Aug/September, 1988

Richardson, P., I. Visco and C. Giorno, 'Predicting the Evolution and Effects of Asian Crisis from OECD Perspective', OECD Economics Department Working Paper no. 236, 2000

Rix, Alan, *Japan's Economic Aid: Making Aid Policies*, St. Martin's Press, Macmillan, 1980

Roosa, R.V., *US and Japan in the International Monetary System*, Group of Thirty, New York, 1986

Rosenbluth, F.C., *Financial Policies in Contemporary Japan*, Cornell University Press, Ithaca, NY, 1989

Royama, S., 'Aspects of Financial Restructuring in Contemporary Japan, *Japan Review of International Affairs*, spring 1990

Sachs, Jeffrey and Peter Boone, 'Japanese Structural Adjustment and the Balance of Payments', Working Paper no. 2614, NBER, June 1988

Sakakibara, E., 'The Internationalization of Tokyo's Financial Markets', in A.H.H. Tan and Basant Kapur (eds), *Pacific Growth and Financial Interdependence*, Allen and Unwin, Sydney, 1986

Sakakibara, E., 'Moving beyond the Public Works State', *Japan Echo*, Tokyo, February 1998

Sakamoto, Y., 'NIC's Economic Adjustment and Asia's Division of Labor', *Mitsui Bank Monthly Review*, 34(36)

Sargen, N. and K.L. Schoenholtz, 'Japanese Adjustment Miracle and its Implications for the Yen', *Japan and the World Economy*, 1990, pp. 283–93

Sato, Hideo, *Japan as an Emerging Power in the World Economy*, NIRA Research Output, 1992

Sato, Kazuo, 'The Role of US Balanced and its Macro-economic Implications: the Case of Japan', *Journal of the Japanese and International Economies*, 1988

Sato, Kazuo, *Transformation of the Japanese Economy*, M.E. Sharpe, New York, 1996

Sato, Ryuzu, 'The US–Japan Trade Imbalance from the Japanese Perspective', Working Paper no. 2479, NBER, Jan. 1988

Sawabe, N., 'The Basle Accord and Accounting of Investment in Securities', *Shooken Keizzai, Financial Economic Review*, no. 189, Sept. 1994

Sawai, Y., 'Internationalization of the Yen: a Progress Report', *Tokyo Financial Review*, November 1989

Schaede, Ulrich, 'Black Monday in New York; Black Tuesday in Tokyo', *California Journal of Management*, 1991

SenGupta, Arjun, 'What Is To Be Done with the Japanese Surplus', *Finance and Development*, September 1988

Seth, Rama and A. Quijama, 'Japanese Bank's Customers in the US', *Federal Reserve Bank of New York Quarterly Review*, spring 1991

Sheard, P. (ed.), *Japanese Firms, Finance and Markets*, Addison-Wesley Longman, NSW, Australia, 1996

Shigehara, K., 'Japan's Experience with the Use of Monetary Policy and the Process of Liberalization', *Bank of Japan Monetary and Economic Studies*, March 1991

Shigehisa, Kasahara, 'A Rescue Plan for the Post-Bubble Japanese Economy', UNCTAD Discussion Paper, June 1994

Shimamoto, R., 'Monetary Control in Japan', in P. Meek, *Central Bank Views on Monetary Targeting*, Federal Reserve Bank of New York, 1993

Shinkai, Y. 'The Impact of Japan on Asian Pacific Markets, the Macro-evidence', AJRC, ANU, Canberra Conference, 1987

Shinkai, Yoichi, 'Japan's Positive Role as the World's Banker', *Economic Eye*, Tokyo, summer 1990

Shirakawa, Masaki, 'Monetary Policy under Zero Interest Rate Constraint and Balance Sheet Adjustment', *International Finance*, 4(3), winter 2001

Snowden, P.N., 'Prolonged Stagnation, Hesitant Recovery; Japan from an Austrian Perspective', *The World Economy*, 2001

Somel, Cem, 'Finance for Growth: Lessons from Japan', UNCTAD Discussion Paper no. 44, July 1992

Stockwin, J.A., *Dynamic and Immobilist Politics in Japan*, Macmillan, 1988

Suto, M. 'New Movements in Japanese Corporate Governance: the Role of Corporate Pension Funds', Nissan Institute, Oxford, 1999, mimeo

Suzuki, Y., *Money and Banking in Contemporary Japan, Theoretical Setting and its Application*, Yale University Press, 1980

Suzuki, Y., *The Japanese Financial System*, Clarendon Press, Oxford, 1987

Suzuki, Yoshio, 'Changes in Financial Asset Selection and Development of Financial Markets in Japan', *Bank of Japan Monetary and Economic Studies*, Tokyo, October 1989

Svensson, Lars, 'The Zero Bound in an Open Economy: a Foolproof Way of Escaping from a Liquidity Trap, *Monetary and Economic Studies*, Institute for Monetary and Economic Studies, Bank of Japan, 2000

Taguchi, Hiro, 'A Survey of the International Use of the Yen', BIS Working Paper 6, Basle, July 1982

Takagi, Shinji, 'Recent Developments in Japan's Bond and Money Markets', *Journal of Japanese and International Economies*, 2(1), 1988

Takagi, Shinji, 'The Japanese Equity Markets, Past and Present', *Journal of Banking and Finance*, 13, 1989, pp. 537–70

Takagi, Shinji, 'Structural Changes in the Japanese Long-term Capital Flows', in M. Okabe, *The Japanese Economy*, Macmillan, 1995

Takeda, M., *Why do Japanese Firms Issue Bonds Abroad*? Basle, July 1991

Takeda M. and Turner, 'The Liberalization of Japan's Financial Markets: Some Major Themes', BIS Economic Paper no. 34, Basle, November 1992

Takenaka, H., *Economic Incentives for Industrial investment: Japanese Experience*, Institute for Fiscal and Monetary Policy, Ministry of Finance, Japan, Feb. 1986

Takeuchi, K., 'Does Japanese FDI Promote Japanese Imports from Developing Countries?', Working Paper no. 458, The World Bank, Washington, DC, June 1990

Tamura, T., *Changes in Corporate Fund-raising and Management in Japan's Financial Markets*, 29, FAIR, Foundation for Advanced Information and Research, Tokyo, 1987

Tandon, Rameshwar, 'Yen Internationalization or Tokyo Financial Centre', IDPAD Working Paper, IMWOO, The Hague, December 1995

Tandon, Rameshwar, 'Japanese Financial Deregulation', UNCTAD Discussion Paper no. 114, Geneva, April 1996

Tandon, Rameshwar, *Japanese Financial Surplus and the World Economy*, Indo-Dutch Program on Alternatives in Development (IDPAD), The Hague, Vikas Publishing House, New Delhi-2, 1997

Tatewaki, Kazuo, *Banking and Finance in Japan*, Routledge, London, 1991

Tatsuno, S.M., *Created in Japan*, Harper and Row, New York, 1990
Tavlas, G.S., 'On the International Use of Yen as International Currency', IMF Working Paper no. WP/91/2, IMF, Washington, Jan. 1991
Tavlas, G.S. and Yuzuru Ozeki, 'The Japanese Yen as an International Currency', IMF Working Paper 91/2
Teramura, Y., *Japan in the 1990s*, Cambridge University, Oriental Studies, Cambridge, 1998
Teranishi, Jurio, 'Catch-up Process, Financial System and Japan's Rise as a Capital Exporter', *Hitotsubashi Journal of Economics*, 27, Special Issue, October 1986
Teranishi, Jurio, 'Financial System Reform after the War', Discussion Paper series no. 244, Hitotsubashi University, Institute of Economic Research, Tokyo, 1991
Teranishi, J. and Y. Kosai (eds), *The Japanese Experience of Economic Reforms*, St. Martin's Press, New York, 1993
Terrell, Henry S., Robert S. Dohner and Barbara R. Lowrey, 'The Activities of Japanese Banks in the US and UK, 1980–88', *Federal Reserve Bulletin*, Washington, Feb. 1990
Tesar, Linda, *International Equity Transactions and the US Portfolio Choice*, NBER, Cambridge, 1994
Teufel, H., 'Domestic Savings, Investment and Capital Flows', Kiel Institute of World Economics Working Paper, 1988
Thorn, R.S., *The Rising Yen*, Institute of Southeast Asian Studies, Singapore, 1987
Thurow, L., 'Asia: the Collapse and the Cure', *The New York Review*, 5.2. 1998
Tokyo Financial Review, 'Internationalization of Yen: Where We Are', 6(3), March 1991
Tsuru, S., *Essays on the Japanese Economy*, Kinokuniya, Tokyo, 1958
Tsurumi, T., *The Japanese Are Coming*, Ballinger, Cambridge, Mass., 1976
Tsutsui, Y. *Japan's Banking Industry, Collusion under Regulation*, Japanese Economic Studies, Armonk, New York, 1990
Turner, Philip, 'Capital Flows in the 1980s: a Survey of Major Trends', BIS Economic Paper no. 30, Basle, April 1991
Ueda, K., 'Japanese Capital Outflows', *Journal of Banking and Finance*, Amsterdam, 1990
Ueda, N., 'Stock Inflation and the Japanese Economy', *Long-Term Credit Bank of Japan Economic Review*, Tokyo, no. 97, December 1989
UN Centre on Transnational Corporations, *World Investment Report, 1994*, The Triad of FDI, New York, 1995
Viner, Aron, Inside Japan's Financial Markets, Economist Publication, London, 1987
Walton, R. and Trimble, 'Japanese Banks in London', *Bank of England Quarterly Bulletin*, London, November 1987
Watanabe, T., 'Helping the NICs Helps the World Economy', *Journal of Japanese Trade and Industry*, no. 4, 1990
Whittaker, D. Hugh and Yoshitaka Kurosawa, 'Japan's Crisis; Evolution and Implications', *Cambridge Journal of Economics*, 22, 1998, 7611–771
WIDER, *Mobilizing International Surplus for World Development, A WIDER plan for a Japanese Initiative*, Study Group Series no. 2 Tokyo/Helsinki, May 1987
Wilson, Dominic, 'Japan's Slowdown: Monetary versus Real Explanations', *Oxford Review of Economic Policy*, 16(2), 2000

Wolff, E., 'Has Japan Specialized in Wrong Industries?', in M. Blomstrom, B. Gangnes and S.J. La Croix (eds), *Japan's New Economy, Continuity and Change in the 21st Century*, Oxford University Press, 2000

World Bank, *Annual Report*, several years

Worthington, P.M., *On the Road to European Monetary Union*, Berg Publishers, Oxford and New York, 1992

Wright, Richard W., *The Second Wave, Japan's Global Assault on Financial Services*, Waterlow Publishers, London, 1987

Wright, Richard W., *A Yen for Profit: Canadian Financial Institutions in Japan*, Institute for Research on Public Policy, Toronto, 1987

Yamada, Tesuji, 'The Effects of Japanese Social Security Retirement Benefits on Personal Savings and Elderly Labor Force Behavior', *Japan and the World Economy*, 2(4), pp. 327–63

Yamaguchi, T., 'Financial Liberalization in Japan', *Tokyo Financial Review*, Tokyo, May 1990

Yamamura, Kezo, 'Success that Soured; Administrative Guidance and Cartels in Japan', in K. Yamamura (ed.), *Policy and Trade Issues of the Japanese Economy*, University of Washington Press, Seattle, 1982

Yamashita, T., *Japan's Securities Markets, a Practitioners' Guide*, Butterworth, Singapore, 1989

Yoichi, S., 'Japan's Role as World Banker', *Economic Eye*, summer 1990

Yoshikawa, Hiroshi, 'On the Equilibrium Yen–Dollar Rate', *American Economic Review*, 80(3), 1990

Yoshitomi, M., 'Japan's Savings and External Surplus in the World Economy', Occasional Paper, Group of Thirty, New York, 1989

Zainuddin, Z., 'Trends in Japan's Portfolio Capital Exports; the Equities Market', in *Towards an Economically Resilient Southeast Asia*, Kuala Lumpur, 1991

Zielinski, Robert and N. Holloway, *Unequal Equities: Power and Risk in Japan's Stock Market*, Kodansha International, Tokyo and New York, 1991

Index

Date Due

	APR 27 2009		

IF YOUR BOOK IS RECALLED YOUR DUE DATE WILL BE SHORTENED. YOU WILL BE NOTIFIED BY MAIL.